D1526438

XENOPHON'S IMPERIAL FICTION

XENOPHON'S

IMPERIAL

FICTION

On *The Education of Cyrus*

JAMES TATUM

PRINCETON UNIVERSITY PRESS

PRINCETON, NEW JERSEY

Copyright © 1989 by Princeton University Press
Published by Princeton University Press, 41 William Street,
Princeton, New Jersey 08540
In the United Kingdom: Princeton University Press, Guildford,
Surrey

Library of Congress Cataloging-in-Publication Data
Tatum, James.
Xenophon's imperial fiction : The education of Cyrus /
James Tatum
p. cm.
Bibliography: p.
Includes index.
ISBN 0–691–06757–0 (alk. paper)
1. Xenophon. Cyropaedia. 2. Cyrus, King of Persia, d. 529 B.C.,
in fiction, drama, poetry, etc. 3. Education of princes in
literature. 4. Imperialism in literature. 5. Political fiction,
Greek—History and criticism. 6. Kings and rulers in literature.
I. Title.
PA4494.C9T38 1989
883'.01—dc19   88–17822
CIP

Publication of this book has been aided by a grant from the Paul
Mellon Fund of Princeton University Press

This book has been composed in
Linotron Trump

Printed in the United States of America by Princeton University
Press, Princeton, New Jersey

For Harry Avery and James Hitt

εὖ γὰϱ μέμνημαι . . .

Except in the abandoned sphere of the dead languages, no one has discussed what part of education has, in his personal experience, turned out to be useful, and what not.

The Education of Henry Adams

Government includes the art of formulating a policy and using the political technique to attain so much of that policy as will receive general support: persuading, leading, sacrificing, teaching always, because the greatest duty of a statesman is to educate.

Franklin Roosevelt, September 1932

Although people are better equipped to judge acting better than any other art, the hypocrisy of "sincerity" prevents them from admitting that they, too, are always acting some role of their own imagination.

Louise Brooks, *Lulu in Hollywood*

CONTENTS

x   CONTENTS

ILLUSTRATIONS

PREFACE

I f you inquire into the
origins of the novel long enough, sooner or later, before De-
foe and the rise of the novel in seventeenth-century Eng-
land, even before Cervantes' ancient masters Heliodorus
and Apuleius, you will come to the fourth century before
our era and Xenophon's *Cyropaedia, The Education of Cy-
rus*.[1] The Cyrus in question is Cyrus the Great, the founder
of the Persian empire celebrated in the Book of Ezra as the
liberator of Israel.[2] His exemplary education furnished later
poets and novelists with, among other things, what they re-
garded as the sentimental love story of Panthea, the fairest
woman in all of Asia.[3] And if you are an altogether different
kind of reader, one looking for a Machiavellian moment be-
fore Machiavelli, sooner or later you will trace your way
back to the same source.[4] For the *Cyropaedia* was also the
most influential of all mirrors for princes. Its fame was at
last obscured by the publication of *The Prince* itself.[5]

This is a study of the way Xenophon intertwined the fic-
tional and the political in a single text. My aim is to recover
Cyrus and his education for contemporary readers and make
the *Cyropaedia* a twentieth-century text rather than a re-
mote historical document; to explain how Xenophon came
to the writing of it, how he put it together, and how the
ensemble works. Above all, I want to understand how one
and the same work could instruct and inspire poets and nov-
elists as much as it did political philosophers, princes, and
the tutors of princes. The range of its influence is exempli-

fied by the ancient Greek novelists and Edmund Spenser, as well as Alexander the Great and Elizabeth I of England, and Cicero, and Machiavelli.

Approaching Cyrus and his education entails, first of all, a recognition of the role that theories of reception can play in the recovery of classical literature.[6] Like readers in every other age between Xenophon's and ours, we have our own historical position which must be recognized.[7] We need to realize that the *Cyropaedia* has been read and reread in ways that point to the elusive truth of what Xenophon created. This truth cannot be reduced to a single and determining point of origin (Chapter 1).

Then there is that blend of romance and politics: easy to declare, but also something of a paradox. In common parlance romance signifies a turn away from the political and the real, to the ideal and unreal. Romance promises dreams realized, wishes fulfilled, a story in which the world goes the way of the imagination rather than the way of history and actual experience. But for Xenophon, this displacement of Greek political problems into an exotic Persian realm marked the creation of a mode with great potential for instruction about political power, as well as a mode for creating political power itself.[8] He was not imitating a literary form that already existed; he was engaged in a creative process that had its beginnings in his response to other works, in his rethinking old questions in a new way.[9] Instead of relegating *The Education of Cyrus* to a marginal status, as earlier histories of literature have tended to do, this conception of the political uses of fiction centers it, just as Xenophon centered the *Cyropaedia* in his own writing.[10] Reading *The Education of Cyrus* as a politically engaged romance allows us to recognize its multiple determinations and origins,[11] as well as the many paths it later took, becoming at one time the plaything of a poet or a novelist, and at another the paradigm for a royal education (Chapter 2).[12] What he says at the end of the story is equally significant. Having created a romance in the *Cyropaedia*, he then turns into its earliest critic. This book will end with a study of the way Xenophon ends his (Chapter 10).

The chapters in between (3 through 9) are an essay on how to read *The Education of Cyrus*. Throughout, the method is to proceed in multiple crossings, so that we engage the political and the fictional in a single reading. I take the social and political structures that Xenophon represents to be, equally, fictional structures. Cyrus's rise to power is portrayed through his encounters with other people. The education of Cyrus is not a static prescription but a dialectical exchange between the ideal monarch and his present and future subjects. These subjects prove to be members of his own family, as well as citizens of the foreign nations he subdues. For Xenophon, the art of fiction largely consists of the invention of the people whom Cyrus meets. If Cyrus is a paradigm of the ideal ruler, they are themselves the exemplary targets of that monarch's imperial designs. He always wins, and, in the end, they always obey. The reader is encouraged to imitate Cyrus. Many readers did. But many others chose to imitate Xenophon himself, preferring to follow the example he set as a writer, rather than the example he intends us to admire in his account of the education of Cyrus the Great.

In these ways we gain a position from which we may interrogate the text we read. For the questions we ask of the *Cyropaedia* must be of different kinds. Try to place it in any single category and you will find that it can be, alternatively, a pedagogical novel, a historical novel, a romanticized biography, a mirror for princes, an ideal romance, a novel before the novel, or a contribution to Greek constitutional theory (*politeia* literature). These are some of the things modern readers have called *The Education of Cyrus*; none of them is inaccurate, and the sum of all these terms comes closer to the truth than does any single one of them.[14] One of the pleasures of this text is the way in which it does and does not fit its readers' expectations.[15] Not the least of its ironies is the way it continually breaks the rules of the very genres it is thought to have inspired. And what frustrates the historian is what artists like Spenser and Chariton most relish.

To become readers of *The Education of Cyrus*, we need

a certain flexibility in our approach to it, a variety of critical methods of the kind that have been brought to such kindred texts as *The Faerie Queene* and *The Golden Ass.*[16] What follows will place the *Cyropaedia* in the context of current literary theory and history through a study of its reception, a philological analysis of some points of detail in its text, and an intertextual and structural description of its narrative. Read sympathetically, the nearly forgotten work of a philologist like Gustav Eichler (1880) can be as illuminating to our present reading of the *Cyropaedia* as are the theories of M. M. Bakhtin or Wolfgang Iser. It is not loyalty to my own discipline of classics that leads me to say this. On the contrary, the term "classic" raises the first of several questions we shall have to explore if we are to read the *Cyropaedia* once again, because, considered as a classic, the *Cyropaedia* has virtually ceased to exist.

ACKNOWLEDGMENTS

THIS BEGAN as a project for the Center for Hellenic Studies in Washington, D.C. Originally conceived as a contribution to the study of narrative technique in the Greek romance, it soon metamorphosed into something altogether different from an analysis of Xenophon's narrative technique in the *Cyropaedia*. The broader scope of the present book owes much to Bernard Knox, the former Director of the Center, as well as to my colleague Fred Berthold. He saw that the Dartmouth Humanities courses were instituted and he gave me the opportunity to teach in them.

Dartmouth has supported my work in many ways, leave for research and writing being only one of them. I am grateful to Patricia Carter, Virginia Close, John Crane and Sue Marcoulier of Baker Library for their obliging help at every stage of my work. During a briefer time at the Warburg Library in the University of London, I found it as hospitable, and educational, as ever. Gail Patten has been an invaluable collaborator in processing and reprocessing the words of the manuscript. A fellowship from the John Simon Guggenheim Memorial Foundation helped me find a way to bring the project to a conclusion.

Such refinements as there may be are due first to the patience and criticism of those who heard earlier drafts of this work as it was in progress. Practically nothing I wrote for those earlier occasions remains unchanged. My thanks to audiences of the annual meetings of the American Philological Association (San Francisco) and the Classical Association of New England (Providence); to Charles Segal for an invitation to a conference at Brown University on Romance in the Ancient and Medieval Worlds; to Romuald Turasiewicz and Stanisław Stabryła for their hospitality and the opportunity to address the Polska Akademia Nauk at the University of Cracow; and to Rudi van der Paardt (Leiden) and Ben Hijmans, Jr. (Groningen) for their invitation to offer a paper about my work in its earliest stages. This last occasion resulted in an address about the merits of the *Cyropaedia* to a bemused but exquisitely courteous session of the *Symposium Apuleianum* at the Rijksuniversiteit of Groningen.

In a more distant way I think I must even be grateful to that traditional foe of finished books, academic administration. Undoubtedly the time spent chairing a program and a department took time away from Cyrus and his education, but in the long run it was time well spent. However pale a simulacrum of real political power such academic offices may be, they do teach a basic lesson of the *Cyropaedia* supremely well: human beings resist no one so quickly as the person they see trying to rule over them. The gap between theory and practice is vast and instructive. I should quickly add that no colleague or student ever confronted me with anything remotely like the challenge Cyrus finds in the Evil King of Assyria, the Most Beautiful Woman in All of Asia, or the Eunuch Prince Gadatas.

For illuminating advice about the relationship of this classical project to literary theory I am much indebted to Jonathan Goldberg. Equally important was the help from other friends and colleagues who answered questions about specific problems that arose in the manuscript: Paul Woodruff, Robert Fogelin, Louis Renza, Gene Garthwaite, Michael Ermarth, Joy Kenseth, Paul Rahe, Liselotte Kurth, Michael Maas, William Cook, Hoyt Alverson, Christine Zarbin, Nancy Vickers, and Gordon and Jay Williams. Joanna Hitchcock and her colleagues at Princeton University Press have encouraged me at every stage of editorial review and production. Jane Lincoln Taylor worked wonders in editing the final copy. For the arduous task of reading and commenting on the entire work I owe a great deal to Jack Winkler, Bryan Reardon, William Higgins, Stephen Hirsch, Robert Connor, and Christian Wolff. My deepest thanks of all to Jack Harvey and Bill Noble.

With as many acknowledgments as these, a dedication may seem beside the point, but I have not spent time in the company of the greatest memoirist of the classical world for nothing. Memory has a way of reordering the past, so that people who were at one time of critical importance recede into the background. Permit me then to leap over the many names here and go to two of my first teachers in classics. They were very different presences inside and outside the classroom, and I owe both of them a great deal. While I sat enthralled in Austin at the discovery of Petronius' *Satyricon* and Aristophanes' *Clouds*, they patiently set in motion another impulse, one which would lead eventually to a book about *The Education of Cyrus*. Only those who know nothing of the mysteries of teaching will be surprised at this development.

I

APPROACHING CYRUS AND HIS EDUCATION

CHAPTER ONE

The Classic as Footnote

No man forgets his original trade: the rights of nations, and of kings, sink into questions of grammar, if grammarians discuss them.

Johnson, *Lives of the English Poets* (Milton)

Our conception of what constitutes Greek or Latin literature may be no narrower than that held in any earlier time. It is surely as particular. Nothing reveals more clearly the arbitrary nature of our notions of classicism and the classic than books that are classics in an ironic sense: works of great age that have survived, only not to be read. At present the *Cyropaedia* is just such a book: a footnote to literary history, in a literal as well as a figurative sense. If it were not for footnotes, today's reader of *Tristram Shandy* might never smile at an account of Mr. Shandy's attempt to undertake his son's education.[1] Tristram says that his father sat down to write a *Tristra-paideia*, an *Education of Tristram*. His aim was to save his son from being taught by his mother, by his nurse, and by women generally. By collecting his scattered thoughts and notions, he hoped to bind them together into a paternal institute for the government of his son's childhood and adolescence.

Mr. Shandy imitated Xenophon scrupulously. He worked with caution and diligence, scrutinizing every line he wrote. The result was that after three years of indefati-

3

gable labor he had completed scarcely half the project he
had envisioned. And while this great work was in progress,
so was young Tristram:

> The misfortune was, that I was all that time totally ne-
> glected and abandoned to my mother; and what was almost
> as bad, by the very delay, the first part of the work, upon
> which my father had spent the most of his pains, was ren-
> dered entirely useless—every day a page or two became of
> no consequence. (*The Life and Opinions of Tristram
> Shandy*, 5.16)

So much for Tristram's sad education. Sterne writes in a
grand tradition of learned wit—*Gargantua and Pantagruel*,
The Anatomy of Melancholy, the *Satyricon*. But the joke is
more than a scholarly burlesque of the classics. By the time
the fifth volume of *Tristram Shandy* appeared in 1761, the
Cyropaedia was also becoming, page by page, a classic of no
consequence. Sterne was inspired to write his chapter on
the *Tristra-paideia* by what was actually happening to the
Cyropaedia itself. During the second half of the eighteenth
century the *Cyropaedia* ceased to be regarded as literature
of any consequence. There were some exceptions to this
general trend. David Hume admired the *Cyropaedia* for its
elegance and was unconcerned that it was "altogether a ro-
mance."[2] But Cyrus and his education offended the greatest
historian of the century, and his judgment was influential:
"The *Cyropaedia* is vague and languid: the *Anabasis* cir-
cumstantial and animated. Such is the eternal difference be-
tween fiction and truth." It is appropriate that Gibbon ren-
dered his verdict in a footnote.[3]

I

There are several ways to turn Gibbon's footnote back into
something more substantial. The first course has already
been charted by historians. They have never mistaken the
Cyropaedia for history, but neither have they neglected the
important role it once played in intellectual and political
life. If Gibbon found it vague and languid, for example, this

opinion did not prevent him from using *The Education of Cyrus* for all it was worth in an essay in French on the Medes.[4] There he treats Xenophon respectfully, but as a *philosophe* rather than an *historien*.[5] Gibbon had ample reason to be so liberal.

There is an anecdote in Plutarch about Demetrius of Phaleron, the librarian of Alexandria: he advised King Ptolemy to read as many books as he could about kingship and leadership, because they contained wisdom that the friends of a king would not dare give him face to face.[6] If Ptolemy followed this advice, he would have been an early beneficiary of a development in Greek literature that was to have important consequences for the political and philosophical history of the west. The fourth-century Greek world saw a proliferation of utopias, and an idealization of civilizations that actually existed: in Greece there was Sparta, and in the east there was Persia. And there were ideal monarchs: the nameless philosopher kings of Plato, and such great leaders of past or present history as Cyrus the Great, Philip of Macedon, and Alexander.

Xenophon's fellow Athenian Isocrates stands at the beginning of this literature, with his *logos symbouleutikos*, or advisory discourse for monarchs. His *Nicocles* legislates for monarchs, and his prose encomium *Evagoras* enumerates the virtues of an exemplary king of Crete, in chronological order. In intention, if not in literary form, the *Cyropaedia* is linked to such developments. The tradition can be traced through Philostratus' *Apollonius of Tyana* to the end of classical antiquity, extending to Eusebius' *Life of Origen* and the Byzantine courtier Cecaumenos' *Strategicon*.[7] The *Cyropaedia* was revived in the western Renaissance, as soon as classical texts were available to the tutors of princes. Plato's *Republic* is now the most familiar example of this new direction in fourth-century Greek literature, but Machiavelli and many others concerned with the education of their own princes thought just as highly of Xenophon and the *Cyropaedia*. Machiavelli in fact cites Xenophon more often than he does Plato. The first Latin translations by the humanists Poggio (1440) and Filelfo (1476) reflect the desire of many in the Renaissance to aim for much the same kind of government and education that Xenophon had described two millennia before.[8] With a characteristic desire to link their present world with that past one, they saw Xenophon as they saw themselves. (Illustration 1.) The acme of his influence was in the sixteenth century, which began with a whole generation of mirrors for princes provided by Machiavelli (1513), Erasmus and More (1516), Elyot (1531), and Budé (1540), and ended with the *Cyropaedia*'s most vigorous apologist of all in the Renaissance, Sir Philip Sidney.

This preference for monarchy and for literature of advice about how it could best be achieved reflected developments in the actual political experience of classical antiquity and the Renaissance. Monarchy was not a theme new to Greek literature. Herodotus reports a speech by the Persian Otanes, who argues that democracy is much preferable to monarchy, because one man is not liable to give an account of his actions, even when they are irresponsible. Otanes does not prevail; Darius becomes king, as he had intended to be from the first.[9] When Isocrates, Plato, and Xenophon turned away from democracy, they followed a general tendency in the culture of the fourth century and later to look for the single great ruler. They wanted to influence men of power, and frequently they did. Plato's seventh letter is the most famous account of the difficulty of finding an ideal ruler; not even he was able to reform Dionysius, the tyrant of Syracuse, whom he tried to instruct in person. It is the classic story of the right teacher and the wrong prince.[10]

However sharp a departure it might seem from the democratic ideals of fifth-century Greek literature, the discovery of the value of writing for princes, real or imagined, was not unique to the Greeks or their successors in the Renaissance. The wisdom literature of the Old and Middle Kingdoms of ancient Egypt anticipated this Hellenic development by one and a half millennia. King Amenemhet I (ca. 1990) instructed his son Sesostris I to "trust no brother, trust no friend," a lesson recorded by the misanthropic scribe Akhtoy.[11] Ferdowsi's *Book of Kings* (*Shahnameh*), the Turkish *Wisdom of Royal Glory* (*Kutadsu Bilig*) by the

1. Xenophon Composing His *Cyropaedia*. From the *Traitté des faiz et haultes provesses de Cyrus* of Vasque de Lucène (1470).

central Asian poet Yusuf Khass Hajib (1069), and the Iranian mirror for princes (the *Gabus Nama*) by Kai K'us 'Bn Iskandar (1082), are each the beginning of a major literary tradition under Islam.[12] Xenophon's own work could have been influenced by an ancient Iranian tradition of teaching on kingship, but any such sources he may have had are lost; their traces are accessible (if at all) only through intermediary works like the *Shahnameh*.[13]

Western European writers in and after the Renaissance thought that their own work would have been impossible without the example of Xenophon and other ancient models. And it is true that Elyot and others go to some pains to point out how their advice to princes revives classical wisdom.[14] The best of these courtiers do this not only by direct literary imitation and citation, but by an assimilation of classical learning that goes far beyond the means of any index or concordance to measure. Anyone who knows the *Cyropaedia* will be astonished to see how thoroughly Machiavelli has mastered Xenophon's text and expressed much of its essence in far briefer scope, with so much else besides.[15]

Yet it is also worth realizing that a mirror for princes could be written without any reference at all to classical antiquity. During the Carolingian era, the princess Dhuoda wrote a *Manual Addressed to Her Son William* (841–843) without Xenophon or Plato, but with a great deal of St. Jerome and the Church fathers.[16] The point is that we should not conceive of Xenophon's work too narrowly, as a project that could only have been invented by Greeks in a particular time and place. Mirrors for princes and other kinds of utopian literature regularly appeared wherever there was a monarch to instruct, or to please.

In these ways the *Cyropaedia* figures as an important document in the history of western political theory and education.[17] The historian of Renaissance and modern Europe has as much claim to its Latin and vernacular translations as the ancient historian has to its Greek. Xenophon provided humanists with a crucial text for princes and their tutors, just as he already had instructed the dynasts of ancient Greece and Rome.[18]

2

There is another way to recover *The Education of Cyrus*, and it does not avoid the problematic opposition of history and fiction that Gibbon discerned. On the contrary, to turn this footnote to the classics into a recognizable literary text, it should first be understood that the opposition of history and fiction that Gibbon speaks of is not original to him or his followers. This view was first articulated by Cicero, and the opposition was not invidious. Xenophon portrayed Cyrus, he says, not in accord with historical truth, but as a model of a just ruler.[19] Because of the prestige of Cicero, this opinion has exerted great influence. Wrenched from its original context in a long letter to his brother Quintus, Cicero's testimony can also be most misleading. For Gibbon, in disparaging the fictions of the *Cyropaedia*, dismissed the very thing many readers before him had embraced. Cicero valued *The Education of Cyrus* precisely because it was fiction that served a highly political purpose.

For Cicero's often-quoted invocation of Cyrus is no passing allusion. The *Cyropaedia* inspired both the didacticism and the heavenly length of *Ad Quintum Fratrem* 1.1.[20] His reading of Xenophon prompted him to turn a letter to his brother Quintus into a *Quintopaedia*, an education in the art of being a proconsul. Cicero spent much of his career near supreme power, gaining it for himself only once, as consul in 63; even then, he had the great good luck to have Catiline for an enemy. He was often tempted to offer advice to Romans far more illustrious than his brother, and ones far more powerful; among others whom he sought to cultivate were Pompey and Julius Caesar. Even for Cicero the present enterprise was bold. The office of proconsul was one Quintus had already held for two years, and one Cicero himself would not hold until ten years later. Then he would discover how difficult it could be to emulate the *Cyropaedia* when one must confront political realities.[21] Nonetheless, he has a great deal of advice to offer, as he always does.

Quintus, his brother says, has the virtues of Cyrus. Cicero draws this flattering parallel so that he can advance his one criticism without offense. Quintus has a short temper and needs to learn how to control it. The way to do this is to realize that he is engaged in an office which is essentially a theatrical enterprise. He is a Roman proconsul playing before an audience of Greeks. They may be provincials in Cilicia, but they are Greeks all the same:

> Since therefore you have been assigned a theater such as this, crowded with such multitudes, so ample in its grandeur, so subtle in its criticism, and by nature possessed of such an echo that its demonstrations of feeling and ejaculations reach Rome itself, for that reason I implore you, struggle and strive with all your might, not merely to prove yourself to have been worthy of the task allotted to you, but also to prove that by the excellence of your administration you have surpassed all that has ever been achieved in Asia. (42)

The metaphor of theater is a much-used characterization of Roman political life. The dying Augustus asked for a review of his performance in the mime of life (*mimus vitae*), and exited like an actor from the comic stage—in Greek.[22]

> Since you have been well pleased, give me your applause,
> And all depart in high spirits, well pleased.
> (Suetonius, Augustus, 94)

Quintus never played a role as complex as Octavian's metamorphosis into Augustus, but he was in the same profession. Accordingly, Cicero ends his letter by returning to this familiar metaphor for a successful political career:

> I end my letter by imploring and urging you that—after the fashion of good poets and hard-working actors—you should take particular pains with the last phase and finale of your office and employment, so that this third year of your rule may, like the third act of a play, be recognized as having been the most highly finished and brilliantly staged of the three. You will do this most easily if you imagine that I,

the one man whose approbation you have desired above
that of the whole world, am always at your side, taking
part in everything you say or do. (46)

The peroration is characteristically felicitous. In effect Cic-
ero offers to serve as both director and critic of Quintus' per-
formance on that provincial stage.

To conceive of a political office as a dramatic role was
natural for Cicero, and not for him alone. Serving in a public
office and playing a role in the theater are related profes-
sions, because neither is a spontaneous expression of a per-
son's true self. Suetonius' anecdote about the exit of Augus-
tus carries with it the implication that his success depended
on an ability to subsume the private person within the pub-
lic roles of Octavian and Augustus. Such role-playing is an
instinctive part of political life. Since ambitious political
leaders think they are making history rather than writing it,
and since indeed they often are, they will ask of a book like
the *Cyropaedia* not that it be true to history, but that it be
useful for their future projects. Thus Cicero is not only
happy to acknowledge Xenophon's fictions; his real aim is
to encourage his brother to create his own fictions in turn.
Political power is in some fundamental sense achieved by
creating and living fictive roles. Quintus' term in the office
of proconsul was a role to be played, with the third year of
office a final act in a drama before an audience. Cyrus in the
Cyropaedia is a fictive leader whose life is meant to be im-
itated and adapted to the needs of present political life, and
not only in Rome.

So long as they were close enough to princes and their
power to influence them, or so long as they thought they
were, Xenophon's readers could use the *Cyropaedia* for just
this kind of political education. They could learn the arts of
his ideal ruler Cyrus and put them to their own use by at-
tempting to imitate him. Like Cicero, they read the *Cyro-
paedia* for many of the same reasons that moved Xenophon
to write it.

The precise way these monarchs learned from Cyrus's
example is beyond my ability to measure. It has been sug-

gested that Alexander's later career reflects as much famili-
arity with the *Cyropaedia* as with the *Anabasis*.[23] That the
tutors and courtiers of later princes had a high regard for
Xenophon is beyond doubt. They taught his Greek, they
translated him, and they hoped he would make the mon-
arch they served the better for knowing him. Of course
there were mixed results. Roger Ascham seems to have
done very well by the young Elizabeth, but the Portuguese
humanist Vasque de Lucène did not teach Charles the Bold
of Burgundy to be less *téméraire*.[24] James I of England knew
the Greek *Cyropaedia*, though he was unmoved by the pa-
thetic story of the castration of Prince Gadatas, ordinarily
regarded as one of the book's more poignant episodes; he
imitated the form of Xenophon's work in his own manual
on kingship, the *Basilikon Doron*.[25]

Many of Xenophon's readers have preferred to use him
rather than to comment on him. Montaigne knew the *Cy-
ropaedia* and had as high a regard for it as for any other work
he cited.[26] Sir Philip Sidney was an important exception to
what Montaigne and others took for granted. He explained
why Xenophon was a classic writer, and he explained how
to read him. Xenophon's greatest influence in and after the
Renaissance lay roughly between Machiavelli and Elyot
(1513–1534) and the translations of Philemon Holland
(1632) and François Charpentier (1659). Sidney lived his
comparatively short life approximately in the center of this
period (1554–1586). He was typical of the Renaissance in
that he regarded the *Cyropaedia* as a work of self-evident
importance; fortunately for our present purposes, he was
more aggressive on this point than any other reader we
know of. A brilliant poet and classical scholar, Sidney goes
on the offensive about the uses of literature in *The Defence
of Poesy* (1582), an Horatian epistle in prose, graced every-
where with a pugnacious argument that owes much to Ar-
istotle's *Poetics*. In a blend of felicity and rigor, Sidney is
thinking as much in Greek as in English. His "poesy" is
simply a transliteration of *poiêsis*, not restricted to the
sense of "poetry" in modern English usage but expressing
the root idea of the Greek *poiein*, "to fashion" or "to create"

something. His theme could be glossed as "creative writing," "fine arts," or "imaginative fiction."[27]

Sidney begins with Cicero's comments on the *Cyropaedia* but moves far beyond them. He has a courtier's view of historians and philosophers; in that context, he finds the Xenophon of the *Cyropaedia* a poet, and more efficacious than the historians and philosophers are. Sidney's poet is far superior to them in the instruction of princes and their courtiers, because his "feigned examples" have greater power to teach than true ones. His poet is more efficient than the historian, because he need not adjust his lessons to the unavoidable failures and compromises of human history. And he is more useful than the philosopher, because his lesson is not so difficult and is more intelligible to a wider range of readers. Thus courtiers and scholars can learn as well from Xenophon's fictions as from any historian's verities. Nor is that all. Contrary to the disposition of modern literary historians, Sidney can in one sentence praise the *Cyropaedia* with Heliodorus' *Ethiopica*, a work now regarded strictly as a novel.[28]

For Xenophon, who did imitate so excellently as to give us *effigiem iusti imperii*, "the portraiture of a just Empire," under the name of Cyrus (as Cicero saith of him), made therein an absolute heroical poem. So did Heliodorus in his sugared invention of that picture of love in Theagenes and Chariclea; and yet both these wrote in prose, which I speak to show that it is not rhyming and versing that maketh a poet, no more than a long gown maketh an advocate, who though he pleaded in armor should be an advocate and no soldier. But it is that feigning notable images of virtues, vices, or what else, with that delightful teaching, which must be the right describing note to know a poet by, although indeed the Senate of Poets have chosen verse as their fittest raiment, meaning, as in matter they appeared all in all, so in manner to go beyond them, not speaking (table-talk fashion or like men in a dream) words as they chanceably fall from the mouth, but peizing (sc. weighing) each syllable of each word by just proportion according to the dignity of the subject. (*The Defence of Poesy*, IV)

The fluidity of boundaries in literary genres is a typical debate in the Renaissance.[29] Although Tasso does not comment so extensively as Sidney on the *Cyropaedia*, he makes much the same point about Xenophon's work by arguing that he is a philosopher and historian, and at the same time something of a poet. What makes him poetic is his mingling of the true with the false and the feigned. Tasso saw just this mingling in Horace, Plutarch's *Life of Theseus*, commentaries (Macrobius on the *Dream of Scipio*, Servius on Vergil), and the *Cyropaedia*.[30]

Sidney lived in an age hospitable to this view of literature. After Elizabeth I, English monarchs never again succeeded in being patrons of the intellectual life. James I made the attempt and met with ridicule. By temperament his subjects were suspicious of the kind of Mediterranean sophistication the *Cyropaedia* represents.[31] Our history of its reception in English would very nearly have stopped here, if Paris and Scotland had not been more imaginative. Yet this insular environment did not prevent the tutors and counselors of princes—and sometimes their poor relations—from attempting to impress Xenophon's virtues upon the next generation of readers.

How was a classical scholar now to make his way in a world without princes? And what would be the point of instructing a prince even if there were one, especially if one were not paid for it? The Oxford scholar William Barker supplied Tudor England with its first English translation of the *Cyropaedia* (1567), but he has never been admired for this service. He is remembered chiefly as the prisoner in the Tower of London whose sworn testimony proved fatal to his patron Thomas Howard, the Fourth Duke of Norfolk. Norfolk and history dismissed him as an "Italianated Englishman."[32]

His successor Philemon Holland earned a more enduring reputation. This impoverished scholar from Coventry was the most accomplished translator of his age.[33] He dedicated a translation of Livy to Elizabeth in 1600, then undertook a translation of Plutarch's *Moralia* for the same monarch, and switched its dedication to James I when Elizabeth died in

1603. He turned to the *Cyropaedia* last of all. He worked long and carefully, comparing his version with ones already published in Latin and French. He was eighty years old at the time of publication in 1632 and too infirm to see the book through the final stages of publication. His son Henry assumed control and turned the Holland version of the *Cyropaedia* into a tribute to his father, and dedicated it to Charles I.

Henry designed the title page. (Illustration 2.) Although not the artistic equal of the title pages of Rubens, it is eloquent about the way Holland and his contemporaries conceived of their reading of the classics.[34] The two monarchs frame the page, the ancient exemplar "Cyrus the Greater, King of the Persians and Monarch of the World" on the left, and "Charles, By the Grace of God King of the Britons and Monarch of Great Britain" on the right. Cyrus's spear and shield represent the education he offers in warfare and wisdom, and Charles's scepter and shield with its royal coat of arms symbolize the authority of his reign. The ancient author Xenophon is in the middle at the top, and the modern interpreter (translator) Holland is below him.

The portrait links the ancient and modern worlds in several ways. Xenophon is in profile, in the style of an ancient medallion or commemorative coin; he looks left, back into history, at his subject Cyrus. Cyrus himself has the stance and costume of an ancient statue, looking straight across to King Charles, his implied successor. While Cyrus stands on a pedestal with an engraving that depicts an ancient battle with spearmen in phalanx formation, Charles appears above a battle scene with ranks of men with firearms. Both scenes fix in an image the metaphoric foundation of a prince's power, his ability to wage war.

The portraits of translator and monarch are more detailed and lifelike, as befit living contemporaries. Both Holland and King Charles look straight toward the reader: Holland, because he is the translator whose work we are about to read, and Charles, because he is the monarch who governs us. Charles appears as his friend Van Dyke often represents him; Holland's likeness was probably engraved from

2. Title Page to the Translation of Philemon Holland (1631).

an existing portrait as well. The ensemble appears on a triumphal arch. Roman architectural structures were much used on title pages in this period.[35] Everything we see serves as a prelude for what we are about to read. In the empty space beyond the arch appears the title: *Cyrupaedia or The Institution and Life of Cyrus King of Persians, Written in Greek by Xenophon, Translated into English by Philemon Holland, Dr. in Physick, Anno Domini 1632.*

There were great hopes for the translation. Thomas Farnaby provided a patriotic epigraph closer to W. S. Gilbert than to Machiavelli:

> And why should Spanish, French, and other nations
> Rather than we use have of such translations?
> And why should not courtiers read what courtiers write?
> And soldiers know what soldiers do recite?

Another commemorative poem was more political. Beginning with a pun on the *phil-* of Philemon Holland's first name, it prophesies long life for his patron:

> Love's Tree, decay thou cannot, or if dead
> Yet from thy mast how many shall be fed,
> Who thy translation read? If King Charles give
> Grace to thy work, King Charles shall ever live.

History swiftly imposed an ironic reading on the whole enterprise. Philemon Holland was looking backward to the past rather than forward to pressing necessities. So was Charles. Although new versions of the *Cyropaedia* continued to appear, they became little more than exercises in a genre that had outlived its usefulness. The *Cyropaedia* has little to say to those bent on revolution. It represents as well as any single book could the kind of political order a popular revolution would seek to overthrow.[36]

But all was far from lost for Cyrus and his education. There have been plenty of times when there are no princes to teach, in antiquity as well as the early modern era. Monarchs could be so insignificant, or so remote, that no one thought of writing to gain their favor. Even if no one had reason to turn to Xenophon for instruction in the art of rul-

ing others, his text remained, and audiences with less polit-
ical ambition could read it for their own purposes. They
were attracted to the *Cyropaedia* because it was fiction.
One is reminded of a character in a novel by Mary Mc-
Carthy, who recommends we read the Book of Common
Prayer for its style. Another part of Xenophon's readership
turned to the *Cyropaedia* wanting neither an education in
the art of gaining power, nor instruction in the administra-
tion of an empire. More and more readers came to it because
they were just looking for a good read.

3

So far as the *Cyropaedia* is concerned, this response is one
from which we have not yet recovered. It induces a kind of
literary schizophrenia, where Xenophon's readers find it
more and more difficult to comprehend what increasingly
comes to seem a confused text. The sharper the distinction
between history and fiction becomes, the more the *Cyro-
paedia* seems to offer: simultaneously, austere political in-
struction and a few oases of romantic fiction. Ultimately it
will become uninteresting even as didactic fiction and will
find few readers of any kind, for any purpose.

Antiquity anticipated these difficulties in several ways.
After Cicero, we can only guess at what use those in power
made of the *Cyropaedia*. The emperor Julian might have
profited from Cyrus's example; Greek novelists in the Ro-
man empire such as Chariton were engaged in the develop-
ment of an art form Xenophon did much to inspire. Julian
himself scorned such fiction as a sham of history.[37] Philo-
stratus modeled his *Life of Apollonius of Tyana* in part on
the *Cyropaedia*.[38] The novelist Xenophon of Ephesus and
the historian Flavius Arrianus (Arrian), the biographer of
Alexander, both approved of the first Xenophon's example,
and each sought to enhance his prestige by calling himself
"Xenophon."[39] This much can be traced from the scanty an-
cient evidence relevant to the question.

The story can be told in much greater detail when we

turn to more recent history. The pattern that emerges is much the same as in antiquity: first Xenophon is the property of princes and those who would instruct them; then he is abandoned to the novelists and the poets. With the classicizing tendencies of the Renaissance well behind them, historians and novelists in the later modern era tended to emancipate themselves from classical examples. The firmer their ideas about what constituted proper history and fiction, the less compelling the *Cyropaedia* seemed to be, and the more tentative, even primitive, its novelistic techniques. The work of classical writers such as Thucydides and the Greek novelists seemed more useful to these modern readers than what was increasingly perceived as an uneasy combination of fiction and politics in the *Cyropaedia*. Gradually even those classics would be displaced by the classics of the new age. Why should princes read three hundred pages of Xenophon when they could read a hundred pages of Machiavelli, and with more profit? Thus literature came to neglect a work of considerable originality, once the arts it had invented were carried beyond whatever its author seemed to have achieved.

The reason for this development is easy to see. If politically ambitious readers could lose interest in the *Cyropaedia*, novelists and poets could be no less particular in their purposes. In the end they tended toward just as partial a reading. The *Bibliothèque Universelle des Romans* for December 1775 concludes its survey of the *Cyropaedia* with the death of Panthea (7.3). So far as Paris was concerned, there was nothing more of interest in the remaining ninety pages:

> Here finishes the novelistic part, considered as such, of the *Cyropaedia*, a work which contains a good deal more than what its title announces. For besides that which pertains to the childhood of Cyrus, up to his sixteenth year, we find again all that he did after his fortieth year up to his death. There are additionally some later events which seem to belong properly to history, such as the reduction of Caria and Phrygia.

The *Bibliothèque*'s reviewers had firm ideas about their subject. To qualify for inclusion, a book needed amorous intrigue; this was the essence of a novel. If there wasn't any romance (the human condition), there wasn't any romance (the literary form).[40] About the same time as the *Bibliothèque* offered its appreciation of the *partie romanesque* of the *Cyropaedia*, it published discussions of other ancient romances: Cupid and Psyche (July 1775), *The Golden Ass* (July 1779), Xenophon of Ephesus (May 1776), Achilles Tatius (November 1775), and Heliodorus (April 1776).

Because they were engaged in the creation of their own fictions, novelists could afford to be just as arbitrary in their reading of Xenophon as were his critics. They took whatever their fancy required and discarded the rest. For the most part, this meant they used the episodes in which Cyrus, Panthea, Araspas, and Abradatas appear (Books 5, 6, and 7). In a striking parallel to the Cupid and Psyche story of Apuleius' *Golden Ass*, Panthea and Abradatas acquired a life of their own and became familiar to many who had otherwise never read a word of Xenophon.[41] Either with their original names Panthea and Abradatas, or in another guise, they can reappear in a romance with a comic or a tragic ending; everything depends on whether the story stops with an account of Araspas' prudent renunciation of any claim on Panthea (6.2), or continues past that point to Abradatas' death in battle and Panthea's suicide over his body (7.5). The tragic death of Panthea is celebrated by Philostratus and her escape is retold as late as the five-act drama *Araspas und Panthea* (1759), written by Goethe's contemporary Christoph Martin Wieland.[42] Best known now for his *Agathon* (1766) and its influence on the German *Bildungsroman*, the young Wieland admired the *Cyropaedia* so much that he was inspired to compose a heroic poem about Cyrus and his education. The invocation at the beginning of Book 4 will give some idea of the challenge this enthusiasm aroused.

Nenne mir erst, Xenophontische Muse, die Menge der Völker
Mannichfaltig an Sprach und Gestalt, an Sitten und Waffen,

Die aus entlegnen Zonen der Erde von herrschenden Winke
Babels gerufen, sich neben einander zu sehen erstaunten.
Nenne sie, melde die Sitten der Männer, dann gib sie, O Göttin,
Ihrem Schicksal!

(Name me first, Xenophontic Muse, the multitude of peo-
ples manifold in speech and visage, in morals and weapons,
who from remote realms of earth by masterful means of
might to Babylon were summoned, who themselves did
there at one another marvel. Name them, declare the mor-
als of men, and bestow on them, O Goddess, their fate!)

The *Xenophontische Muse* is a prosaic goddess. Wieland
never completed his *Heldengedicht.*

As we have seen, whenever later readers turned to *The
Education of Cyrus* with some political goal in mind, they
shared a basic aim of Xenophon: to learn how to create and
maintain an empire. The course of novelistic (mis)readings
is not much harder to predict. Philostratus' *Word Pictures*
(*Eikones*) are especially important, because they offer us an
early view of a romantic reading of the *Cyropaedia*—that is,
a reading altogether oblivious of its political dimensions.[43]
The *Word Pictures* are lectures Philostratus says he deliv-
ered to a ten-year old boy at a rich man's villa in the Bay of
Naples. A crowd of young men looks on, and everyone pres-
ent is Greek; therefore, says Philostratus, they are addicted
to cultural conversations. We must now add as well that
they are a typical audience of the Second Sophistic.[44]
Whereas Xenophon had described Panthea's character
(*êthos*), the painting Philostratus wants to describe rendered
her soul (*psychê*). This Panthea and Abradatas are not Xen-
ophon's characters. His Abradatas was a man reminiscent
of Hector, so mangled in battle that his body was virtually
in pieces; the sophist's hero has become a beautiful youth
graced with the cliché of Greek erotic literature, the downy
cheeks of a first beard.[45] The mangled body in Xenophon is
now a coordination of colors; flecked with blood of hyacin-
thine hue, Abradatas' corpse contrasts nicely with the shin-
ing gold of his armor.[46]

Panthea is the real focus of Philostratus' ecphrasis. She

surpasses mythological heroines like Laodameia and Evadne, with a beauty that is at its most intense at the moment of death. Even her wound is a cause for admiration:

> She has already driven the dagger through her breast, but with such fortitude that she has not uttered even a groan at the thrust. At any rate she lies there, her mouth retaining its natural shapeliness and a beauty (by Zeus) the bloom of which so rests upon her lips that it shines forth clear, silent though she is. She has not yet drawn out the dagger but still presses on it, holding it by the hilt—a hilt that resembles a golden stalk with emeralds for its branches—but the fingers are more charming still; she has lost none of her beauty through pain, and indeed she does not seem to suffer pain at all but rather to depart in joy because she sends herself away. (*Word Pictures*, 2.9.4–5)

This lapse into romance and erotic fantasy would be repeated in the Renaissance, within a century of the *Cyropaedia*'s first service as a mirror for princes. Then Panthea was once again an object of male admiration, most especially in her death.[47]

Not surprisingly, the only innovation in the long history of male admirers of Panthea was achieved by a woman. Published from 1649 to 1653 under the name of her brother Georges de Scudéry, Madeleine de Scudéry's *Artamène ou le Grand Cyrus* carried the romanticization of the *Cyropaedia* to astonishing length. The first edition runs to 12,886 pages. So long as *Le Grand Cyrus* was in process, it swamped admirers and detractors alike.[48] Not only its magnitude impresses the reader. *Artamène* is perhaps the most original adaptation of Xenophon after the Renaissance. At least it is the most deliciously perverse. In ancient sources Mandane is never anyone but Cyrus's mother; here she is his wife and partner, for those 13,000 pages, as well as a thinly fictionalized representation of the Duchesse de Loungeville, to whom the work is dedicated. (Illustration 3.) To whom could the great Cyrus more fittingly come than to the beautiful Duchess, before whom he lays down palms and trophies in adoration?

Moins d'éclat auoit dans les yeux,
Celle pour qui les Grecs firent dix ans de guerre:
Et vous n'auez Hommes et Dieux,
Ni rien de plus beau dans les Cieux,
Ni rien de si beau sur la Terre.

F. Chauueau in.   N. Regnesson fecit.

3. La Duchesse de Loungeville, dedicatee of *Artamène ou le Grand Cyrus* (1649–1653).

Moins d'esclat avoit dans les yeux,
Celle pour qui les Grecs firent dix ans de guerre:
Et vous n'avez, Hommes et Dieux,
Ni rien de plus beau dans les Cieux,
Ni rien de si beau sur la Terre.

(Less power had she on men's eyes, she for whom the
Greeks waged ten years of war. And you, you mortals and
gods, have nothing more beautiful in the heavens, nor any-
thing so lovely on the earth.)

Mlle de Scudéry maintains some names drawn from Herod-
otus and Xenophon, but little else. Her Cambyses is an evil
king whose beautiful daughter Mandane falls in love with
Cyrus. The plot advances like an ancient Greek romance,
by abductions and accidents. A king of Pontos kidnaps Man-
dane; Cyrus disguises himself as Artamène, takes the king-
dom of the Lydian king Croesus, and recaptures Mandane.
Then the King of Pontos uses the ring of Gyges (!) to abduct
Mandane again. Aryante, brother of Tomyris, removes her
to the land of the Massagetae. When Cyrus kills Aryante,
Tomyris vows revenge. A severed head is brought to her;
Tomyris avenges her brother Aryante by plunging the head
into a bucket of blood. Mandane faints. But the head ac-
tually belonged to a look-alike of Cyrus named Spitradates.
Cyrus is alive, and the couple is reunited. Let no one sup-
pose this summary does justice to *Le Grand Cyrus*.

Naturally Mlle de Scudéry had her predecessors in ro-
mance. The most proximate inspiration was Honoré d'Ur-
fée's *L'Astrée* (1607–1610); a more searching list would
oblige us to include Ariosto and others.[49] But no writer of
romance even begins to rival her in the lengths to which she
was prepared to exploit the conventions of the form. Once
she was esteemed only for her reflection of the world of the
précieux and *précieuses* at the Hôtel de Rambouillet.[50] Now
it is more apparent that writing romance and reading it were
complementary acts for Mlle de Scudéry; she and her read-
ers could share in the creation and the sustaining of a ro-
mantic world for the space of the text she created. Romance
was an alternative to ordinary life, and a powerfully seduc-
tive one.

In this vicarious way *Le Grand Cyrus* enabled its first generation of readers to share in Cyrus's adventures for over five years. The ten volumes of installments constituted both a serialization of the text of the romance, and a serialization of the romantic experience. Once begun, it could be sustained as long as its end was postponed. From the very beginning one wondered not what the conclusion would be, but rather what the next adventure might be. No critic was able to interrupt the project, so long as it was in process. Neither Molière's one-act *Les Précieuses ridicules* nor Boileau's Lucianic dialogue *Les Héros de Roman* caused Mlle de Scudéry a moment's regret about her confident project.[51] Not even the authority of Herodotus or Xenophon held any terrors for her.

> I have sometimes followed the one and sometimes the other, according to whether or not they have been more or less appropriate to my design. And sometimes as I followed their example I have said some things that neither of them said. After all, it is a fable I am composing, not a history that I write. And if this reasoning does not utterly satisfy the scrupulous, they need do nothing more to calm themselves than imagine that my work comes from an old Greek manuscript from Egypt in the Vatican Library, but one so precious and so rare, that it has never been printed—and never will be. There you are, dear reader. That is all I have to say to you.

A fine disregard of scholarly convention, this witty apology is of course utterly conventional. It is a delightful variation of Apuleius and other novelists who write prologues.[52]

Some male authors did not admire *Le Grand Cyrus*. Dryden was neutral, Pepys was less patient. His wife was a great enthusiast of Mlle de Scudéry and drove him to distraction by reciting her version of tales she had read in *Le Grand Cyrus*.[53] Possibly because of the Old Alliance, the Scotsman Sir George MacKenzie was inspired to write an imitation, *Aretina, or The Serious Romance* (1660). Boileau had complained that Mlle de Scudéry was the kind of writer who could not enter a room without giving you an inventory of its furniture.[54] Now MacKenzie tried to translate the French

of the *précieux* and *précieuses* into English for the delecta-
tion of "English and Scotish ladies":

> The hard-hearted ice had now dissolved itself in tears,
> through rage to see itself conquered by its enemy the Sun,
> who advancing to his former height, from which that rebel
> Winter had degraded him, was sending forth his beams in
> troops, to subdue Winter's auxiliaries; and in that sweet
> month of May, wherein the Earth, as a badge of her grate-
> fulness to the Summer, begins to put on its livery; and
> when the air lays aside that veil of thick mist, wherein it
> lapped itself during the coldness of the Winter, in a sweet
> morning of that sweet season, the two ladies Agapeta and
> Aretina, who had lain together the last night (resolving to
> overtake the Sun in bed) did rise very early, leaving their
> waiting-maids lying in Morpheus' embraces, who was be-
> getting on them that bastard babe called Laziness; and so
> were necessitated to play the handmaid to each other,
> which was notwithstanding no great task, seeing their
> clothes seemed most willing to hang upon them, as if they
> knew how much they were honored by being theirs. (*Are-
> tina*, Book 4)

This kind of romance did not last, not even for the audience
for whom it was intended. Charlotte Lennox believed it ad-
dled the brains of female readers, in the same way that
Amadis de Gaul had confused Don Quixote. Her *Female
Quixote, or The Adventures of Arabella* (1752) was admired
by male readers, not the least of them being Dr. Johnson.[55]
So far as the evolution of the novel was concerned, Madame
de Lafayette's *La Princesse de Clèves* (1677) marked a turn-
ing away from Mlle de Scudéry's concentration on the ex-
ternalities of life (chiefly public conversation) to the interior
world of private thoughts and feelings.[56] Perhaps it was not
irrelevant to its success that *La Princesse de Clèves* was
scarcely one-twentieth the length of Mlle de Scudéry's ten
volumes.

   In these ways, *Le Grand Cyrus* was as subversive in lit-
erary politics as it was in literary form. It was a novelistic
equivalent of Machiavelli's *Prince*; while it lasted, it was
just as controversial. The letters of the Englishwoman Dor-

othy Osborne to her future husband Sir William Temple (1652–1654) show how one reader could live out in her own life the romance which Madeleine de Scudéry's characters enacted.[57] She approved especially of the episodes based on Panthea and Abradatas (*Le Grand Cyrus*, 5.1); here was a lady exacting in her search for the ideal lover (*l'honnête homme*) who would devote himself to her and give undivided service. The point of her enthusiasm would not have been lost on her future husband, Sir William. Her sense of self and her expectations of her future husband were frankly strategic matters, inspired by the example of Mlle de Scudéry's fiction.[58]

Le Grand Cyrus marked the last important stage of the *Cyropaedia*'s influence on the literate world. After the seventeenth century, with ever greater frequency, readers of Xenophon tended to respond more and more to one or the other of the two strains that had first appeared in antiquity, and then resurfaced in the Renaissance: they might recommend Cyrus's education for personal moral instruction, or they might dwell on such romance as they could find. The most bizarre of all readings of Xenophon was a remarkable book which attempted to do both these things at once.

Although he published *Les Voyages de Cyrus* first under his French name in 1727, André-Michel Ramsay was born Andrew Michael Ramsay in 1686 and educated at Oxford. He was converted to Catholicism by Fénelon, and from 1724 was tutor to the sons of the Pretender. He made his literary debut by writing a *Discourse on Epic Poetry*, a spirited answer to some criticisms of his master's prose epic *Télémaque*, a moral epic that begins with Calypso's asking Telemachus about his life, continues with his experiencing adventures very like his father's, and concludes with reunion of father and son in Book 24. This story of a virtuous son of a virtuous father was immensely popular throughout the eighteenth century. *Télémaque* inspired Ramsay to undertake a similar project. Just as his master Fénelon had taken advantage of Homer's silence about much of Telemachus' life, so he now proposed to take advantage of a similar silence in the *Cyropaedia*. If you read Xenophon in a way he never meant to be read, it is possible to compute that he says nothing about Cyrus's life from the age of sixteen to the age of forty. Ramsay resolved to fill that gap by writing another narrative about Cyrus, which would be filled with everything Cyrus did between the ages of sixteen and forty that Xenophon had not bothered to narrate. To underscore how closely the new story of Cyrus followed its original, *Les Voyages de Cyrus* was divided into eight books.[59]

Ramsay had all the zeal of a convert to a true religion. His principal aim was to combat atheism and deism. To do this he wrote something his readers found "more a systematic history than a novel." The *Bibliothèque Universelle des Romans* discussed *Les Voyages de Cyrus*, but only to demonstrate why it does not belong there.[60] The anonymous reviewer began by observing that M. Ramsay had forgotten one must sacrifice often to the Graces.[61] He knew the ancient and modern romances reasonably well. In Book I, while Cyrus is at the court of his grandfather Astyages, he meets Princess Cassandane, a distant relation of Cyrus and a daughter of King Farnaspes of the Achemenids. Cyrus has the opportunity of meeting her often, and he gets to know her well. Her conversation does much to influence the character of the young prince, and she gives him a *délicatesse* which he had never known before. (One suspects her of having been schooled in Paris, and of knowing Fénelon.) Of course Cyrus falls in love with her. In this version, his uncle Cyaxares is the same age as Cyrus, and falls in love with Cassandane, too. When Cambyses hears of all this, he summons his son home to Persia, and Farnaspes (on Cyaxares' side) orders Cassandane to stay at Ecbatana. The grief-stricken lovers are at last reunited, after they have confessed all to Cyrus's mother Mandane. By the end of the first book, they have married. Readers of the Greek romances will see the problem at once: Ramsay has removed one of the most essential goals of a romance. In fact, the next seven books of the journeys of Cyrus have nothing novelistic in them. As Ramsay explained in a subsequent public letter answering his critics,

The design of my work is to turn the atheist into a deist,
the deist into a Christian, and the Christian into a Catho-
lic. Aside from atheism, into which I have never fallen, I
have myself passed through all of these degrees.[62]

To achieve this aim, he has Cyrus go on many voyages
which give him an opportunity to depict the religion, mor-
als, and politics of all the countries which Cyrus visits. He
also wants to describe the principal advances in thought and
politics that occur in Egypt, Greece, and the Near East. Even
so, something still more radical was needed if these voyages
were to advance beyond antiquity. Accordingly, in Book 3
when Cyrus returns from his journey with Cassandane and
some satraps, Cambyses asks him to undertake still more
journeys so that he will be the wise ruler the people in Asia
want for their king when his time to rule arrives. Cyrus obe-
diently proceeds to interview Zoroaster, Chilon, Periander,
Solon, Anaximander, Pythagoras, and the Hebrew prophet
Daniel. (Illustration 4.)

Ramsay's public found all of this anything but novel—
ingénieux voyages théologiques, as the *Bibliothèque*'s re-
viewer put it.[63] This theological odyssey culminates in Book
8 with Cyrus at Babylon learning the religion and the cus-
toms of the Israelites. The ensemble is not a success. It
combines romantic material with theological disputations
of such unrelieved gravity that the whole thing breaks
down, asymmetrically, between Book 1 and Books 2–8.
Ramsay read the *Cyropaedia* as something of a novel, to be
sure, but even more as a sermon.

The tendency of the eighteenth century was to read Xen-
ophon as a religious moralist; it was carried even further in
the translation of Maurice Ashley, younger brother to the
Third Earl of Shaftesbury.[64] A contemporary of Ramsay, he
saw Xenophon as a purely religious man, and dedicated his
translation of 1732 not to a prince but to his sister. Ashley
lived on the fringes of power and public life. Although he
strives to give due weight to the political and military as-
pects of Cyrus's education, by temperament he was far
more inclined to stress the careful religious ceremonies Cy-

4. Cyrus Interviewing the Prophet Daniel. Frontispiece to *Les Voyages de Cyrus* (1728).

rus conducts as prelude to every undertaking. A search for
relevance to contemporary English religious life is very pro-
nounced:

> The few instructions with respect to the established reli-
> gion and the priests of those days are not unapplicable to
> our present times. Nor can it be said but that the spirit of
> piety and deference to superior powers which runs through
> the whole, though blended with the established rights,
> does in some measure relate to real religion, and must
> needs be pleasing to those who have a sense of it.

To this translator, Xenophon seems "extremely religious."
He commends Cambyses' long interview with Cyrus (1.6)
as a remarkable example of religious education. Note that
this is the same passage that inspired one of the most noto-
rious of all chapters in Machiavelli: the argument that a
prince may use any kind of lie or trick to gain an advantage
over his enemies.[65] A religious man given to retirement
from public life would naturally be attracted to the *Cyro-
paedia*. So at least Maurice Ashley claimed for himself. To
him, Xenophon was a central author in the Christian's clas-
sical canon.

> There is indeed a plainness and simplicity in this piece of
> Xenophon that may seem childish and contemptible to
> some judgments. But what our Saviour said to his disciples
> when he placed a child in the midst of them (Matthew
> 18.3, 19.14), "Unless you become as little children, you
> shall not enter into the Kingdom of Heaven" and what he
> says in another place, "When his eye is simple, the whole
> body is full of light" (Matthew 6.22) may be applied to the
> disposition of the mind with respect to all other good
> knowledge as well as with respect to religion. Your disposi-
> tion of mind is thus chaste and simple, and you therefore
> will perhaps not be displeased with this.[66]

With the *Cyropaedia* now a handbook not for the education
of a Christian prince, but only for a Christian education
simply conceived, Cyrus and his *paideia* were indeed fit
models for the *Tristra-paideia*.

As Xenophon's presence in literature was reduced to

zero, so was his standing in the eyes of historians. In his *History of Greece,* George Grote relied on the *Anabasis* and *Hellenica* for a narrative of events following the conclusion of Thucydides' history. There was no other comparable source on which to draw.[67] Even then he supplemented Xenophon everywhere with correction and amplification, never taking anything Xenophon reported at face value. The *Cyropaedia* played no great role in his history of the seventh century B.C. Historians since Grote have carried this tendency further. They are distinguished from him by their inclination to believe Xenophon only with heavy qualification, or not at all.[68]

In these ways Xenophon disappeared from the center of the European literary scene. The firmer ideas became about what history and philosophy should be, the less relevant he was to the evolution of either field. Even poets and novelists, once free to exploit the *Cyropaedia* any way that seemed feasible, gradually turned away from it. At a time when Vergil or Euripides could be despised or dismissed, what role could Xenophon play?[69]

Even in his diminished state, Xenophon was far from being the least important of the classical writers. Philologists established critical texts and found a place for the *Cyropaedia* in modern histories of Greek literature. The only complete commentary in English remains the one by Reverend Hubert A. Holden; his and other editions were aimed at undergraduates and other students in the earlier stages of learning Greek.[70] Until the Oxford Classical Text of E. C. Marchant, the German Hellenist Ludwig Dindorf dominated the terrain almost exclusively.[71] The years immediately before the First World War marked a kind of watershed for the *Cyropaedia.* Marchant's Oxford text and Gemoll's edition of 1912 were the editions most readily available, and so they remained, with only minor changes, until 1971. Then a new Budé edition begun by Marcel Bizos and completed by Eduard Delebecque in 1978 reexamined Xenophon's Greek text fundamentally. Beautifully produced as such texts usually are, the Budé edition also underscores the basic irony that was our point of departure in this chapter's examination of *The Education of Cyrus*: it is a classic that seems destined to remain as unread as ever, by just as wide an audience as ever.

Marchant had already wondered whether it was possible to recover Xenophon's Greek at all.[72] The two Budé editors came to the same conclusion. There are so many variants in the manuscripts of the *Cyropaedia*, and the possible readings are so easily interchangeable, and so rarely contradictory or implausible, that one is tempted to ask if Xenophon's own text has not vanished entirely. The variations often turn on synonyms: for example, how can one decide the rightness of one's choice, when the choice lies between "longing" and "love" (*epithumian, erôta*)? "Very much" and "not a little" (*pampolu, ou mikron*)? "Astyages" and "grandfather" (*ho Astyagês, ho pappos*)? "He held the kingdom" and "he took the empire" (*basileian esche, archên elabe*)?[73] The basic difference between the new Budé edition of the *Cyropaedia* and its Oxonian predecessor is that what Marchant rejected and placed in his critical apparatus, the Budé editors now placed in their text; at the same time, they demoted what Marchant had once printed as Xenophon's text, into an alternate reading that now appeared in their new critical apparatus.[74]

4

The present view of the *Cyropaedia* as an elusive puzzle in textual criticism may well change. In the meantime, there are certain aspects of Xenophon's work that we can address with more confidence. First there is the importance of the *Cyropaedia* for history itself—even though it is very clearly not a history. It is as enlightening as any ancient work we have on the formation of the imperial mind, that imagination that creates empires and manipulates others for grand purposes.[75] As we shall presently see, Xenophon himself was obsessed with the question of leadership, and he searched for his ideal ruler in many other works, not only the *Cyropaedia*. Would-be rulers and their subjects found much to engage them here. But it is not necessary for us to share the aims of either Xenophon or his intended audience to appreciate how this text works. To adapt a comment Raymond Aron made about Clausewitz, one need not be an ancient monarch, a Renaissance prince, or an ambitious courtier to share in the adventure of this gifted monarch and the writer who created him.[76]

A second reason for recovering Xenophon's imperial fiction is its influence on novelists and other literary figures. This influence was in its own way as substantial as its impact on a political thinker like Machiavelli. Xenophon was at the center of major developments in political and literary history.[77] Compared with contemporaries and predecessors like Plato and Thucydides, he is not now judged their equal. From another perspective, he is as important as they, and as influential. He appealed to the Hellenistic and Roman worlds and then to the Renaissance because he wrote works that were genuinely prophetic of things to come, both in history and in literature.[78] The originality of the *Cyropaedia* and the boldness of its conception are what most recommend it for reconsideration, and for new readings.

Then there is the matter of power and illusion is a familiar theme in politics and literature.[79] In a wide range of contexts—ancient Rome as well as Elizabethan England—leaders create power on the grand scale by the invention of fictive roles that persuade their future supporters or subjects that their best interests will be served by following the person who creates such roles. Sometimes such a monarch or national leader will be larger than life, more magnificent than ordinary persons; but if democratic or republican sentiments need to be swayed, the leader's role will then be to play the ordinary person, the unexceptionable, the unthreatening. The range of roles runs from leaders as diverse as Augustus, Alexander, and Elizabeth i, to Franklin Roosevelt and Lincoln. The *Cyropaedia* is an illuminating text about any leader who creates such power—even leaders who we can be reasonably sure never studied it at all.[80] What matters in any regime is a leader who knows how to manipulate its power structures. This is the art which Xenophon teaches.

In the course of achieving his own aims, Xenophon also managed to achieve others. Forster's description of the novelist fits him exactly: he is a faker and a cheater, as devious as the character he creates.[81] He does not say that he is writing fiction.[82] Nor does he claim to be writing history. There is never a hint of verification or methodology anywhere in the *Cyropaedia*.[83] He does not name himself, like Herodotus and Thucydides; he prefers most of the time to use an impersonal "we" and a rare "I."[84] Under the guise of describing the deeds (*praxeis*) of his hero and of reporting what "we have found out and think we know" (*eputhometha kai êisthêsthai dokoumen*, 1.1.6), Xenophon creates a Persia and a Cyrus that doubtless owe something to actual fact and personal experience, but even more to the powers of Xenophon's imagination. Character and the sequence of events are fashioned with complete freedom. At the few points where it is possible to compare Xenophon's arrangement of things with the accounts of others, he shows himself to be a writer capable of an extreme, if not indeed perverse, departure from his predecessors.[85] In these ways, Xenophon refashions the world as he finds it. To us, with hindsight, he perhaps most resembles a novelist, yet he maintains a vague profile to the end, never actually declaring *what* it is he is writing, in terms of genre. He exploits our disposition to take prose narratives for granted and believe what an author says. Readers who understand the game will find much to learn, as well as much to amuse them. Unknowing and literal-minded persons are, after all, the chief victims of Cyrus's imperial designs. We observe his manipulation of them with the same pleasure with which we watch a well-made comedy or melodrama. But if Xenophon's readers do not understand his particular game, as they often have not, or if they do, but choose not to play, they may be inclined to dismiss Cyrus and his education altogether. As this account of its reception suggests, the only victim of Xenophon's imperial fiction will then be the *Cyropaedia* itself.

CHAPTER TWO

The Rise of a Novel

There are authors whose end is to tell what has happened.
Mine, if I could attain it, would be to talk about what
can happen.

Montaigne, *Of the Powers of the Imagination*

Novels and romances are by definition such original works that one of the most characteristic responses they have generated in critics of this and the last century is an overpowering desire to explain where they come from. We want to account for the new, to make it less new and more manageable, by demonstrating that a novel is not simply original, not merely the work of individual talent, but the product of social or economic movements, literary exemplars or rivalries, audiences or readers, and many other external factors. All of these things conspire to influence writers of fiction. It is especially gratifying to critics to discover forces at work of which the writers themselves were not even aware. This impulse to write genealogy puts writers in their place, which is not the place they devised, but our place, defined by a broader vision that embraces much more than the world a novelist creates. We can do this as easily to Tolstoy and Cervantes as to the author of the *Cyropaedia*. Only the ephemeral quality of what results should give anyone pause. Somehow this writing about writing does not seem to last quite so long as the writing on which it depends, and which it says it "describes." The reason for this turn of fate is not hard to discover. To judge is not to create.

These considerations underlie the following chapter, which is the second part of our approach to Cyrus and his education. This is neither a sketch of Xenophon's life nor a survey of his works. The *Cyropaedia* is the center of gravity to which everything is drawn. The possible external forces at work on the creator of the *Cyropaedia* are well known, and I shall rehearse most of them for the benefit of those who do not know them. But what interests me just as much are the forces within Xenophon that led him to undertake such a project. Now that we know how some of our predecessors read the *Cyropaedia*, why did Xenophon write it?

In a general way we might observe that much of his career as a writer was devoted to the achievements and the training of ideal leaders of one sort or another. So far as Xenophon was concerned, the leadership of one able person seemed crucial in both public and private life. The search for an ideal leader carried him through many different modes of writing: the philosophical dialogue, the war memoir and the philosophical memoir, history, the technical treatise, the encomium. In the *Cyropaedia* his inquiry into leadership led him into what we now recognize most easily as fiction—a romance, a romanticized biography, an early version of the *Bildungsroman*. Whatever anachronistic taxonomy we may devise for the early history of prose fiction, the *Cyropaedia* quite clearly was meant to carry on this lifelong project in a new mode. Such is one answer to the question, why did he write it?

But another answer to this question has always been before us as well, and it is from Xenophon himself. He gives his reasons for writing the *Cyropaedia* in the prologue to the work (1.1). The prologue is as coherent and as complete an account of the origins and purpose of a text as any that has ever been written. Indeed, it is disarmingly informative. If the importance of the prologue were self-evident, it would not be necessary to turn to a commentary on it; unfortunately it is necessary. Consider this chapter then as nothing but a gloss on the long prologue to the *Cyropaedia*. What follows will not discount well-known theories about the origins of the work, which should not be ignored in any case. The point is simply that none of them is as illuminating to the reader of the *Cyropaedia* as are the comments of Xenophon himself.

I

One long book usually inspires the writing of another. This can happen when their authors are friends, and it is even more likely to happen when they are not. As soon as Plato began to publish the *Republic*, Xenophon is alleged to have set to writing about Cyrus the Great of Persia to correct Plato's idealism with an old soldier's common sense. The notion of a rivalry between the two began in antiquity and has continued to the present day.[1] If there was such a rivalry, Plato won, and by a wide margin. A few historians of Greek literature read the *Cyropaedia*. If they refer to it at all, it is as "*Platon corrigé par Xénophon,*" Xenophon's correction of Plato, a practical handbook for the unphilosophical man who would be king.[2] Xenophon may also have been inspired rather than provoked by the publication of Antisthenes' *Cyrus*; Antisthenes was yet another disciple of Socrates.[3] Unlike the *Republic*, the fragments of Antisthenes' *Cyrus* do not permit us to affirm or deny that he gave Xenophon his theme. These developments, and Isocrates' Panhellenism, suggest that the questions of an ideal *basileus* and *basileia* (ideal king and ideal kingship) were lively topics in Socratic circles, and not only in those circles.[4] Whether the *Cyropaedia* was inspired by a desire to emulate Plato is another question.

At first glance, a battle of Socratic books seems a plausible scenario. Like Plato, Xenophon wrote an *Apology* and a *Symposium*. Both dialogues are shorter than Plato's works of the same title, and very different in character.[5] A number of parallels have been perceived between the *Republic* and the *Cyropaedia*, possibly because Xenophon was replying to Plato, possibly also because he begins with a discussion of tyranny, democracy, and the organization of an ideal state.

Both works are about the rule of one person, and not the rule of a tyrant, but in most respects they use quite different means to create a government Greece had never known. Xenophon removes his narrative to a Persian setting, with a monarch remote in both time and place serving as his paradigm of the ruler. In any case, the *Cyropaedia* is not a dialectical response to the *Republic*.[6]

Consider the way each work treats a familiar theme in Greek ethics. Cyrus is fond of invoking the moral, that it is right to do good to one's friends and harm to one's enemies.[7] His father Cambyses teaches him this lesson (1.6.28), and it is Cyrus's last precept to his own children: "Remember also this last word of mine: if you do good to your friends, you will also be able to punish your enemies" (8.7.28). These last words of Cyrus are one of the first notions about justice to be considered in the *Republic*; there Socrates does not so much reject the idea as examine it with the fluidity that dialectic permits.[8] Polemarchus refers approvingly to a saying he attributes to Simonides, that justice is to speak the truth and give back what one takes. Socrates gets him to agree that Simonides means justice is doing good to friends and harm to enemies (332d). But as the conversation proceeds, he and Polemarchus next discover that justice is, alternatively, useless in the use of each person, and useful in its uselessness; that it is nothing serious if it is useful for useless things; that it is just to injure friends, when they are bad friends, and just to help enemies, when they are good; and finally, that a wise man like Simonides could not have said such a thing, but rather some tyrant like Periander, or a rich man who has a high opinion of what he can do (333d–336a).

Cyrus is quite capable of engaging in this kind of discourse when it suits his imperial designs.[9] Otherwise, dialectical scrutiny of the principles people think they live by is something in which he does not care to indulge. So far as we can tell, neither did the author who created him. In terms of its ethical theory and practice, the *Cyropaedia* concludes by approving of the very issues the *Republic* first questions. It answers the *Republic* in the sense that it pro-

ceeds as if the *Republic* never existed. In most respects the
two works might more accurately be described as ships
passing in the *Attic Nights* of Aulus Gellius and other an-
cient testimonia.

Yet even if the exchange was mostly imaginary, or even
entirely in the minds of later readers, Xenophon was ulti-
mately a loser. As we have seen, however important a role
the *Cyropaedia* played in western intellectual history, it has
been a marginal text since the eighteenth century, if not
earlier. For us, that status is simply underscored by invidi-
ous comparisons with the *Republic*, the very book that sup-
posedly inspired Xenophon to write in reply.

The *Cyropaedia* was not a marginal text for Xenophon.
No other work he wrote is so compendious, none is so evoc-
ative of his other writings. Its enigmatic mixture of fiction
and history released him from the frustrations and compro-
mises that he faced in other, less baffling works. Nothing he
wrote fits easily into contemporary canons of classical his-
tory, philosophy, or literature. And in a career distinguished
by such originality, the *Cyropaedia* proved to be the most
innovative work of all—literally novel.

For these reasons, while the formation of the writer of
the *Cyropaedia* is an old-fashioned theme, it is nonetheless
needed for our approach to the subject. As Xenophon's pu-
tative rivalries with other Socratics may suggest, there is at
present an abiding opinion that he could not write anything
without the stimulus of other and better writers; thus, the
Cyropaedia appeared because of the publication of the *Re-
public*, or possibly Antisthenes' *Cyrus*.

It is more accurate to realize that Xenophon may have
thought well of the works of others, but that he thought
even better of his own. He is the kind of writer who draws
his critics sooner or later into writing about all his works,
rather than any single one.[10] In part this is because he did
not pass neatly from one completed book to the next. He
had a protean imagination, working simultaneously in what
we now regard as different literary forms.[11] And in part it is
also because he was disposed to say the same thing, in dif-
ferent ways, for different purposes. He appears to have had

several projects in progress at once, and he liked to revise and even reject what he had already published.[12] As he was writing the *Cyropaedia*, he may also have been revising or adding to the *Hellenica, Oeconomicus*, and *Memorabilia*. In a sense, his works were in progress as long as he was. And as he neared the end of his career, he turned to writing fiction. The reader of the *Cyropaedia* will not be harmed by a tendentious enquiry into the literary career of the author who produced it. The *Cyropaedia* is not *Platon corrigé par Xénophon*. It is *Xénophon corrigé par Xénophon*.

2

For those searching for the origins of the *Cyropaedia* elsewhere than in Plato's *Republic*, Xenophon's other book with a Persian setting has always seemed a logical place to begin. There are many similarities between the Cyrus of the *Anabasis* and the Cyrus of the *Cyropaedia*.[13] In his summation of Cyrus's character, Xenophon himself points to the parallel: of all the Persians who lived after Cyrus the Great, Cyrus the Younger was the most kingly and most deserving of rule (1.9). It is tempting to infer from what Xenophon says that the association between the older and younger Cyrus later turned into a literary project in its own right, with the Cyrus of the *Cyropaedia* a successful (because fictional) revision of the Cyrus Xenophon knew. In the *Anabasis*, memory of past events shapes the story; in the *Cyropaedia*, Xenophon's imagination is freed to invent what he desires. So the theory goes. It needs some refinement. An unqualified association with the *Anabasis* can affect our reading of the *Cyropaedia* as much as the association with the *Republic*, and in an equally unfavorable way.

As a fictionalization of the life of Cyrus in the *Anabasis*, the *Cyropaedia* seems to make everything that went wrong in history turn out miraculously right through fiction. From the perspective of the *Anabasis*, the *Cyropaedia* seems a flight from reality, an abdication of the role Xenophon had so ably filled in the *Anabasis* when he tried to tell what happened to him and the ten thousand Greeks. If Cyrus in the *Anabasis* is a Cyrus of fact, in the *Cyropaedia* he becomes merely a Cyrus of fancy. Here is the hero of Gibbon's vague and languid romance.

Naturally Xenophon's service in Persia under Cyrus and Agesilaus furnished much of the local color of the *Cyropaedia*—though it is relevant to note that it has nothing like the exotic quality of the lands or the peoples so vividly reported in the *Anabasis*. Possibly because the main focus is on Cyrus and his relationship with other people, the ethnography and topography of the surrounding world recede into the background in the *Cyropaedia*. There is a connection between the *Anabasis* and the *Cyropaedia*, but it operates at a more interesting level than simple literary opportunism.

The parallels between Cyrus the Great and Cyrus the Younger do not explain Xenophon's impulse to write the *Cyropaedia*, because Xenophon himself, not Cyrus, is the central character of that war memoir.[14] In spite of its generous praise of Cyrus, the first book of the *Anabasis* offers a portrait of a man who was a potentially great leader. After the first book, Cyrus and all his promise are only forgotten dreams. Perhaps the calculated objectivity of Xenophon's third-person narration encourages us to think that this self-effacing narrator plays a limited role in the story. But this authorial detachment is a rhetorical strategy: it is an imitation of Thucydides, comparable also to the kind of narrative technique Aristotle so much admires in Homer.[15] Caesar would find it useful to adapt this style to his own war memoirs, the *Commentaries* on the Gallic Wars.[16]

Xenophon himself comes to the center of his narrative only in Book 3 of the *Anabasis*. Some have taken this as a sign of the late composition of Books 1 and 2. Possibly so. If this was Xenophon's original design, however, he makes one of the most well-calculated authorial entrances in literature.[17] Several of his ancient admirers certainly read him this way.[18] His personal story is all the more powerful because of the careful detachment with which it is told. He is brought face to face in the most direct way with the consequences of living in a world governed by men like Cyrus, who is now dead and beyond caring about the consequences of the adventures he once undertook. Serving with Cyrus made Xenophon confront his own mortality at a precocious age, and the experience wonderfully concentrated Xenophon's mind. It is not Socrates, Cyrus, or any of the generals and princes who populate the *Hellenica, Anabasis,* or *Memorabilia,* who has to face the prospect of imminent death, but, according to Xenophon writing about Xenophon, Xenophon himself.

> Why am I lying in bed? The night is passing. As soon as dawn comes the enemy will probably be here. If we fall into the King's power, what is to prevent us from seeing the most terrible things happening, from suffering all kinds of tortures and from being put to death in shame? But instead of anybody bothering to take any steps for our defence, we are lying here as though we could lead the life of leisure. What city then do I expect will furnish the general to tend to all this? Am I waiting to grow a little older? I shall never be any older at all if I hand myself over to the enemy today. (3.1.13–14)

In the *Memorabilia,* Xenophon writes about this kind of experience in a more theoretical way; there Socrates and Aristippus debate whether or not the art of ruling others is a necessary attainment for every person (2.1.8–9, 12–13). In the *Anabasis,* Xenophon has no time to debate the matter at all. He has to translate his nocturnal reflections into public action at once.

> But perhaps there are others who feel the same as I do: by the gods, let's not wait for other people to come and call upon us to do great deeds, but instead let's be the ones to summon the rest to courage and honor. Show yourselves the bravest of captains, with more of a right to be generals than the generals themselves. As for me, if you are willing to take the lead in all this, I am ready to follow you. But if you want me to be your leader, I'll make no excuses about my age. I think I am already grown up enough to act in my own defence. (3.1.24–25)

The Greeks have no more choice than Xenophon does. They rally behind him, and the march is underway. The army fights its way through the encircling Persian army and other barbarian tribes, through the winter passes of central Anatolia, to the sea.

The famous cry *thalatta thalatta* ("the sea the sea," 4.7) marks the resolution of Xenophon's first problem and leads him straight to his second. His refugee army has become the most powerful military force on the coast of the Euxine Sea. Once the furious concentration on survival is gone, he has time to think about the uses of that power. He thinks it would be a fine thing to found a city there and gain more territory and more power for Greece (5.6). This idealistic scheme might have been profitable, but as a political move, it was naively conceived. Xenophon paid too little attention to the disposition of the men he was trying to lead. The soothsayer Silanus charges that he has invented the idea for his own profit. Half the army is disposed to return to Greece; others hope to remain where they are. Xenophon's good intentions get lost in the recrimination and resentment that suddenly boil up in the ranks. The affair turns into a trial of Xenophon where past benefactions count for nothing. He defends himself well enough, and shortly afterwards, the army begins to see the advantage of having a single commander rather than the coalition of officers that has led them to safety. They ask Xenophon to lead them. He says he was inclined to do so, both for his own advantage and theirs. Sacrifice to the gods indicated otherwise, and he refused (6.1). Even this refusal does not free him from the frustrations and dangers of ruling others.

Near the end of the *Anabasis*, Xenophon and his men are in an uneasy alliance with King Seuthes of Thrace. Spartan envoys arrive with the proposal that the Greeks join Sparta in an attack on Tissaphernes and the Persian empire. They say the pay promised would be substantial. Xenophon is attacked yet again for political and personal reasons. This time his disillusionment is total. The glorious achievement of the march out of Persia is as remote and dead as Cyrus the Younger himself.

Whenever we were in difficulties, you with your remark-
able memories, this was not how you felt. Then you used
to call me "father," and promised that you would always
remember me as your benefactor. (7.6.37–38)

By the end of the *Anabasis*, Xenophon discovers that what
matters in command is not so much what one does for
others, as what they perceive one has done. The attempt to
maintain a distinction between truth and illusion in the ex-
ercise of political power is amusingly beside the point. Save
for his eloquence and the probable fact that he was as good
a leader as he says he was, Xenophon's hard work for his
men could just as easily have amounted to nothing. Com-
manding the army of the ten thousand Greeks introduced
him to the frustrating art of political manipulation as well
as the art of war.[19] At the beginning of a lifetime spent ob-
serving and sometimes participating in political affairs,
Xenophon discovered that men will oppose no one so
quickly as the person they think has designs on ruling
them. Reflection on this enduring truth of political life is
the point of departure for the narrator of the *Cyropaedia*,
not a desire to recover whatever it was that Cyrus the
Younger had lost at Cunaxa some forty years before.

3

The beginning and end of the *Anabasis* are instructive
about Xenophon's originality as a writer. His narrative leaps
into the midst of things, with an account of the events in
the Persian royal family that led up to the expedition of Cy-
rus and the disaster at Cunaxa. Xenophon himself emerges
as a central character in his narrative of the march of the
Ten Thousand only at the point where he begins to play an
important role. The *Anabasis* ends when he leaves the
army. The economy of its design allows for as much as we
need to know about his personal involvement, and nothing
more.

When Xenophon undertook to write a general history of
his times, this kind of coherence in narrative design was not
so easily achieved. The fourth century is notorious for its

confusing political and social turmoil. It was an age when Xenophon and many other writers were searching for the right king. Demosthenes awoke early to the realization that Philip of Macedon might succeed in becoming that king. Unlike Isocrates, the ardent champion of Philip's ascendancy over Greece, Xenophon did not live to see Philip's success.[20]

The work we know as the *Hellenica* is Xenophon's chronicle of these events. Its contours are fundamentally different from those of the *Anabasis*. Xenophon begins by finishing Thucydides' defined period of the Peloponnesian War (431–404), and ends with the battle of Mantinea in 362, a battle which in his view and also in the opinion of later historians was singularly inconclusive. He may have written a preface which somehow bridged the gap between what Thucydides left unfinished, and the point where he begins.[21] As it stands, the opening is not really an opening at all, but a continuation of another writer's narrative:

> After these things, not many days later, Thymochares arrived from Athens with a few ships, and the Spartans and Athenians immediately fought another naval action in which the Spartans, under the command of Agesandridas, were victorious. (1.1.1)

The immediate events to which "after these things" (*meta de tauta*) refers remain obscure. Thucydides' history breaks off in the middle of a sentence recounting the Persian satrap Tissaphernes and his activities near the Hellespont: "He went first to Ephesus where he made a sacrifice to Artemis" (8.109). But Xenophon's general aim is clear enough: he is writing a continuation of Thucydides' history.[22] Historiographers have been dubious about the result.[23] I would like to stress here only one aspect of this project.

Writing about his dramatic but incoherent world seems to have frustrated Xenophon at two levels. Not only was it hard for him to develop a coherent theme in his chronicles of political and military events; he found it equally difficult to create a text that itself had coherent literary form. If the *Hellenica* plunges *in medias res*, it closes just as abruptly;

at issue are the crises of Greek political life that seemed to have no perceivable beginning or end. As in Tacitus or Sallust, two writers who knew this work very well, it is often the style of people that attracts our interest as much as anything they accomplish, or fail to accomplish.[24]

Few episodes conclude as satisfyingly as young Xenophon's service in the *Anabasis*. Sometimes justice is served. Dercylidas the Spartan punishes Meidias for the murder of Mania, his mother-in-law, and her young son (3.1.14–27). More typically, the best people of the time cannot alter the course of events, and some of the worst earn ironic praise for their style. As the tyrant Theramenes is dragged off to his execution, he gives a lover's toast to his enemy Critias with his cup of hemlock. Xenophon intervenes for editorial comment:

> Of course, I am not unaware that these remarks are not
> really worth recording, but I do think it admirable in the
> man that even when death was hanging over him his spirit
> lost neither self-control nor witty playfulness. (2.3.56)

Style, or the lack of it. When a corrupt Spartan Euphron is assassinated at Thebes, there is a perfunctory law-and-order speech from the prosecution (7.3.6), but a far more interesting one from one of his assassins. The defense consists entirely of an eloquent *catalogue raisonné* of Euphron's vices. The Thebans acquit the murderers, in what seems a fitting end to the story of Euphron. Then Xenophon undercuts his tidy conclusion with another editorial comment:

> Euphron's own citizens thought of him as a good man and
> brought his body back and buried it in the market place,
> and they honor him as the founder of their city. And in-
> deed, it seems to be the case that most people call their
> benefactors "good men." (7.3.12)

The account of these two deaths is notably ambivalent. Basic terms of moral discourse such as "good" and "bad" become a source of ironic confusion when a tyrant can be admired for the style of his death, and a corrupt official of no consequence can be alternately condemned and praised by people who speak the same language.

Describing this world affords some grim pleasures. One of Xenophon's more complex characterizations is Jason of Pherae. He has many talents, but self-knowledge and self-restraint are not among them. Xenophon underscores his failure to sense the limits of power, first by emphasizing Jason's greatness—which might also be printed Jason's "greatness." As so often in Xenophon, the touch is not a light one.

> When he returned to Thessaly, he was a great man indeed, both because he had been made *Tagos* [Lord] of Thessaly and because he controlled a great many mercenaries, both infantry and cavalry, and because these forces had been trained to the highest pitch of efficiency. He was greater still in the number of his allies, many being already allied with him and others being anxious to do so, too. Considering that he was not taken lightly he was the greatest man of his time. (6.4.28)

This appraisal is a significant variation of Xenophon's usual summations of character. Whereas he praises and criticizes the Greek generals and Cyrus after their deaths (*Anabasis*, 1.9, 2.6), here he underscores Jason's power before his fall in order to make the ironic reversal even more forceful. Jason's impiety at Delphi brings about a peripety as sudden as the climax of a tragedy:

> Then this great man with all his designs for so many great things had just finished holding a review and inspection of the cavalry from Pherae, and was taking his seat, and was giving his answers to those who came to him with any request, when seven young men came up to him pretending that they had some quarrel among themselves, and they struck him down, and they killed him. (6.4.31)

It is also as contrived. One long sentence accomplishes the complete undoing of Jason.[25] It begins with "this great man" (*têlikoutos*) and ends with the double verbs "is cut down and is killed" (*aposphattetai kai katakoptetai*). Xenophon's satisfaction at this sudden reversal of Jason's fortune is scarcely concealed. The story of Jason then trails off into the predictable progress of a tyranny, with his brother Tisiphonus on the throne at the time when Xenophon is writing (6.4.37).

The battle of Mantinea is the culmination of the *Hellenica*. It is also the end of Xenophon's efforts to write a general history of his times. In an uncanny echo of the death of Cyrus the Younger at Cunaxa, Epaminondas of Thebes conceived a brilliant strategy, but was slain in the assault. His army failed to follow through with the victory he had designed, even though they had defeated a coalition of Sparta, Arcadia, Achaea, Elis, and Athens. Epaminondas' death robbed Thebes of any advantage in that victory.

> The result of this battle was just the opposite of what everyone expected it would be. Nearly the whole of Greece had been engaged on one side or the other, and everyone imagined that, if a battle was fought, the winner would become the dominant power and the losers would be their subjects. But the god so ordered things that both parties put up trophies as though they had won and neither side tried to prevent the other from doing so; both sides gave back the dead under a truce, as though they had won, and both sides received their dead under a truce, as though they had lost, both sides claimed the victory, but it cannot be said that with regard to the acquisition of new territory, or a city, or a kingdom, either side was any better off after the battle than before it; in fact, there was even more uncertainty and confusion in Greece after the battle than there had been before it. (7.5.26–27)

A sublimely despairing passage, this brings the narrative down to a situation even more hopeless than the one Athens faced at the end of the Peloponnesian War.[26] Now there is not even a clear winner or loser; if such a thing is conceivable, the future is even more uncertain than the future of Athens appeared to be in 404.

The last sentence of the *Hellenica* breaks off the narrative in a significant way:

> Let this be the end of my narrative; what happened after these things will perhaps be the concern of another. (7.5.26)

It is a sardonic invitation to the reader to attempt what Xenophon himself had tried to do in writing the *Hellenica*: to take up the thread of Greek history where a predecessor left off. Thus we come full circle to the point of reference with which we began the *Hellenica*, and we come back via the same phrase, *meta tauta*, "after these things." The puzzle of the opening sentence finds its analogue here, if not its "solution." As for Xenophon, he himself has now attained much the same status as Thucydides; that is, he also is the author of an incomplete work. There is one difference. While we can assume that death interrupted Thucydides in mid-sentence, despair silences the historian of the *Hellenica*. Its ending is a perfect reflection of the incoherent world Xenophon has tried to describe.

4

One place and one person inspired him to attempt more than chronicles of the passing scene. Sparta organized political life differently from Xenophon's native Athens. But in Athens he also found his other ideal, on the personal level. If the time and place of one's coming into being were accidents of birth, beyond individual control, the philosophical life Socrates embodied offered a way of transcending such circumstance. In Sparta and from Socrates Xenophon learned how to live the good life in both the public and private spheres.

Xenophon's enthusiasms for Sparta and Socrates do much to illuminate his impulse to write the *Cyropaedia*. Again and again the sharp contradiction of experience imposed itself on Xenophon as historian and biographer. There is everywhere a tension between what he would like to have happen, and his obligation to tell what actually did happen. Socrates was executed, the battle of Mantinea was fought, Agesilaus did die, and nothing Xenophon wrote could change these unavoidable facts. For him there is always a counterpoint between the virtues of the people he admires, and the progress of every narrative about them toward such debacles as Leuctra, Cunaxa, Mantinea, and the trial of 399.

Still, if Xenophon could not rewrite history, he could preserve what he admired in different works, with different themes. The *Constitution of the Lacedaemonians* and the encomium *Agesilaus* escape the frustration and compromise of experience and reflect on the perfection of the Spartan constitution that Lycurgus had created.

> As I was reflecting once that Sparta, though among the most thinly populated states, was the most powerful and most celebrated city in Greece, I wondered how this could have happened. But when I considered the institutions of the Spartans, I no longer wondered. (1.1.1)

This process of reflection is much like the programmatic opening of the *Cyropaedia*. What Xenophon reflects on here in the *Constitution* is essentially historical fact, not unlike the situation he reflects on in the *Anabasis* after Cunaxa.[27] However perfect Sparta may have been, its glory lay in the past. The *Constitution of the Lacedaemonians* was written with full consciousness of contemporary Sparta, whose ancient values were supposed to lift this treatise out of the merely archival. And it did. It remains an important source for legal and cultural history, but it never achieved what the *Cyropaedia* was to achieve.

An encomium of the Spartan King Agesilaus opened up a similar avenue for Xenophon's imagination. Like Isocrates in the *Evagoras*, he creates a life for his hero that has a beginning, a middle, and an end, with all his achievements marshalled in pleasing order.[28] The encomium is by its very nature relieved of the burdens history imposes on writer and subject alike. This Agesilaus can be what Xenophon wants him to be, the great man who perfectly realizes the potential of his noble birth and character. His perfection contrasts sharply with the character of the same man in the *Hellenica*. There Agesilaus is patriotic, but not swayed by the rhetoric of patriotism to rush into a battle too hastily. Although he says at more than one point that he will obey any order Sparta gives him, he is also capable of distancing himself from needlessly risky or unprofitable ventures.[29] He can even be duplicitous. When the Spartans execute a gov-

ernor who had abandoned the Acropolis in Thebes and order
mobilization for war, Agesilaus plays two roles at once: the
dutiful, submissive Spartan, and the canny politician who
refuses to risk his neck in a dubious campaign.

> Agesilaus said that it was more than forty years since he
> reached military age, and pointed out that just as other
> men of his age were no longer compelled to go on foreign
> service, so the same rule should apply to kings also. This
> was what he said, and so he did not serve on this cam-
> paign. But this was not the reason why he stayed behind.
> The real reason was that he knew very well that if he took
> command the Spartans would say that Agesilaus was turn-
> ing the state upside down because he wanted to help ty-
> rants. He therefore left them to make whatever decisions
> they liked about the whole affair. After listening to the
> men who had been driven out of Thebes after the massa-
> cre, the ephors sent out Cleombrotus on his first command
> in the middle of winter. (5.4.13–14)

This calculation reflects the compromise that actual politi-
cal life demands. However problematic the *Hellenica* may
be as a source for fourth-century history, we sense a canny
politician here who never appears in the catalogue of virtues
that is the *Agesilaus*.[30]

The other Spartan for whom Xenophon expresses great
enthusiasm is Agesilaus' brother Teleutias, admiral of the
Spartan fleet. He particularly marvels at the personal loy-
alty Teleutias was able to develop with the sailors in his
charge (5.1.3–4). One secret of Teleutias' popularity was the
care he took to see that his men were well paid and well
supplied with ships. His speech could be exchanged with
any number of Cyrus's speeches in the *Cyropaedia*.[31]

> You know well that when I command you I pray no less for
> your lives and safety than I pray for myself. As for food and
> drink you may be surprised if I tell you that I would rather
> see you supplied than myself. I swear by the gods that I
> would rather go without food myself for two days than
> have you go without for one day. (5.1.14)

Teleutias creates his hold on his men by persuading them
that he cares for them more than for himself. Whether he

really felt this way does not matter. His men performed prodigies for him, including a daring raid on the Piraeus in 388 that succeeded in disrupting the Athenian fleet.

Yet with what result? No amount of admiration for Sparta could undo the obvious fact of Leuctra. There was also an inherent limitation in being the best of the Spartans. Xenophon admires Agesilaus and his brother because they respected the limits which Spartan generals and admirals were expected to observe; but the very virtues which saved them from the fate of Alcibiades, Epaminondas, or Jason of Pherae also seem to have prevented them from being anything more than the best of their kind.[32] In the *Cyropaedia*, by contrast, Cyrus's ambitions extend to far more than being the best of the Persians.

One reason Xenophon appealed so much to the Romans and later readers at the center of power was that his ideals seemed so clearly a distillation of the practical experiences he had had and of the people he had known. Hence the vital importance of the other ideal in his intellectual and artistic life. To vindicate Socrates of the charges against him, and to preserve his teaching for posterity, Xenophon was, he says, drawn into writing a memoir of Socrates. Nothing in the *Hellenica* or the *Anabasis* quite prepares us for the text that was the result.

What we traditionally call the *Memorabilia* is Xenophon's apology of Socrates writ large.[33] It is the master text of his Socratic writings.[34] It opens with an indignant complaint about the charges against Socrates.[35]

> I have often wondered what arguments Socrates' prosecutors could ever have used to persuade the Athenians he deserved to forfeit his life to the state. For the charge against him was as follows: "Socrates is guilty of not paying respect to the gods whom the city respects, of introducing new divinities; and he is guilty of corrupting the young."
> (1.1.1)

The first two chapters of Book 1 are a systematic refutation of these charges; the procedure is reminiscent of a courtroom defense by an Attic orator like Lysias. But then (1.3) Xenophon turns to an account of Socrates' words and deeds,

a series of biographical sketches that continues to the end
of Book 4, where he ends with an account of the death of
Socrates and a final eulogy for his teacher and friend:

> Of all those who knew Socrates and what he was like, all
> those who seek virtue continue to long for him even now,
> for he was most helpful to them in the quest for virtue. But
> to me, as I describe what he was like, he was so reverent
> that he could do nothing without counsel from the gods; so
> just that he never hurt anyone at all, but was immensely
> helpful to all who dealt with him; so self-controlled that
> he never chose pleasures in place of something better; so
> prudent that he never erred in distinguishing what was bet-
> ter from what was worse, and he never needed anyone's ad-
> vice but was independent in his decisions about good and
> evil; he was skilled in arguing and in defining good and
> evil, skilled in testing others, showing them their mis-
> takes, and urging them toward virtue and true nobility; he
> seemed to be what the noblest and happiest man would be.
> And if anyone is not satisfied with this, let him compare
> the character of other men with what I have described, and
> then let him judge. (4.8.11)

This peroration is similar to the conclusion of the *Apology*
(34). If the *Memorabilia* begins as an apology (in the original
sense of a formal defense), it ends as an encomium.

Between these polarities of indignation and praise lie all
the recollections that constitute the *Memorabilia*. Some-
times cited as an important precursor of biography,[36] Xeno-
phon's memoir of Socrates just as easily anticipates the
infinitely expandable contours of romance.[37] Socrates' per-
sonality had as many facets as the sum of the people he met.
No one person was able to draw out all of his qualities as a
teacher, no single occasion adequately represented him in
his entirety. And it is a curious paradox that no readers of
Plato or Xenophon ever sense anywhere that they know
Socrates any better than they know Socrates from the comic
parody of him in Aristophanes' *Clouds*. Even in his one mo-
ment of public discourse, the speech before the jury in Ath-
ens, he is at his most elusive. He is destabilizing to our or-
dinary patterns of thought about personality and the events

in a life, just as he unsettles our conventional ways of thinking and exposes our unexamined assumptions. Unlike Agesilaus, or Epaminondas, or even Xenophon himself, his life and his activities have no perceptible chronological progression or development.

At first glance neither do the *Memorabilia*. They seem a series of disconnected vignettes covering a wide range of philosophical topics, and even some topics that are not philosophical at all. Socrates' badinage with the courtesan Theodote is a striking example of the range of Xenophon's recollections; it would not be alien to the dialogue of New Comedy or a Roman comedy like *Truculentus*.[38] But what begins as an apology for Socrates gradually evolves into a recreation of his character through brief scenes depicting his encounters with a wide range of people. These episodes are completely absorbing separately, surprisingly coherent when recalled together. Our memory of someone we have known can, by our conscious effort, proceed in chronological order, but we can just as easily rearrange that person in our thoughts by other kinds of associations; so the Socrates in the *Memorabilia* begins and ends as the Socrates who is executed in Athens in 399. In the spaces in between, enclosed by that trial of 399, exists the Socrates whom Xenophon wants us to know, the Socrates whose discourse he is determined to preserve.[39]

In this way the character of Socrates structures the narrative of the *Memorabilia*. While Agesilaus lived at all times a life that could be measured by his accomplishments in government and war, Socrates occupied an entirely different sphere. He was a citizen of Athens, and claimed to be as responsible and patriotic as any other.[40] But he had no desire to rule others. With no high offices or empires in the picture, the only way for Xenophon to defend Socrates and recover his character and personality would be to portray him at work, teaching. Unlike the campaigns of a general or the diplomacy of a statesman, his teaching was always in progress, never perfected. There was no preconceived order in which he met people, just as there is no order or scheme to the persons most people meet in life. It is thus possible to

write about Socrates with a randomness that would make
no sense in the biography of a general and statesman.
Socrates lived in history, and he dealt continually with
historical personages like Meno and Alcibiades; and yet,
paradoxically, we always sense that the essence of Socrates
lies outside chronology. It is not accidental that the only
points in his life that yield up even approximate dates are
those moments when he is forced into his role as a citizen
of Athens: his military service, his conduct in office under
the Thirty, his trial in 399, and, more indirectly, his exploi-
tation in Aristophanes' *Clouds*. The sum of his life was phi-
losophy. He seems at once aged and ageless. We find it hard
to imagine the childhood or the youth of Socrates. And
everywhere *paideia* is the central theme of Xenophon's So-
cratic writing. It separates success from failure. It spills over
into his practical treatises on the arts of hunting, household
management, and the cavalry commander. Not surprisingly,
paideia also becomes the key to the process whereby a great
leader is produced: the leader for whom Xenophon so ar-
dently searched all his life.[41]

At the end of the *Oeconomicus* (*Household Manage-
ment*), Socrates' friend Ischomachus is talking about an
ideal master who makes his servants want to work for him.
He makes an imaginative leap from the manager of a house-
hold to the king of an empire:

> "But Socrates," he said, "if the master—who can harm the
> bad workers and honor the eager ones to the greatest de-
> gree—himself appeared at work and the workers did noth-
> ing remarkable, I would not admire him, but if on seeing
> him they were stirred and every one of the workers was
> filled with spirit and a love of victory and an ambition to
> outdo the others, then I would assert he had something of a
> kingly character. And this is the greatest thing, it seems to
> me, in any work where something is achieved by human
> beings, in farming as in any other. I do not say that it is
> possible to learn by seeing it or by hearing of it once, but I
> do assert that the one who is going to be capable of it needs
> a good nature, and, most of all, he needs to become divine.
> For it seems to me that this good—to rule over willing sub-

jects—is not altogether a human thing, but, rather, divine;
it is clearly given only to those who have genuinely been
initiated into the mysteries of restraint and self-control.
Tyrannical rule over unwilling subjects, it seems to me,
they give to those whom they believe worthy of living like
Tantalus in Hades, who is said to spend unending time in
fear of a second death." (21.10–12)

The idealism of Ischomachus is plain enough. Whether or
not the ruler he envisages would ever appear in actual his-
tory remains an open question, so far as the *Oeconomicus*
is concerned. But Xenophon was not disposed to wait on
events. He could also bring Ischomachus' ideal ruler and his
paideia to life. This is essentially what Xenophon does in
the *Cyropaedia*. He turns the problems that his Socratic and
historical writings had disclosed into the theme of his new
work. Instead of writing his way through to the hard ques-
tions to which these other works lead us, he writes his way
toward an answer to those questions. The text that results
from this process is not a flight from Socrates and history,
but an answer to the problems that history and Socrates
pose.[42]

It was the generic flexibility of prose itself that enabled
Xenophon to move so easily across the boundary between
history and fiction. It is true that this move has not been so
easy for some of his readers to make. But it is important for
us to realize what was available to Xenophon when he
turned to writing *The Education of Cyrus*. Like any prose
writer, he was engaged in the invention of his own genre as
he went along. To ground an exemplary education in an in-
dividual character was nothing new to him or Greek litera-
ture; for example, Socrates, the wisest of men, replaces
Achilles, the best of the Achaeans. Nor was it a new idea
for Xenophon to find a solution to the instability of political
life by focusing on leadership. What was new was that this
exemplary ideal of education was now created in a non-
Greek space, with a model ruler who was alien to Greek
history and political experience. By displacing the problems
of Greek public and private life to the *barbarikos topos*, the
place where those who do not speak Greek dwell, and by

making his exemplary ruler as remote in time as he was in space, Xenophon was able to represent that good that is "not altogether a human thing, but divine": the ruler of willing subjects.

To describe the process in more practical terms, ones related to Xenophon's other literary works, it is as if Socrates were given the role of Cyrus the Younger, or Agesilaus, or Teleutias to play, but in disguise. In such a role he would be a leader who could read the world and its people as expertly as ever, but he would also take care never, ever to reveal his designs. He would be the paradigm Xenophon so ardently pursued throughout his career, but his true purpose would be obscure to those about him; it would be essential that his design for power remain concealed from those at whom it was aimed. He would be everything Ischomachus desires at the end of the *Oeconomicus*. He would succeed where Cyrus the Younger and the Spartans had failed. And, unlike Socrates, Cyrus the Younger, or Epaminondas, he would transform his world, rather than be destroyed by it.

Such a leader as this does not exist in the world Xenophon lives in. Nor could any history written about that world tolerate such an invention, and remain history. But if he could create that leader from his imagination, he could impose the power of his imagination on at least that fictive world. This would be an intriguing alternative to acquiescing in the world's usual tendency to impose itself on him. There would be no limit to what author and character might accomplish.[43] In this way the characters and events of the *Cyropaedia* arise out of Xenophon's reflections (*ennoia*). While the narrative to come will address the same political problems he confronts elsewhere, the process of writing now flows in a new direction. Where *ennoia* is a consequence of events in other works, it is now their source. Xenophon had discovered what Montaigne would later term the power of the imagination.

5

For the formation of the novelistic narrative of the *Cyropae-dia*, then, the most important consideration was not another literary genre, but Xenophon's experiences in history and in writing.[44] He gave much thought to the reasons he wrote the *Cyropaedia*. What he says deserves our closest attention. He is at once developing a new project and telling us how we should read what he writes.

> The reflection [*ennoia*] once came to us how many democracies have been overthrown by people who preferred to live under any form of government other than a democracy; and again, how many monarchies and how many oligarchies in times past have been abolished by the people; and how many of those individuals who have aspired to tyranny have either been deposed once for all and then very quickly, or if they have continued in power, no matter how short a time, they are objects of wonder as having proved to be wise and happy men. (1.1.1)

Unlike the reflection that opens the *Constitution of the Lacedaemonians*, which led to an account of a *politeia* that really existed, this reflection sums up Greek political experience generally. It is not tied to any specific nation or government, nor is it fixed in any specific time. The adverb "once" (*pote*) places these thoughts at an unspecified moment in the past; for example, at the same time as Xenophon's imaginary dialogue between Simonides and the tyrant Hiero of Syracuse, which also takes place "once upon a time" (*pote*). In this rapid survey of political institutions, there is neither progress nor decline. The narrator is not so much concerned with which form government takes, as with the inherent instability of any system; any one is fated to be overthrown and replaced by something else. What else is a matter of indifference both to the narrator and to the citizens, or subjects. The absence of any preference for one kind of government over another is a striking contrast to discussions of constitutions in Plato and Aristotle.[45] Instability in public life is the theme that links each observation to the next.

The meditation on government then expands into a related perception about governance of the *oikos* (household) of private life.

> Then too we had observed, we thought, that even in pri-
> vate homes some people who had more than the usual
> number of servants, and some also, who had only a very
> few, were nevertheless, though nominally masters, quite
> unable to assert their authority over even those few. (1.1.1)

The shift from the public to the private sphere is typical of
Xenophon's disposition to trace the interconnections be-
tween the two. Public and private, city and household (*polis*
and *oikos*) are organized according to the same principles.[46]
But now these connections are outlined only to deepen the
negative comment on public government. In this way the
reflection becomes more pointed. Whether one is concerned
with a grand house or a small one, the same problem of re-
sistance to authority pertains. The real theme that is emerg-
ing is the intractability of human nature. Like the forms of
government and the size of households, the particular status
of the governed is a matter of complete indifference: they
can be citizens, subjects, servants, or slaves. The point is
that in public and private life, resistance to rule is the rule.

There follows an even longer analogy. In this instance,
it is linked to what precedes and follows in more than a fig-
urative way.

> And in addition to this, we reflected that cowherds are the
> rulers of their cattle; that grooms are the rulers of their
> horses; and that all who are called herdsmen might prop-
> erly be regarded as the rulers of the animals over which
> they are placed in charge. Now we noticed, we thought,
> that all these herds obeyed their keepers more readily than
> men obey their rulers. For the herds go wherever their
> keeper directs them, graze in those places to which he
> leads them, and keep out of those from which he excludes
> them. They allow their keeper, moreover, to enjoy, just as
> he will, the profits that accrue from them. And then again,
> we have never known of a herd conspiring against its
> keeper, either to refuse obedience to him or to deny him
> the privilege of enjoying the profits that accrue. At the
> same time, herds are more intractable to strangers than to
> their rulers and those who derive profit from them. Human
> beings however conspire against none sooner than against
> those whom they see attempting to rule over them. (1.1.2)

This chain of analogies exchanges the attributes of human beings and animals. Human beings are conceived of theriomorphically, as bad property; animals are anthropomorphically good citizens. Cows, sheep, and horses are spoken of with approval; their good service to their keepers makes them into ideals of the faithful subject, for loyalty and faithfulness are human qualities, and these "subjects" are praised for their good citizenship in resisting strangers and shunning rebellion. Correspondingly, cowherds, shepherds, and grooms are elevated into rulers, as if they were *archontes* (rulers) of human beings. For their part, human beings are implicitly demoted below the level of animals, because they are not so controllable as cows, sheep, and horses. As specimens of the political animal, men are inferior to the animals they rule. The prologue thus delights us by inverting the roles of ruler and ruled in the human and animal kingdoms: the "society" of animals is "faithful" to its "rulers," the "herds" of human beings "disobey" their "shepherds." The ancient metaphor of the king as a shepherd of a people is reduced to a matter of literal fact.[47]

Our reflective narrator then comes full circle back to where he began, with this implicit moral drawn from the excursus into animal husbandry: if the art (*technê*) of grooms, herdsmen, or shepherds works so well with their "subjects," why couldn't a similar one be devised for dealing with human beings?

> When we reflected on these things, we were inclined to conclude that for man, as he is constituted, it is easier to rule over any and all other creatures than to rule over men. (1.1.3)

This accords very well with Xenophon's own experiences in the *Anabasis*, as well as the experiences of the generals and statesmen he writes about in the *Hellenica*. What lifts it above the commonplace is its analogy with more docile creatures. One senses the exasperation of the author of technical treatises on hunting, the cavalry commander, and horsemanship. He is at once political and technical in this epistemology of authoritarianism. The prologue shows signs of becoming an introduction to a handbook on human husbandry.

But then our reflective narrator turns away from a world where animals are better subjects than human beings, to a specific example remote from Xenophon's Greece in both time and place:

> But when we reflected that there was Cyrus the Persian, who reduced to obedience a vast number of men and cities and nations, we were then compelled to change our opinion and decide that to rule men might be a task neither impossible nor even difficult, if one should only go about it in an intelligent manner [*epistamenôs*]. (1.1.3)

The ideal ruler Ischomachus describes at the end of the *Oeconomicus* seems at last to have been found. But the *Hiero* and the *Oeconomicus* show that successful rule is not in itself the entire picture; a tyrant who succeeds in holding power for even a brief time is regarded with wonder.[48] What is most urgently required is that the people so ruled want to be ruled by the person who leads them. Recall that this quality is what Agesilaus' brother Teleutias possessed to so extraordinary a degree—though he ruled only the sailors of a fleet, not an empire. Now Xenophon declares that he has found just this necessary quality in Cyrus.

> At all events, we know that people obeyed Cyrus willingly, although some of them were distant from him a journey of many days, and others of many months; others, although they had never seen him, and still others who knew well that they never should see him. Nevertheless they were all willing to be his subjects. (1.1.4)

The empire of Cyrus was vast, extending over all nations, even ones that did not speak his language. His power extended to all the world that mattered. And the proof of that power was that

> he was able to cover so vast a region with the fear which he inspired, he struck all men with terror and no one tried to withstand him. He was able to awaken in all so lively a

desire to please him, that they always wished to be guided
by his will. (1.1.5)

Here is the ideal leader, and the reason why we want to
study him. The extravagant powers of Cyrus are due in no
small measure to the kind of social orders that existed in
the Persian empire. When Xenophon wrote, it would have
been very hard to imagine the collective city-states and al-
liances of the Greeks jumping up to salute an authority as
quickly as this. Yet this very displacement of the narrative,
away from the realities of time and place in present-day
Greece, to the remote world of Cyrus the Great, is what en-
ables the project to take place at all. And so the program of
the *Cyropaedia* is at last announced:

> We then have investigated this man as one who is worthy
> of all admiration, looking into who he was in his ancestry
> [*genea*], what natural endowments he possessed [*êthos*],
> and what sort of education [*paideia*] he had enjoyed, that
> he so greatly excelled in governing men. Accordingly, what
> we have found out, or think we know concerning him, we
> shall now endeavor to present. (1.1.6)

The themes are clearly laid out in the reference to *genea*,
êthos, and *paideia*. Research, here described as not only
things actually learned (*eputhometha*) but also things *pos-
sibly* learned (*eisthesthai dokoumen*), will tell the story.
There is no claim here or anywhere else about the truth or
falsity of this story.

The special character of the *Cyropaedia* is already evi-
dent in its elaborate complaint about the instability of hu-
man nature, the praise of animal husbandry, and the extrav-
agant achievements which Xenophon gives as reasons for
his choice of Cyrus as an object lesson. All the political in-
stitutions and divisions of the household are the conven-
tional means we have for defining codes of social conduct
in both the public and private spheres, yet in each instance
these institutions are undermined by humanity's innate re-
sistance to another's rule. Within Cyrus's empire, a perfect
kind of place, that imagining can create, subjects are loyal
"who are distant either many days, or many months; who

have never seen him, and who know they never will see him; and even ones who cannot speak his language." In this world everything that would serve to make any government lose control over its citizens becomes merely one more way to measure how firm a control Cyrus has over all within his power.

The contrast between unstable human beings and reliable animals also suggests where Cyrus's power originates: in his communication with others—or more accurately, his lack of it. To move from democracy to animal husbandry, as the prologue has done, is to move from one extreme of communication to another: from the discourse of a democracy, where every citizen must be heard, through its progressive diminutions in oligarchy, monarchy, and tyranny, to the mute obedience of animals who have only the most rudimentary understanding of what their masters say. A herdsman speaks the language of animals, in a sense, in that he communicates well enough to get them to do what he wants them to do. Although Cyrus's language has yet to be heard, we already know that he was as skillful in ruling men as herdsmen and shepherds are skillful in ruling their animals. The analogy of the arts of governance in animal husbandry implies that Cyrus had a certain detachment about human beings that was crucial to the creation of his empire.

As an analogy of government, Xenophon's much-obeyed herdsman recalls something Thrasymachus says at the beginning of his speech in the *Republic* (1.343b–344c). There he says that Socrates is a silly baby who should have his nose wiped:

> Because you suppose shepherds or cowherds consider the good of the sheep or the cows and fatten them and take care of them looking to something other than their masters' good and their own; and so you also believe that the rulers in the cities, those who truly rule, think about the ruled differently from the way a man would regard sheep, and that night and day they consider anything else than how they will benefit themselves. (*Republic*, 1.343b)

Xenophon seems to glance at this more cynical view of herdsmen, then bypass it. He is not advocating a Thrasymachean notion that injustice is the right or duty of a ruler, but neither is he being Socratic. Nothing whatever is said here about whether or not such rulers should be just. The epistemology of rule is a technical matter devoid of ethical content. Xenophon neither affirms nor denies the kind of arguments that Thrasymachus attempts to advance. But there are some implications to this analogy that Thrasymachus might appreciate. To spell out some of them, we may conclude this study of the *Cyropaedia's* opening reflection with a reflection of our own.

Loyalty and affection are desirable traits in animals if they are to be used as horses and dogs are, for warfare and hunting. But it is well known that animals raised to be eaten cannot acquire such an identity. Above all they should not be named; if they are, they become friends (pets), and sentimental owners will find it difficult to slaughter them. To eat chickens, ducks, pigs, and cattle, there must be a certain distance between the governor and the governed. To apply this art to human beings who speak a language, it will only be necessary to hold back the whole truth, to pretend to be less than what one really is. In short, it is only necessary to be an actor. As in acting, the same arts can work to beguile those at close range, as well as those far away.

Furthermore, while the herdsman who raises animals for profit is not truly their friend, they need to be persuaded that he is, by being fed and cared for. Like the shepherd or cowherd, the would-be ruler must not seem to be what he really is. He will require, as Xenophon says, a thorough knowledge and understanding of his subjects, but he will also need to be detached from them in order to practice his art as successfully in his sphere as the herdsman or shepherd do in theirs. The expectation is that Cyrus will practice an art that enables him to treat other people as animal husbandry teaches human beings to treat animals. In this way the prologue tells us how to begin to read *The Educa-tion of Cyrus*: so long as we regard everyone Cyrus meets as a person to be controlled, as someone potentially useful for the future course of his empire, we shall be of the same mind as Cyrus and the writer who created him.

II

THE EDUCATION OF CYRUS

In order to be the ruler Xenophon desires, Cyrus needs a supporting cast who will be responsive to his designs. So Xenophon invents them, either by making them up entirely, or by adapting characters known to him but not to us, or by transforming actual historical personages like Cyrus, Croesus, and Astyages so thoroughly that for all practical purposes he might just as well have invented them altogether. They are conjured up to serve as ideal subjects of an ideal prince who himself was invented to exemplify an abstract ideal.

The argument of Chapters 3 through 9 is organized according to the characters of the *Cyropaedia*. Encounters with these fictive persons are the education of the prince; for Xenophon's present readers, these characters are also the place where the two strands of the novelistic and the political intersect. Every person in the book has a double aspect: each is at once the product of Xenophon's imagination, and the object of Cyrus's imperial designs. In order to understand Cyrus's father Cambyses and his role in his son's education, for example, we need to explore how Xenophon uses him and his two appearances in the *Cyropaedia* to organize the entire work. In essence, the ethical pattern of Cyrus's life determines the structure of the narrative: where it starts, and where it stops (Chapter 3). To appreciate the political significance, as well as the charm, of Cyrus's first appearance as a little boy, our reading of Xenophon is much enhanced by reference to the first appearance of Cyrus in Herodotus' *Histories* (Chapter 4). Cyrus's jealous uncle Cyaxares tests his precocious nephew's abilities, and his patience, from the time he is a boy in Media to the middle of the war with Assyria. Save for that of Cyrus himself, Cyaxares' is the most sustained characterization in the *Cyropaedia*. Through him the ideal ruler learns that kinship requires as much attention as any external foe (Chapter 5). A childhood friend, Tigranes, presents him with an amusing challenge in Socratic dialectic. But their anachronistic exchange serves no genuine philosophical purpose; what their encounter actually reveals is the essential difference between the private activity of philosophy and the public life of the ruler of an empire, where the options to

engage in the philosophical life are, evidently, strictly limited
(Chapter 6). To see the political dimensions of Cyrus's meeting
with Croesus of Lydia, and not only its intertextual aspect as a
revision of scenes in Book 1 of Herodotus, we must realize that
Xenophon's account of the meeting is set within a context funda-
mentally different from anything to be found in the *Histories*
(Chapter 7). Such considerations obtain for every character, and
nowhere more than in the episodes in which Panthea and Abrada-
tas appear; their story is at once the story of Wieland and Philo-
stratus, sentimental and romantic, and Machiavelli's kind of text,
intensely political in both its design and its implications (Chapter
8). And even those who serve Cyrus without hesitation require
his care. Loyal lieutenants like Chrysantas and Pheraulas, and
grateful allies like the refugee king Gobryas and the eunuch
prince Gadatas, are good friends, but he does not take even them
for granted (Chapter 9).

At the end of Cyrus's education all of these characters blend
back into the nameless generality from which they came, and
only Cyrus matters. We read about them not for their own sake,
but to learn how Cyrus used them for his own purposes. Such are
the *archomenoi*, the ones whom Cyrus ruled. The *Cyropaedia* is
not a story about things that happened, but an account of things
that could happen, an elaboration of the abstract desire of the au-
thor of the prologue to learn how to create power and maintain it:
ên tis epistamenôs touto prattêi, "if someone were to do this in-
telligently." In this epistemology of power, the focus is never on
what Cyrus achieved, but on how he achieved it. A summary of
what Xenophon terms the achievements of Cyrus (*praxeis*,
1.2.16) shows that there are absolutely no surprises in store for
the reader of the *Cyropaedia*. (I also offer it here as an aid to
those who are not familiar with its basic plot.)

> Cyrus is the son of Cambyses, king of Persia, and Mandane, daugh-
> ter of Astyages the king of the Medes. He is raised according to the
> laws and customs of the Persians. While he is still a boy, Mandane
> takes him to the court of Astyages, where he becomes the favorite
> of his doting grandfather and everyone else. He learns to hunt and
> distinguishes himself as the best in this art and every other. When
> the Assyrians invade his grandfather's kingdom, he proves himself
> a brave if impetuous young warrior. At this point his father Cam-
> byses summons him back to Persia, where he completes his
> course of study. In the meantime, his grandfather Astyages has

died, and Mandane's brother and Cyrus's uncle, Cyaxares, suc-
ceeds to the throne of Media.

On his way to the Assyrian campaign, Cyrus has a long conver-
sation with his father in which they review Cyrus's past education
and preparation for the arts of war and kingship. Cyrus joins his
uncle Cyaxares in the war against the Assyrians. As soon as Cyrus
is on his own, he immediately puts into practice everything his fa-
ther taught him. He reorganizes his army and gathers about him a
number of loyal lieutenants: the nobleman Chrysantas and the
commoner Pheraulas. Boyhood friends like the Medes Araspas and
Artabazus also help out. He takes care to cultivate the friendship
or alliance of others as well: he wins back the rebellious Armenian
king and his son Tigranes, persuades the distant king of India to
become an ally, and through his open show of magnanimity and
generosity even causes some subjects and allies to desert the As-
syrian king. Thus he wins the friendship of the aged king Gobryas,
whose son the cruel Assyrian king had murdered; the eunuch
prince Gadatas, another victim of that king; and the most famous
of his converts, Panthea and Abradatas of Susa. Cyrus's conduct
toward Panthea is so respectful that she persuades her husband to
desert the Assyrians to come over to his cause.

Cyrus's prosecution of the Assyrian war is entirely successful.
He captures Croesus of Lydia, the Assyrian king's most formidable
ally, forgives him his past actions, and finds a place for him in his
court. When Cyrus takes Babylon, Gobryas and Gadatas have the
satisfaction of killing the Assyrian king himself. But these victo-
ries are not without their costs. For much of the campaign Cyrus
must contend with the envy of his uncle Cyaxares. In the end he
wins him over completely. But the greatest loss is Abradatas of
Susa: he is killed in the battle before Babylon, and his wife Pan-
thea commits suicide rather than survive him. Cyrus erects a
monument to their memory.

The organization of the post-war world is swift and complete.
Cyrus decides to use his army as a model for the organization of
his empire. He establishes a court and surrounds himself with
elaborate ceremonies. Everything he does serves to create awe and
obedience in his subjects. Then he returns to Persia with gifts for
his mother and father. Cambyses warns Cyrus and the Persians
that they must remain loyal to one another in the future if the
newly won empire is to last. Cyrus marries the daughter of his un-
cle Cyaxares, disposes of his friends' and subjects' lives equally
well, and continues to expand Persia's hold on the world by many
more campaigns. The story then jumps many years ahead, to the
death of Cyrus. Warned in a dream of his approaching end, he
summons his sons and friends about him, awards the throne to his
eldest son Cambyses, and warns both Cambyses and his brother

Tanaoxares to avoid fraternal strife at all costs. And with that said, he dies.

Cyrus's reign was as good as promised, but his successors did not live up to his example. In the last chapter we learn that the Persian empire went into decline with the succession of Cambyses, and that this degeneracy has continued to the present day.

Cyrus is exactly the kind of ruler the prologue says he will be, and it is here that we may perceive the particular genius of *The Education of Cyrus*. Running in strict counterpoint to this bland success story is that activity I have already alluded to: Cyrus's constant manipulation of everyone he meets. Even when he is in the company of his father Cambyses, he is never simply what he seems; his every word and deed have a design behind them that looks past the present moment to some future goal, often one no one else is aware of. His serene rise to power subverts the world into which he was born. Persia expands into a vast empire, but only because he bends the laws and customs of the Persians to serve his own interests. He is the most dutiful and obedient of sons to his father Cambyses, yet he somehow becomes a ruler incomparably more powerful than anything his father's precepts or example provide for. His uncle Cyaxares first loses all authority over his own army, then his kingdom as well. The clients and subjects of the Assyrian king exchange their bad master for a good one, but subjects they remain. Abradatas is drawn to Cyrus's service by the force of his noble personality, and dies fighting for him; Abradatas' widow Panthea is not consoled by this noble death, and says so. In these ways Cyrus remakes the world into an empire of which he is the center, and he achieves all this at other people's cost rather than at his own. After him, nothing is as it was.

Cyrus accomplishes everything as much by instinct as by careful study. At no point does he achieve anything by accident. To discern the strategic thought that ripples beneath the surface of this success story is the aim of the following chapters. It is the greatest pleasure of this particular text. Although the broad divisions of family, friends, and enemies are real enough, we shall find it hard to see any difference in Cyrus's treatment of his family, friends, or enemies. At every stage of his career, and at every level of involvement with others, he has a curious detachment about other people, even as he makes himself famous throughout the world for his kindness and his generosity, through calculated shows of philanthropy.

FAMILY

CHAPTER THREE

The Curious Return of Cambyses

I am not a leader, nor do I aspire to become one. Com-
mand, obey, it's all one. The bossiest of men commands in
the name of another—his father—and transmits the ab-
stract acts of violence which he puts up with. Never in my
life have I given an order without laughing, without mak-
ing others laugh. It is because I am not consumed by the
canker of power: I was not taught obedience.

Sartre, *The Words*

As soon as Xenophon turned
to writing fiction, he created another challenge for himself
that in some ways was as daunting as the continuation of
Thucydides in the *Hellenica*. The romantic project he had
conceived now imposed its own constraints, because the
possible designs of the narrative to follow were limitless.
Escape to romance is not necessarily the easier path for a
writer, nor does it guarantee an audience for all time, or
even temporary success. *Les Voyages de Cyrus* and *Aretina*
exemplify the possible results—to say nothing of Gibbon's
opinion of the *Cyropaedia*.[1]

It is important to be aware of the challenge Xenophon's
new project posed, because the survey of his career as a
writer in Chapter 2 might leave the impression that the *Cy-
ropaedia* wrote itself. Xenophon's turn away from history to
romance seems such a cutting of the authorial Gordian knot
that we might imagine the writing of it was easier for him

than the writing of history or philosophy. His theme is how Cyrus succeeds, rather than what he achieves. From the prologue onward it is clear Cyrus will win his empire and rule it well. And it is also clear that any account of the education of such a ruler might reasonably begin with his origins. That much is easy to see. Anyone can *start* a romance. But it is far less obvious where this imperial fiction will stop, now that it is underway. Since it is not the life story of Cyrus that is the theme, the grave need not be the goal. Even if it were—and Xenophon did find Cyrus's death a convenient way to stop—how much did he need to tell about everything that came in between?

This chapter is about the taxonomy of the *Cyropaedia* as a literary text.[2] It offers an overview of Xenophon's narrative technique that aims to expose the simplicity of his designs. What I aim to uncover are some of the ways he managed to create a rich and complicated texture out of relatively simple means.

I

The least predictable part of any novel or romance is its ending. At the end of the *Cyropaedia* Xenophon confronted a problem later authors in the genre would find equally vexing. Marriages of heroes and heroines are common solutions. It is also possible for the narrative to break off in the middle of some significant episode; it can even break off in the middle of a sentence.[3] The more we know about Xenophon, the less surprising his own solution should be. And if we dare to criticize him, we might also recall how Homer ended—or did not end—the *Odyssey*. No one links that poem with the *Cyropaedia*, yet the ending Homer devised is as problematic as anything we shall observe at the end of the *Cyropaedia*.[4]

After the capture of Babylon and the end of his war with the king of Assyria (7.5), Cyrus turns to the organization of a court and a newly won empire. The remainder of the *Cyropaedia* is a lesson in how to follow up a military victory with the reorganization of a post-war world. A model for future princes, Cyrus returns to Persia and Persepolis with lavish gifts for his mother and father. Then comes a sudden pause in his otherwise unbroken rise to supreme power. His father Cambyses summons an assembly for a formal welcome.

> Men of Persia, and you, Cyrus, I am naturally well disposed to both of you; for I am your king, and you, Cyrus, are my child. I have every right to say openly what, as I think, is for the good of both of you. (8.5.22)

Cambyses reminds the assembly that everyone owes a great deal to Cyrus for bringing them a new empire. Without Cyrus, they would be the poorer. If both they and Cyrus continue to act in the future as they have in the past, there will be much prosperity for both. But he also has a word of warning about exploitation (*pleonexia*) to add to this praise.

> But if you, Cyrus, get puffed up by present good fortune and try to exploit the Persians for your own advantage the way do other people, or if you citizens envy his power and attempt to depose him from rule, I assure both of you that you will hinder one another from receiving many good things. (8.5.24)

They will avoid such problems by pledging common support in a covenant sealed by a vow and a sacrifice. He concludes with a matter-of-fact observation about present and future occupants of the throne.

> So long as I am alive, the kingdom of Persia is mine; when I die, it is clear that it will be Cyrus's, if he is alive. (8.5.26)

The Persians follow Cambyses' advice; and, as Xenophon often says in his desire to link Cyrus's romantic world with present-day Persia, so do they even now.[5] Cyrus says nothing in reply. He returns to the Medes and marries his cousin, the daughter of his uncle Cyaxares. There is nothing exceptional in this scene. It is only one more episode in the extended happy ending of Cyrus's march to power. Its utility is another matter.

   The son whom Cambyses lectures so sternly has already vastly expanded the Persian empire and given every indication that he is fit to govern it. Moreover, he has done this without the aid or even the presence of his father. Cambyses has not appeared in the *Cyropaedia* since the end of Book 1, yet here he is now, determined to establish firmly that he, not Cyrus, is the king of the Persians. Nor is that all. The conqueror of Assyria is still his child (*pais*). He ends with a warning to Cyrus—of all people—about the dangers of tyranny. No less deserving a target for such advice could be imagined. Cyrus takes extraordinary pains to insure his subjects' loyalty. His reputation for generosity contributes much to his widening power. Both what he has attained and what he will hold in the future depend to a great extent on his ability to make the self-interest of those he rules coincide with his own—or at least seem to coincide.[6] He has already performed in a more thorough and imaginative way than his father's generalized admonitions even begin to suggest. Cambyses' warning is actually a commonplace on the dangers of tyranny.[7]

The entire experience of Cyrus up to this point shows that he is incapable of committing the kind of crude errors his father describes. In this sense, while Cambyses has been heard politely by Cyrus, both his advice and his return to the narrative are superfluous. Naturally Cyrus's return to Persia would lead to a return to his father Cambyses. But logic in geography is one thing, logic in narrative quite another; and from the standpoint of the narrative, the return of Cambyses to the story serves a symbolic rather than a practical purpose. It is both a political act and a sign of the agreeable, romantic world Xenophon created for Cyrus to subdue. Some further reflection on the curious return of Cambyses can help us discern the larger design of the story to which Cyrus's father so briefly and unexpectedly returns.

2

The public ceremony of welcome is an adaptation of political institutions from Sparta and Persia.[8] Cambyses' exhortation to Cyrus and the Persians resembles the covenants (*synthêkai*) Xenophon describes in *The Constitution of the Lacedaemonians*:

> as they then reached a covenant on these things, so the Persians and their king still continue to this day to act toward one another. (8.5.27)

> I wish also to give an account of the compact made by Lycurgus between King and state. For this is the only government that continues exactly as it was originally established, whereas other constitutions will be found to have undergone and still to be undergoing modifications. (*Constitution*, 15.1)

Although Xenophon's Persians are, as always, blandly Greek-speaking, and more than a little reminiscent of Spartans in their outlook, the covenant which Cambyses enforces also resembles the *mithra* or alliance sworn between king and subjects in ancient Persia.[9] The evidence for ancient Iran is scanty, but in general it seems that Xenophon could blend *synthêkai* and *mithra* together because both Persian and Greek institutions provided for the kind of contract Cambyses establishes in the *Cyropaedia*.[10] The religious aura of this reunion of father and son is distinctly Persian rather than Greek. The word *mithra* is formally indistinguishable from the name of the god Mithra, who among his many duties functioned as the god of contracts, as for example in the Avestan Hymn to Mithra (mid-fifth century):

> The knave who is false to the treaty, Spitamid, wrecks the whole country, hitting as he does the truth-owners as hard as would a hundred obscurantists. Never break a contract, O Spitamid, whether you conclude it with an owner of falsehood, or a truth-owning follower of the good religion; for the contract applies to both, the owner of falsehood and him who owns truth.[11]

But sources are just the beginning of interpretation; while they show that an important moment in the narrative is based on actual political institutions, they do not account for the momentary reappearance in Book 8 of a character

who has otherwise played no role since Book 1. The signif-
icance of Cambyses' return to the narrative may be better
understood by examining the role he plays elsewhere. While
his return demonstrates Cyrus's submission to paternal au-
thority, it is not his function to serve as yet one more epi-
sode in an ongoing encomium on the good character of Cy-
rus. He reappears because he defines precisely the present
status of his son: for all his conquests and his skillful organ-
ization of a new empire, Cyrus is still his father's child, still
capable of being taught by him: *su de, o Kyre, pais emos ei*
(8.5.22). In Greek the connection between "child" and "ed-
ucation" is an etymological bond as well: Cyrus the *pais*
(the stem is *paid-*) is still subject to his father's *paideia*.[12]
Cyrus's education and his identity as a person depend on
this bond, and when Cambyses returns to the narrative, we
realize that the bond is as strong as ever.

It is a classic example of ring composition: the narrative
ends by returning to where it begins. Cambyses is thus im-
portant for what he can do for Cyrus, but even more impor-
tant for who he is. His return to the narrative at the end of
the Assyrian campaign reveals the ethical pattern that un-
derlies the *Cyropaedia*. While Cambyses is peripheral to
most of its events in a literal sense, in another way he is the
central figure in Cyrus's education. He also plays a central
role in Xenophon's design of the entire work.

Cambyses' appearances at the beginning and the end of
the Assyrian war are framing scenes for his son's excursion.
Cyrus goes off to battle thoroughly his father's son, and he
comes back from battle, willing as ever to be his father's
son. Education and moral authority extend outward from
the father to the son; thence from the son to lieutenants,
soldiers, client and subject nations, and even to the enemies
he wins over to his side. Everywhere the key role is "father"
(*patêr*), the word by which Cyrus was known in his own
lifetime, according to other ancient sources.[13] In a series of
rhetorical questions summing up Cyrus's virtues, Xeno-
phon asks

> Of whom else is it said that by the munificence of his gifts
> he makes himself preferred above even brothers and par-

ents and children? Who else was ever in a position like the
Persian king to punish enemies who were distant a journey
of many months? And who, besides Cyrus, ever gained an
empire by conquest and even to his death was called "fa-
ther" by the people he had subdued? For that name ob-
viously belongs to a benefactor rather than to a despoiler.
(8.2.9)

As Cyrus's lieutenant Chrysantas observes, a good ruler (ar-
chôn) is no different from a good father (8.1.1). Paternalism
conceived in a broad sense is the solution to the problem
Xenophon raised in the prologue. Cyrus can obey Cambyses
without a word in reply because he has already articulated
the duty of a ruler in his conversation with his father in
Book 1: "And the many laws seem to me to teach these two
things above all else: to rule and to be ruled" (archein kai
archesthai, 1.6.20). As Cambyses observes,

> My son, have you forgotten the things which I and you
> once talked about? We said that it was a considerable and
> good task for a man, if someone could undertake to be
> proven a good and noble man, to be able to provide suffi-
> ciently for himself and his household? Also, that since it is
> a great task, that he understand how to govern other people
> so that they might have all they need in life in abundance
> and that they might all become what they ought to be?
> And that this seemed to us to be worthy of all admiration?
> (1.6.7)

There Cyrus also agreed completely with everything his fa-
ther said.

> Yes, by Zeus, father, I do remember your saying this, and I
> agreed with you that it was an exceedingly difficult task to
> govern well. Now I think the same way when I consider
> the matter and reason about the principles of governing.
> (1.6.7)

This exchange echoes the prologue's description of Cyrus,
who is worthy of all admiration because he so excelled in
his ability to rule others (to archein anthrôpôn, 1.1.6). By
the time Cambyses and Cyrus are reunited in Book 8, they
have talked their way through all the issues raised by the
prologue, and Cyrus has learned how to rule other men.

Every other person we shall encounter in the *Cyropaedia* is but a specimen of the problems that confront the ideal ruler. If Cyrus is the embodiment of the ideal ruler, he has mainly his father to thank for that attainment. The first and most important setting for Cyrus's rise to power is dynastic, in the royal families of Media and Persia. The formation of the ideal ruler of men depends to some degree on the Persians' education, but most of all on Cyrus's family, where his father is the central figure of authority.[14] In his relationship with Cambyses, Cyrus is the antithesis of the recalcitrant subjects Xenophon says human beings are disposed to be. The seemingly effortless way he comes to rule others is shaped by a complementary and equally effortless submission to the power of his father.

When Cyrus rules others, he becomes father to his army and subjects in a figurative sense. For Xenophon, paternal identity in the political sphere is the handiest way to reconcile others to the rule of one. To be subjects of a "father" implies that subjects can think of themselves as in some sense demoted to the status of children. It is hard for those who think they are your equals or your superiors to submit to your authority without a sense of injured merit. The discourse of the ideal ruler is thus like the speech of a parent to a child; like a genuine father, a king can take special delight in this role, because his "children" cannot understand everything adults say. Thus is tyranny made palatable; compare Sophocles' *Oedipus Tyrannus*, where Oedipus speaks of the citizens of Thebes as his "children." Cyrus's rise to supreme power over his army and his allies is alternately a political paternalization or infantilization of everyone he meets.

Cyrus's authority could be summed up another way, by changes in grammar. In this romance of rulers and ruled, the narrative shifts from the middle/passive voice of *archesthai* ("to be ruled"), where Cyrus is ruled by others, above all his father, to the active voice of *archein* ("to rule"), where Cyrus is the agent. At the same time, this shift from *archesthai* to *archein* is not a simple shift from childhood and youth to maturity, nor does this shift occur only once. From the very beginning Cyrus exhibits an ability to submit and a disposition to rule, simultaneously. Perfect submission is for him a means to an end, because he realizes from the first moment we see him that he will rise to supreme power by obeying those who legitimately have power over him: his mother, father, and grandfather. The difference between Cyrus's submission to his father and the submission of others to him is that his obedience is a means to an end that is the very opposite of obedience.

3

Sartre's account of his disinclination to pursue power points up the political uses of this kind of filial submission. Someone like Cyrus undertakes it because he knows that this kind of obedience will one day enable him to impose the same kind of control on others in turn. The power relationship of father and son that Sartre finds so ludicrous is not a joking matter to Xenophon. He never questions it anywhere in the *Cyropaedia*; he uses it to shape both Cyrus the character, and the narrative in which he appears.

The importance of Cambyses can be measured by considering what would have happened to Cyrus if his father had not been there to guide him. Before Cyrus leaves Persia for his campaign against the Assyrian king he delivers a formal speech to his troops. In this first effort at public speaking in Book 1, he pours everything he knows about Persian education into his exhortation for war. The speech is an exemplary specimen of hortatory rhetoric.[15] It begins with a *prooimion* whose studied artificiality (chiefly hyperbaton) is not easy to capture in translation:

> My friends, I have chosen you, not because I now see your worth for the first time, but because I have seen from your boyhood onwards that the things which the state regards as good, you eagerly work to complete, and those that it considers wrong, you altogether abstain from. Because of this, both the reason I have assumed this office not unwillingly, and the reason I have called you to me, I now want to make clear to you. (1.5.7)

Although Cyrus will occasionally turn to this more formal style, on the whole he prefers a less ornate kind of discourse and rarely delivers speeches of such obvious rhetorical calculation.[16] He is always calculating, but his plans lie elsewhere than in oratorical display. Here he seems to be straightforward enough, praising his men for their readiness, because they are *pepaideumenoi*, and abusing the Assyrians for their lack of education in warfare, because they are *apaideutoi*:

> For they are not yet valiant warriors, who, however skillful in the use of bow or spear and in horsemanship, are still found wanting if it is ever necessary to suffer hardship. Such persons are mere tiros (*idiôtai*) when it comes to hardships. Nor are those men valiant warriors who are found wanting when it is necessary to keep awake; these also are tiros in the face of sleep. Nor yet are they valiant warriors, who have these qualifications but have not been taught how they ought to treat comrades and how to treat enemies. It is evident that they also have no experience with the most important branches of education. (1.5.11)

After further praise of his men, Cyrus adds a brief epilogue (*ti dei eti legein*, "What more need I add?"), in which, incidentally, he utters the first concrete command of the entire speech:

> Choose your men and get them together, and when you have made the necessary preparations, advance into Media.

The army does what Cyrus orders it to do. There is not a hint anywhere that he has been inadequate. For the moment, he seems to have complete control of the situation. But if we examine the speech more critically, apart from its admitted elegance, it becomes clear that the speaker himself is something of an *idiôtês* in the matter of waging war.

As a speech for men departing for war, this one is completely backward-looking. It is smug about the superiority of Persian institutions, facile in its caricature of the enemy. This self-congratulation is doubly dangerous. If not corrected at some point before he engages the Assyrians, Cyrus's flattery of his men might tempt him and them to a fatal complacency about their readiness for the approaching war. Worse still, this lack of self-knowledge is compounded by an ignorance of the strengths and weaknesses of the enemy. Invective and contempt replace observation and facts.[17] For all its rhetorical polish and praise of Persian institutions, Cyrus's speech is idealistic and quite uncontaminated by practical observation or preparation for actual battle. If the orator of this exhortation went forward with no more practical sense than is evident here, he would find himself at the head of an army distinguished perhaps for excellent academic marks, but one also quite innocent of what real battle can do.

No one but Cambyses knows Cyrus well enough to be so analytical about his imperial designs. As we shall see in Chapter 4, his grandfather Astyages is captivated by Cyrus's charms. His mother Mandane is a shrewd, unsentimental observer of Cyrus while he is a boy, but she plays no role in his later education. And his uncle Cyaxares is a special case: intuitively aware of Cyrus's imperial schemes, he is not energetic enough to devise any countermeasures. For him this will be doubly unfortunate. Cyrus gains no such ascendancy over his father. Cambyses is the only person in the *Cyropaedia* who combines a power to analyze Cyrus's actions with an equal ability to point out where Cyrus has not mastered his art. He is the only person who even partially shares Cyrus's imperial perspective. He does not teach Cyrus how to win a world empire, but he does more than any other person to help Cyrus attain it.

4

Aside from Cambyses' brief reunion with Cyrus in Book 8, Xenophon shows us this most important teacher of Cyrus in one long scene at the end of Book 1, in a conversation between Cyrus and Cambyses when Cyrus is on the point of leaving his father and departing for the war against the Assyrian king. Here, as everywhere else, we have no continuous narrative of Cyrus's life and education, but only emblematic scenes that suggest what that life and education might be. Much is compressed into this single meeting. At the point Cyrus leaves for war, he is already among the *teleioi andres* (Persian citizens at least twenty-five or twenty-six years of age). Xenophon captures the sum of all of Cambyses' teaching, both what Cyrus learned and how he learned it.

The scene takes the form of a dialogue based on Cyrus's memories of his past education with his father.[18] As narrative strategy, it is not such a bad move. The character Cyrus rather than the narrator carries the burden of organizing and recollecting the sum of past experience. Cambyses concentrates his entire attention on what Cyrus can tell him, now, about his past education, in a flashback to earlier events.[19] Like Socrates, Cambyses controls the direction of the dialogue. This is one time in the *Cyropaedia* where Cyrus relinquishes control of a situation; the other is when his father reappears at the end of Book 8.

The conversation begins and ends with reflections on the gods, the uses of piety, and the importance of sacrifices and omens (1.6.1–2, 1.6.25–27). There are important differences between these opening and closing remarks that indicate far more than simple piety on the part of Cyrus and his father. Cambyses begins by noting Cyrus's careful attention to omens and sacrifices; all these signs from the gods have been auspicious, and presumably mark the beginning of a successful campaign against the Assyrian king. Yet Cyrus is sufficiently inexperienced in his pious enthusiasm to think that the gods are his friends (1.6.4). At the end of their conversation, Cambyses will return to the topic with a more searching comment.

> So we see that mere human wisdom does not know how to choose what is best any more than if any one were to cast lots and do as the lot fell. But the gods, my son, are eternal and know all things, but what has been and what is and what shall come to pass as a result of each present or past event; and if men consult them, they reveal to those to whom they are propitious what they ought to do and what they ought not to do. But if they are not willing to give counsel to everybody, that is not surprising; for they are

under no compulsion to care for any one unless they will.

(1.6.46)

The dialogue before this fatalistic conclusion is animated and of very different character. Cambyses is a stern and persistent questioner and Cyrus is never able to throw him off the track. Particularly striking is the way he seizes on one complacent answer after another. Resumptive and emphatic particles drag Cyrus through a cross-examination that is unlike anything else in the *Cyropaedia*: *oukoun nun* ("do you not now then?" 1.6.4), *ti gar . . . memnêsai ekeina ha pote edokei hêmin* ("indeed then . . . do you remember those things which we once concluded?" 1.6.5). The questioning can be impatient and pressing: *ekeinon de . . . epelathou ha pote ego kai su elogizometha* ("but have you forgotten those things which once upon a time I and you reasoned about?" 1.6.7), *alla toi* ("but let me tell you," 1.6.9), *toutois de su . . . pisteuôn erchêi* ("relying indeed on *these* things are you marching?" 1.6.9), *homôs de toutois pisteueis tois adêlois* ("but nevertheless you trust in *these* uncertain things?" 1.6.9), *erôtais pou an apo sou poros prosgenoito* ("you're asking where provisions might be procured for you?" 1.6.10). Toward the end of their conversation, Cambyses' comments become longer and longer, until he concludes with a speech that ranges over everything a commander of an army must have in mind when going against his enemy (1.6.37–46). This princely education is the most overtly didactic part of the whole work; cross-examination in the end gives way to lecture.

What strategy can Cyrus devise to deal with this most formidable of all persons? Cambyses is not his opponent. Harmony between father and son is basic to the design of the ethical pattern that informs every action of Cyrus in the *Cyropaedia*. This encounter amply demonstrates why Cambyses merits such obedience. But there may be something more here than a show of obedience in the royal family of Persia. If there is any perceivable strategy in Cyrus's conduct with his father other than simple obedience, it is that he projects everywhere an awareness that his father must be taken seriously as a teacher. Accordingly, he strives to show a good memory for his father's teaching in the past. A pattern of eager assent is as pervasive in Cyrus's replies, and as repetitive, as those pressing particles in Cambyses' questions: *kai mên dê memnêmai gar akousas pote sou* ("and in fact I do indeed remember once hearing you," 1.6.3), *panu men oun* ("yes absolutely," 1.6.5), *nai ma Di' . . . memnêmai mentoi toiauta akousas sou* ("yes by Zeus, I do indeed remember hearing you," 1.6.6), *kai gar oida se legonta aei* ("for I very well know that you always used to say," ibid.), *nai ma Di' . . . memnêmai kai touto sou legontos* ("yes by Zeus, I do remember your saying this also," 1.6.8). Cyrus's instinct with members of his family is unerring. Even with the person who has the most power over him, he strives to be not only a son obedient and respectful of his father's teaching, but the ideal of such a son.

Throughout this long catechism, Cyrus never resists correction or amplification; he grasps instantly every point his father raises. He is an ideal student of the kind few teachers ever encounter in their experience—it is not in the experience of Socrates, for example. Cambyses himself is fierce and unsentimental. He never relaxes into mere praise of his son, the easiest thing any teacher of superior students can do. Rather he remains focused on doctrine to the end of their conversation, so that although he shows everywhere that he is solicitous of Cyrus's welfare, he is even more concerned to test his grasp of the totality of the art of ruling others. Unlike Astyages, Cambyses never permits himself any great show of affection. But then an affectionate nature is not what needs to be cultivated in those who will someday rule an empire.

Thus Xenophon brings Cambyses back near the end of Book 8 to signal the return of Cyrus to the origins that had shaped him. The design is so simple that it might tempt us to think it simpleminded. But these framing scenes of father and son delimit the romantic world within which Cyrus exercises his powers; and if the boundaries of Xenophon's romance are simple, the education Cyrus acquires while he is away from his father is far from simple. So far as Xenophon was concerned, the rupture of familial bonds was the stuff of which history and tragedy were made. Recall how the *Anabasis* begins, with an account of the discord within the Persian royal family. There we have not a word of introduction, perhaps because the disruption of family ties at that level required no further comment. The consequences of the rivalry between Cyrus the Younger and his older brother Artaxerxes were terrible and not long in coming.

5

In these ways paternal identity is central both to Cyrus's conception of himself and to Xenophon's design of his text. The bond between father and son is so important to the program of the work that once it has been reaffirmed by this politically self-conscious appearance of Cambyses (8.5), Xenophon finds it possible to bring his account of the education of Cyrus to a rapid conclusion. Cyrus leaves the company of his father, returns to Media, marries the daughter of his uncle Cyaxares, and organizes his empire (8.6). Cambyses plays no role in any of these actions. Indeed his mission in 8.5 may be even more redundant than I have supposed. After this interruption, Xenophon goes on to describe Cyrus's conquests and other institutions of his empire, and there is not another word from his father. Xenophon then writes this transition:

> When his life was far spent amid such achievements and Cyrus was now a very old man, he came back for the seventh time in his reign to Persia. His father and his mother were, as one would expect,[20] long since dead. Cyrus performed the customary sacrifice and led the Persians in their national dance and distributed presents among them all, as had been his custom. As he slept in the palace, he saw a vision; a figure of more than human majesty appeared to him in a dream and said, "Make ready, Cyrus, for you shall soon depart to the gods." When the vision was past, he awoke and seemed almost to know that the end of his life was at hand. (8.7.1–2)

The first sentence of this passage compresses most of Cyrus's life into a single sentence: by means of two participial constructions (*houtô de tou aiônos prokexôrêkotos, mala dê presbutês ôn)*, we are brought instantly from Cyrus as a young man, on the threshold of ruling his empire, to Cyrus in old age, at the point of death, with his mother and father long since dead. Like the return of Cambyses to the narrative from which he was so long absent, this metamorphosis of Cyrus into an elder statesman acquires different meanings depending on the questions one asks of it. Naturally, in a literal sense, if Cyrus is an old man, his parents will be long since dead. But what is not at all natural in the narrative is this transformation of Cyrus into an elderly person even older than the father whose company he has just left. All he has left to do is to instruct his sons as his father had once instructed him. After a prayer to the gods, he does so. He defines the succession, and then he dies. There is a similar strategy in the symmetrical opening and closing of the *Memorabilia*.[21]

The coincidence of narrative structure and ethical pattern in Cyrus's life has important implications for our estimation of the *Cyropaedia* as a work of literature. Not the least consequence of this design is that the Greek title *Kyrou paideia* is an accurate description of the entire work. Some scholars have objected that it is not. After all, Cyrus ceases to be a *pais* from 1.5.1 ("When he had passed through this education [*paideia*] and had now entered the class of youths") and becomes an "ephebe," the next stage in the Persian system of education and social order described briefly in 1.2. And since *paideia* is appropriate to children, not men, so the argument goes, "The Education of Cyrus" seems to describe only part of Book 1 (1.1–4), not the rest of the work. For a similar inaccuracy, one might compare the title of the *Anabasis*, where *anabasis* ("the march up") applies literally only to Book 1.[22]

The often cited reference to the education of Cyrus in Plato's *Laws* ought to have been sufficient evidence that Xenophon entitled his work *Kyrou paideia*, or at least that it could be referred to, in a general way, as "the *paideia*." If it had to be summed up in a single word, what other word would do? As Higgins has observed, its educational purpose appears on every page.[23] Furthermore, for these Persians, education is a continuing process that goes on at every stage of life and is not confined to the young. Cyrus was educated in the laws or customs of the Persians (*epaideuthê ge mên en Persôn nomois*, 1.2.1), and these laws cover every age in life. "The Education of Cyrus" is an appropriate title because Cyrus remains a *pais* until his sudden transformation into an old man at the end of Book 8. The *Cyropaedia* is coherent and disciplined in both its theme and its structure. Indeed it is disciplined to the point where artifice veers into artificiality.

For us, there is an even more interesting consequence of this design. It helps us better appreciate the relationship between the *Cyropaedia* and earlier Greek literature. Although it is possible to see Cyrus and his education as an implicit counter-statement to the doctrines of the *Republic*, a more relevant negative image of Xenophon's positive project can be found in the *Iliad* and in the *Histories* of Herodotus. Down to the death of Cyrus himself (8.7), *The Education of Cyrus* rewrites the tragic pattern of human life that both the *Iliad* and the *Histories* exemplify. Only at the end of his poem when he sees his own father in Priam does Achilles begin to think the patrilineal thoughts that Cyrus thinks from beginning to end of the *Cyropaedia*. The disruption and violence of Cyrus's life in Book 1 of Herodotus are in startling contrast to the happy never-never land into which Xenophon's Cyrus has the luck to be born.[24] Herodotus' Cyrus is a tragic figure whose rise and fall are foretold in his parentage and his character.[25] We are reminded of the advice Solon gives King Croesus: "One must look to the end of every matter, how it will come out" (1.32.9). Cyrus's happy end is foretold and firmly in place from the narrator's opening reflection (1.1) to the end of his life (8.7). Up to that point, the text and its hero achieve romantic completeness and perfection in no small part because the author who creates them looks to the end.[26]

6

With these polarities in ethical pattern and narrative structure between Books 1 and 8 established, Xenophon wanted a mechanism for what would happen in between. In fact this was not entirely a literary option. War was the only possible choice. His subject demanded it; empires are created through wars. He knew more about war than about any other subject; strategy, and more often the lack of it, is at the center of his *Hellenica* and *Anabasis*, the technical treatises, and long passages in the Socratic writings. Since the Cyrus of history really did subdue Assyria, war became the engine whereby Xenophon could move his plot, from the first aggression of the Assyrian king (1.4) through the fall of Babylon (7.5). The utility of this war can be measured by what happens after it is concluded. Once it is over and Cyrus has nothing to do but establish his control over his newly won empire, the pace of the narrative begins to falter. In Book 8 Xenophon frequently resorts to the lamest kind of transitions from one topic to the next, in a style reminiscent of the transitions in the *Agesilaus*.[27]

As for his opponent, Cyrus finds an ideal enemy, somewhat like the unifying demon Hitler presented to the Allies in World War II, or, for that matter, the unifying threat of Persia itself when Cyrus's descendant Xerxes invaded Greece in 480. The Assyrians are leaders who lead without any virtues whatever. In his speech at 3.3.44–45, the Assyrian king appeals to his army's self-interest, mentioning lives, land, homes, wives and children. Victory will save everything, defeat will lose it all. The peroration is a lesson in how to be everything Cyrus strives not to be.

> Therefore, if you desire victory, stand and fight. It would be folly for men who desire to win a battle to turn their backs and offer to the enemy the side of their body that is without eyes or hands or weapons. Anyone who wishes to live would be a fool if he tried to run away, when he knows that it is the victors who save their lives. Those who try to run away are more likely to meet their death than those who stand their ground. And if any one desires wealth, he also is foolish if he submits to defeat. For who does not know that the victors not only save what is their own, but take in addition the property of the vanquished, while the vanquished throw both themselves and all they have away? (3.3.45)

In the context of the *Cyropaedia* this is remarkably bad rhetoric. It evokes most vividly the specter of defeat and the consequences the defeated will face. It is a perfect speech for a tyrant; for example, Sallust adapted it for a speech of Catiline.[28] Since the Assyrian king rules by fear, the only way he knows how to inspire his army is by trying to make them fear defeat so much they will desire victory all the more. Cyrus has an easy time contending against this kind of foe. The advantage for his imperial designs is that the eyes of everyone are focused first of all on the evil Assyrian rather than on Cyrus. He can win the affection and loyalty of others precisely because he offers so clear an alternative to the Assyrian king.

In other respects, both the Assyrian king and his wicked son are vague figures, never called by any other name than "the Assyrian."[29] The main distinction between them is that the son is an unworthy, degenerate heir of a better father (6.1.45). He commits many atrocities, such as the castration of the young prince Gadatas and the murder of the innocent son of Gobryas.[30] Both Gadatas and Gobryas flee to Cyrus as refugees from this ogre, and both become loyal and useful subjects in the new empire Cyrus is creating. Apart from the good service he performs by bringing on a war that never was, the Assyrian king provides a nice example of the futility of attempting to rule an empire by terror.

Thus the Assyrian war enables the romantic empire of Cyrus to flourish easily. If empires are made by wars, as they generally are, this particular war assumes a character entirely different from anything that had been seen in Greek literature before the *Cyropaedia*. Homer, Herodotus, and Thucydides had each made war the center of their works. Beginning with the *Iliad* and its sympathetic portrait of Trojan and Greek alike, however, it was never the tendency of the Greeks to create melodramatic villains on the order of the Assyrian king and his depraved son. Of course they bear some resemblance to actual Assyrian monarchs; the younger king's cruelty is redolent of the calculated frightfulness that the Assyrians made part of their statecraft. These Assyrians are simpler than anyone in Homer or history because they are constituted in the first place as dialectical opposites to Cyrus, being everything that he is not. They are supremely bad, but so vaguely present at the very margins of the text that they serve mainly as the polar opposite of Cyrus, evil rulers from whose example everyone may happily flee. They turn Cyrus's campaign into a quest, somewhat like the great adventure that gives literary form to later romance.[31]

With this kind of war as the basic motivation for his story, Xenophon made the heart of his narrative Cyrus's encounters with other people; in essence, these encounters are his education.[32] As we have seen, Cambyses gives Cyrus his identity, and a pattern to impose on his own subjects and sons in the future. Everyone else, including his mother and grandfather, merely offers one more opportunity for Cyrus to learn about the exercise of power. All of them appear to come in contact with Cyrus in the same way that people come in contact with one another in ordinary life, not so much by design as by accident. This is no more than a semblance, a representation of the truth. When writing history, Xenophon had no choice but to deal with people as he found them. He could make them better than they were, or worse than they were; and he could try to ignore them, if he chose. The fundamental fact of their existence could rarely be evaded entirely. But in the new world he was creating for Cyrus, the rules of the game change fundamentally. He introduces only those characters who will contribute to his main theme. Although it is the particular achievement of his fiction that he creates a world not unlike the one he had described in his earlier writings, Cyrus nonetheless inhabits an Asia created entirely by Xenophon's imagination. And the people he encounters are as fictive as Cyrus is.

There is also a fundamental difference between them. Cyrus is a constant, unvarying figure, a static embodiment of success. He moves through a world that is endlessly variable, but in which he remains unchanged. His education consists of dialectical encounters with other people. And in them there is also a polarity of design. This kind of symmetry is typical of romance in all periods, from the *Odyssey* onwards, where pairs of opposites are the rule: light and dark, bad and good, honest and dishonest, clever and stupid.[33] We can see such a design easily by stepping back from the text and thinking about it in a different way. When we actually read the *Cyropaedia* as Xenophon organized it, without such schemes, the symmetry of its characters is not so blatant as this list will imply.

1. The polarity may be remarked first of all in Cyrus's mother and father; here, as elsewhere, there is an imbalance in ability, character, and usefulness to Cyrus. Cambyses is the crucial figure in his education, and Mandane a firm but distant partner in it. Where he is Cyrus's most important teacher, she serves mainly as a foil to the young Cyrus when he is at his grandfather's court amongst the Medes.

2. Cyrus's Median relatives through his mother Mandane: his grandfather Astyages and uncle Cyaxares. The first of them is doting and indulgent, the second of them fatally blessed with the same character. Astyages' insouciance costs him nothing but the gifts he gives Cyrus, and he does genuinely love his grandson. But Cyaxares is not only made jealous because he is displaced by Cyrus in his father's affections; ultimately he surrenders him his kingdom and gives his daughter to Cyrus in marriage.

3. Cyrus's lieutenants: Chrysantas the noble peer (*hômotimos*), of the same rank in Persia as Cyrus, balanced by the commoner (*dêmotês*), Pheraulas, who rises to a position as powerful as any nobleman because of his capable service to Cyrus.

4. Two Medes, childhood friends of Cyrus, both of them afflicted by Eros: Artabazus, who loves Cyrus, and Araspas, the would-be lover of Panthea.

5. The incompetent King of Armenia (unnamed) and his son Tigranes, who is far more capable and intelligent.

6. Cyrus's allies: Gobryas, a king whose son (unnamed) was murdered by the Assyrian king, and a daughter (also unnamed); and a fellow suppliant to Cyrus, the eunuch prince Gadatas, who was castrated by the Assyrian king, who has a father (unnamed) and perforce no children in prospect. Gobryas finds a substitute son in Cyrus, while Gadatas finds in him both a substitute father and child.

7. Abradatas of Susa and his wife Panthea, converts to Cyrus's

service; both of them die heroic deaths. In extreme contrast are his former enemy Croesus of Lydia and his wife (unnamed), who are contented but not altogether trustworthy survivors.

Each of these persons reappears through Cyrus's campaign. In several instances, notably the pair of Araspas and Artabazus, their relevance to his education will not be apparent for a very long time. Taken together, his family, friends, and foes create the education of Cyrus. For novelist and monarch, the ultimate focus of the creative act is other people. The one invents them so that the other may use them. In some such way, Xenophon conceived of the design of the romantic world of the *Cyropaedia*.

CHAPTER FOUR

The Grandson of Astyages

More had long conditioned himself to ask himself on all
public occasions, "What would 'More' say about this?"

Stephen Greenblatt, *Renaissance Self-Fashioning*

T HE FIRST victims of the new
prince were his mother Mandane and his grandfather As-
tyages. They are Cyrus's family and we might presume that
they would play an important role in his education; in fact
they do, but as the first persons to experience his genius for
manipulating others to suit his own purposes. Although Cy-
rus is renowned for his obedience to authority and for his
strict discipline at every stage of life, these childhood scenes
at the court of the Medes are nothing less than a sustained
test of wills. It is a test Cyrus passes on every occasion. He
always resists doing whatever his mother or his grandfather
wants him to do, he always manages to do whatever they
do not want him to do, and he manages to achieve all this
in such a genial fashion that neither Mandane nor Astyages
finds it possible to resist him. At the same time, he is busily
ingratiating himself with children his own age as well as
other adults: Tigranes, Artabazus, and Araspas are child-
hood acquaintances who prove useful to Cyrus the adult.
The conquests of the grandson of Astyages will not long de-
tain us. They are as important as any part of his education,
though, because they are the earliest signs of a young prince

who seems to have known almost by instinct how to excel in the art of ruling others.[1]

I

However contrived Xenophon's evil Assyrians and their war may be, they cannot be subdued by a tiro. They demand more of Cyrus than anything the happy accident of his royal birth or an education under the laws and customs of the Persians can supply. Xenophon outlines these *nomoi* after his prologue. The Persians see to it that the public interest is served by every male citizen at every stage of life: "the best citizens are educated citizens" (*beltistoi politai . . . pepaideumenoi*).[2] But these laws are not in themselves a solution to the problem of ruling others, nor do they show how to win an empire. No one better illustrates their limitations than Cyrus's father. Cambyses is a good king and an exemplary teacher, but he will never be a world ruler. To become as powerful as Cyrus eventually becomes requires exploitation of the very laws and customs which Cambyses serves so well. Here then is the paradox of Xenophon's portrayal of the childhood of a prince: Cyrus is an ideal pupil, seemingly obedient to every law; at the same time, from the moment he first appears as a little boy in the court of his grandfather Astyages, he is ruthlessly self-serving and subversive of the status quo.

Given the claims made for Cyrus in the prologue of the *Cyropaedia*, we should expect nothing less. Unlike children in later times, and especially children in modern literature, children in Greek literature are adults writ small. Often they are the victims of adult evil. The artistic exploitation of childhood's innocence begins in the *Iliad*, in the parting of Hector and Andromache, and continues to be a favored theme in the tragic poets, particularly Euripides.[3] For philosophers as well as later Greek and Roman biographers, the child was an embryonic version of the adult. The evolution of the adult personality is present from the first page onwards.[4]

The first appearance of Cyrus is emblematic of everything to come. We first encounter him when he is a young boy paying a visit with his mother Mandane to the court of his grandfather Astyages, king of the Medes. As soon as he sees his grandfather, he kisses him with great affection. Then he notices Astyages' colorful robes and cosmetics; the Medes affect more luxurious dress than do the members of the austere court of Persia. He is much impressed and blurts out

> O Mother, just look how handsome grandfather is! (1.3.2)

The first words of Cyrus are the last spontaneous thing he will utter in the *Cyropaedia*. He quickly learns what happens to people who say what they think. His mother asks,

> Who is the handsomer man: your father, or your grandfather? (1.3.2)

Mandane hands her son a nice courtier's dilemma. By choosing his grandfather, he will please Astyages but slight his absent father; yet, if he praises his father at the expense of the king before him, he will be exposed as a flatterer too easy with a compliment.

Cyrus's embarrassment would amount to nothing more than a moment's entertainment for the adults of the court, were it not for the level of calculation that underlies his reply.[5] He at once shifts from the invidious comparison his mother has contrived, by awarding first prize to both his father and grandfather:

> Mother, by far the handsomest of the Persians is my father. But of the Medes, so many of them as I have seen both in the streets and here at court, the handsomest man by far is my grandfather. (1.3.2)

Neither Astyages nor the absent Cambyses could possibly take exception to what Cyrus has said. The only person who could be disappointed is Mandane: Cyrus has not answered her question. Astyages is not so analytical. He showers presents on his grandson, as any doting grandparent would. Cyrus is precisely the creature Xenophon promised he would be. Already disposed to love his grandson, Astyages is made to love him even more. This is not a bad debut in the art of ruling others. We learn that power comes to those who master details.

Mandane's question contained a trap. If Cyrus answered her on her terms—father or grandfather?—he would spoil the beginning of an agreeable first meeting with Astyages. She took control of the occasion by asking Cyrus to draw a comparison where he had intended none, in effect changing the rules of their conversation; Cyrus regains control of it by shifting from her comparative adjectives to the superlative degree. At one level, this is witty play of no consequence, turning as it does on the progression of "handsome," "handsomer," "handsomest" (*kalos, kallion, kallistos*). But at the level at which Cyrus thinks, and it is apparently by instinct, this exchange is an exercise in the manipulation of others by language. He learns that people can say one thing at one level and have other meanings and other purposes at another. The key to deflecting his mother's question was first to grasp her strategy (invoking a comparison where none had been before), then to turn this same strategy against her. He sees that language can be as much an instrument of power as of communication.[6]

Cyrus's exquisite conduct can be usefully contrasted with the first appearance of the child Cyrus in Herodotus' *Histories*. That earlier account of Cyrus also anticipates the adult ruler who is to come, and he is everything this Cyrus is not. His grandfather Astyages had learned through the portent of dreams that he would lose his throne to the child if he lived. The infant Cyrus was supposed to have been slain at birth, but a series of kind-hearted people saved him. He was raised as the son of a shepherd, and his noble character emerges inevitably: he is by nature a commander who can be ferocious in asserting his right to rule. This Cyrus has been raised as the slave of Medes, and is challenged by the son of a Mede. In short, the dialectical exchange between cultures from which Xenophon's Cyrus so much profits is denied to Herodotus' Cyrus entirely. Once he and other boys were playing the game of "Kings," and it happened that Cyrus, then unknown and supposedly the son of a slave, was picked to be "King" by the boys.

In the course of their game, he was giving his "subjects"
their various tasks—some to build houses, others to be his
bodyguard, one to be the "king's eye," and another his
messenger—when one of the players, who happened to be
the son of a distinguished Mede called Artembares, refused
to do what King Cyrus commanded, and Cyrus ordered his
arrest. The other boys accordingly seized him, and Cyrus
beat him savagely with a whip. (1.114)

When Artembares complains to Astyages, Cyrus and his
herdsman father are brought before the king. This Astyages
is very different from the genial grandfather of the *Cyropae-
dia*. How dare the son of a slave strike a nobleman's son?
Cyrus is bold and unapologetic:

"Master, there was nothing wrong in what I did to him. We
boys in the village—and he was with us—were playing our
game, and they made me king because they thought I was
the best man to hold the office. The others obeyed my or-
ders, but he did not. He took no notice of me—until he was
punished. That is what happened. If I deserve to suffer for
it, I am ready."
      Almost before he finished speaking, Astyages had
guessed who he was, for that was not the answer of a slave;
moreover, the cast of the boy's features seemed to resemble
his own, and he was just of an age to fit the date of the ex-
posure. (1.115)

Herodotus' Cyrus reveals his imperial disposition sponta-
neously, even before he knows his own true identity. This
highly competent player King is very much the father of the
real king to come.
      Xenophon's departure from Herodotus' emblematic
scene is fundamental. He has omitted all the characteristics
that link Herodotus' Cyrus to a mythical hero like Oedi-
pus—the ominous birth, the exposure—because his aim is
political rather than historical or tragic.[7] This Cyrus does
not need to wrest control of empire from anyone. He makes
himself an adorable grandson, thereby increasing his hold
over Astyages, by acting on his analysis of the rules and the
people in the situation in which he finds himself. He has a

fine sensitivity to others. Herodotus' Cyrus exhibits different qualities, both as man and boy.

2

Like his successors in ancient biography, Xenophon does not give a continuous chronicle of Cyrus's deeds, but what Plutarch would later term the "signs" (sêmeia) of a subject's life.[8] There are only two more glimpses of Cyrus as a child. Both reveal his growing ability to manipulate others for his own purposes. It is an art that is already more visible to the reader than to most of the people Cyrus encounters. One ostensible purpose of these later childhood scenes is that they teach Cyrus the differences between the laws and customs of Persia and Media. As always, travel broadens. But Xenophon's purpose is not simply to contrast Median luxury with Persian simplicity. Cyrus plays both sides of the game, first criticizing Median luxury as a puritanical Persian might; then, just as ably, dismissing with Median insouciance such basic Persian virtues as the learning of justice (dikaiosynê) and self-knowledge and self-restraint (sophrosynê). He understands the relativity of cultural values.[9] And he learns that he can do what he wishes to do, rather than what his grandfather or his mother wants him to do.

In the first conversation, Cyrus expounds what will become a favored theme in his adult life: the simplicity and moderation of the Persians. This is more than a lesson in Persian austerity at the expense of the Medes. Cyrus finds himself in a relaxed, even frivolous social gathering, yet he insists on serious conversation. He finds fault with everything his grandfather does. Astyages' banquet is a lavish entertainment in the grand style, with a huge variety of dishes, drink, and servants to attend to every wish. A child in such adult company might be expected to be subdued. Not Cyrus. When his grandfather asks him if he doesn't think this dinner is finer than anything in Persia, he takes the offensive immediately:

No grandfather. The road to satiety is much more simple
and direct in our country than in yours. Bread and meat
take us there; but you, though you make for the same goal
as we, go wandering up and down through many a maze
and finally arrive at the point we have long since reached.
(1.3.4)

Astyages urbanely tries to turn this sermon aside by con-
tinuing the metaphor of the road.

But my boy, we do not object to this wandering about. If
you have a taste, you also will see that it is pleasant. (1.3.5)

Cyrus is not to be deflected. He turns at once to the Medes'
table manners:

"But grandfather," Cyrus said, "I see that even you are dis-
gusted with these dishes."
    "And how did you reach this conclusion?" asked As-
tyages.
    "Because," he said, "I see that when you touch bread,
you do not wipe your hand on anything; but when you
touch any of these other things you at once clean your
hand on your napkin as if you were very displeased that it
had become soiled with them."
    "Well then, my child," Astyages replied, "if that is your
judgment, at least have a helping of meat, so you may go
home a strong young man." (1.3.5–6)

He places a large serving of wild and domestic meat before
Cyrus. An adult might have acquiesced at this point, but
that is not Cyrus's way. He springs up and distributes all his
portion to his teachers and Astyages' other servants. This
action devalues Astyages' hospitality. Cyrus supplants his
grandfather as the host of the gathering, and wins the grati-
tude of his servants in the bargain (1.3.7).
    Another adult pastime elicits an even sharper departure
from good table manners. As an innocent child, Cyrus sees
only the effects of drinking on his grandfather and other
Medes. He supposes it is some kind of poison.

In the first place you kept doing what you never allow us
boys to do: for instance, you were all shouting together at

one and the same time, and none of you heard a word any of the others were saying. Then you began singing, and in a most ridiculous manner at that, and though you did not hear the singer, you swore he sang most excellently. Each one of you kept talking about his own strength, but if you stood up to dance, to say nothing of dancing in time, why, you could not even stand up straight. All of you quite forgot—you were king; and the rest, that you were their sovereign. Then I also discovered for the first time that what you were practicing was your boasted "equal freedom of speech" [isêgoria]. At any rate, none of you were ever silent. (1.3.10)

For Cyrus, the basic problem with drinking is that it interferes with the essential duties of the king. It causes both the ruler and his subjects to forget the roles each of them should play.

Now that he has complete control of the occasion—or at any rate a silent audience—Cyrus finds that the duties of a host have devolved on him. Perhaps he senses that he has gone far enough in lecturing his grandfather, for he abruptly changes roles, dropping the mask of solemnity and taking up the role of a clown. Jokes can be as useful as lectures when one wants to control a situation, and they are particularly effective when employed by a child. Cyrus mimics Astyages' cupbearer Sacas, whom he dislikes because Sacas keeps him from visiting his grandfather whenever he wishes (1.3.8–10). If Cyrus could rule over him for three days, he says, he would return the favor: Sacas would get no lunch, "because it [lunch] is at the baths." If he were very hungry, he would get no dinner, "because it [food] is visiting the women" (1.3.11). Astyages and Mandane are so charmed by this foolishness that they overlook the firm assertion of authority that underlies all these pleasantries. Cyrus displays good will and affection for others in order to acquire power over them. At Astyages' court he reaches the limits of that power very quickly (1.3.12).

It might be objected that he is too precociously serious for one so young, that this kind of conduct is precisely what earned the Cyropaedia its reputation as tedious moral fiction. It is vitally important then to read this first banquet scene in sequence with the departure of Mandane that follows it. For if Cyrus has played the role of an earnest little puritan among Median voluptuaries, he now reverses roles completely. In the next scene, he wants to stay with his grandfather and let his mother go back alone to Perisa; however, he must first answer some stern questions from his mother Mandane about the life of leisure among the Medes. On this point also, his grandfather Astyages is less severe. He tries to bribe Cyrus by promising him all the things a grandson might want: no more Sacas, plenty of grandfather's horses, temperance at dinner parties, animals to hunt, training in hunting, children for playmates, and anything else Cyrus can think of. Naturally Cyrus wants to stay, but it is typical that he singles out only the useful skill of horsemanship to justify staying (1.3.14–15).

Mandane is not so indulgent. She is all Persian, as serious as Cyrus was at the banquet: How is he going to learn justice (*dikaiosynê*) among the Medes when his teachers for that subject are in Persia? (1.3.16). Again the alternatives seem to lead only to invidious choices, and again, Cyrus refuses to play according to the rules of her game. He already knows everything about justice, he says. Once in Persia his teacher asked him for a verdict on the following case. A big boy with a little tunic found a little boy with a big tunic, took it and put his own tunic on the little boy. Cyrus decided that it was better for both that each keep the new tunic he had. For this he received a whipping. His teacher told him that he was not judging sizes of tunics, but justice; and since what is lawful is just and what is unlawful is wrong, the judge must always render a verdict on the side of the law. This is how Cyrus "learned" justice. If he needs any further instruction, he adds, his grandfather will teach him. In short, he evades the question by telling an anecdote. A joke at his own expense does no harm, especially if it enables him to do as he pleases (1.3.17).

This time Mandane is not turned aside so easily. The problem with Astyages as a teacher of justice is that he is a Mede, not a Persian; hence he does not have the same view of justice that Cyrus's father does. Astyages is not a king like Cambyses, but a tyrant; as she observes, one characteristic of tyrants is that they think it is right for one person to have more than all others (1.3.18). Cyrus now replies as if he were a Mede rather than a Persian.

> But your father at least is more shrewd at teaching people to have less than to have more, mother. Why, don't you see that he has taught all the Medes to have less than himself? So never fear that your father will turn either me or anybody else out trained under him to have too much. (1.3.18)

Xenophon does not say whether or not Mandane laughed at this. Her objection about the difference between Median tyranny and Persian kingship is very much to the point, and Cyrus has not answered it. What he has done is reveal how readily he can abandon the norms of one society for another when it suits his purposes. Learning about justice is a serious business among the Persians, and Cyrus has turned the whole enterprise into a joke.[10]

Xenophon sums up the character of young Cyrus by admitting that he was perhaps too talkative at times (*polylogoteros*) (1.4.1). He attributes this characteristic to Cyrus's youth, his keen mind, and the nature of his education, in which he was encouraged to ask questions. Of course Xenophon is being charmingly disingenuous; in effect, he is apologizing to us for something he himself has invented. For his part, the boy Cyrus has been so genial and pleasant that no one has noticed he has played two very different roles, adjusting his performance to what he perceives are the needs of the moment. The young Persian at the banquet (1.3.4–12) would not have hesitated to follow his mother back to Persia. Like his admirer Machiavelli, Xenophon writes for those who will understand; and for those who do, this portrait of the childhood of a prince is more than charming.

3

Transitions in Cyrus's life bring about changes in the art of ruling others. Adolescence proves to be an awkward time for the would-be ruler of men. Cyrus has already shown that he knows power comes to those who perceive their roles in life most clearly—the priggish Persian boy, the adorable grandson, the insouciant Mede. Now his own status is, for the moment at least, ambiguous. He is at once a child and a man, on the point of having power, yet not having it. He gained not-so-childish control over his grandfather by playing to perfection the roles of Persian boy and Median grandson. Now he learns how to achieve what he desires by playing a role based on the ambiguity of adolescence itself; that in-between status of being at once a child and not a child, an adult and not an adult.[11] He faces competing claims on his loyalty and affection now, not simply from his father and grandfather (Persia and Media), but from boys his own age; the context for his imperial designs is widening. While Astyages remains the same, a doting grandparent who would prefer to keep his young grandson forever a child, the charming boy he adores is growing up. Cyrus himself does not understand what is happening to him, but he is increasingly aware that the change is taking place.

> I do not know what sort of person I have become, for I cannot speak to my grandfather or even look at him as I used to. If I keep on at this rate, I fear I shall become a dolt and a fool. When I was a little boy I was thought ready enough to chatter. (1.4.12)

It is as if the character Cyrus had overheard his creator and resolved to be more serious, and at once. Even so, in this transitional stage of life, Cyrus still remains at the center of everything. And he learns that popularity has its costs. He gives such a good account of his adventures on a hunt for wild game outside his grandfather's park that his friends beg him to get permission from Astyages to let them all go on another hunt. The only person who can do this for them is Cyrus, but as he points out, he no longer finds it so easy to talk to adults like his grandfather (1.4.11–12). His friends then go off, quite willing to find someone else if Cyrus cannot do this favor for them. Cyrus is furious, but takes counsel silently.

> When he had summoned up his courage to make the ven-
> ture, he went in to his grandfather, after he had laid his
> plans how he might with the least annoyance broach the
> subject to his grandfather and accomplish for himself and
> the other boys what they desired. (1.4.13)

He is still devoted to his grandfather and wishes to cause
him no trouble; on the other hand, he now also feels the
claim of his peers and is sensitive to the possibility that
they will find somebody else to do his job for him. His prob-
lem is that he must devise a strategy that accomplishes
what he wants; at the same time, it must be one that does
not create enmity.

As in his response to Mandane's question about who
was the handsomer man, Cyrus solves the problem by re-
defining the terms in which it is posed. His dilemma is
rather similar to the one he faced with Mandane, but the
game has become more complex. He cannot disobey his
grandfather, but he also does not want to disappoint his
friends. He wants to do what they want, not what his grand-
father wants. Since grandfather has all the power, grand-
father gets all the attention: somehow Astyages must be
made to change his mind. Cyrus approaches him with hy-
pothetical questions about the punishment of disobedient
slaves:

> "Tell me, grandfather, if one of your servants runs away
> and you catch him again, what will you do to him?"
> "What else but put him in chains and make him
> work?"
> "But if he comes back again of his own accord, what
> will you do?"
> "What else but flog him to prevent his doing it again,
> and then treat him as before?"
> "Then it may be time for you to be making ready to
> flog me; for I am planning to run away from you and take
> my friends out hunting."
> "You did well to tell me in advance. I now forbid you to
> stir from the palace. It would be a fine thing if for the sake
> of a few pieces of meat, I should play the careless herds-
> man and lose my daughter her son."

When Cyrus heard this, he obeyed, and stayed at home.
He said nothing, but stayed downcast and sulked. (1.4.13–
14)

Astyages finally changes his mind because of Cyrus's obe-
dient but resentful conduct, and because this little exchange
is in fact an ingenious trap.

Cyrus first of all makes it plain that, like an adult, he
knows what obedience and disobedience mean. He even
goes so far as to think of two punishments for disobedience.
But when he questions Astyages about his policy of punish-
ing disobedient slaves, he confronts him with an impossible
dilemma. By this analogy, he suggests that if a grandson
wants to run away (in this instance, to hunt game), he must
be some kind of captive to his grandfather, one who needs
to be confined and watched like a slave. Yet his thoughtful-
ness shows he is capable of thinking adult thoughts, grand-
son though he may be. And to treat an adult like a child, to
refuse an adult what is his due, is in effect to treat that adult
like a slave, a creature with no freedom. Such is the rhetor-
ical implication of the analogy; logically of course it is full
of too many errors to be taken seriously. But grandfathers
are not rigorous cross-examiners of their grandsons. Punish-
ing Cyrus is a disagreeable idea and not one that Astyages
could contemplate with any pleasure.

The case of the slave who returns voluntarily for punish-
ment is what clinches Cyrus's specious argument. When
Astyages admits that he would beat the loyal runaway, and
Cyrus says, "Then it is time for you to prepare to beat me,"
Astyages is caught in a syllogism from which he cannot es-
cape. He thinks that the conclusion is that Cyrus must not
leave the palace. What he does not realize is that Cyrus has
anticipated all the prohibitions his grandfather would lay
down, as well as any kind of punishment he could devise.
Not that there was any prospect of such punishment; it is
demonstrable that the king of the Medes would not put his
grandson in irons, or have him flogged. In this way Cyrus
suggests that he has as fully developed a moral conscious-
ness as his grandfather, and along with it, the maturity to

restrain himself even under what he perceives as unfair re-
strictions. By this very submission, he is also implying that
he is being treated like a good slave. His poor grandfather
has no choice but to end his grandson's sulking silence.
There is a happy ending, of course: Xenophon is inter-
ested in the art of creating an empire, not verisimilitude.
The happy hunting grounds of 1.4.5–17 are in pointed con-
trast to the tragic story we half expect could have been writ-
ten. Compare for example the story of Adrastus and Atys,
the son of Croesus, in Herodotus 1.34–45. Things turn out
happily for Cyrus because they must turn out that way, not
because Astyages was incorrect.[12] Astyages is so pleased
that he himself goes hunting with Cyrus whenever possible
and, for Cyrus's sake, he allows the boys to go along as well.
Cyrus has accomplished precisely what he intended to.

Hunting marks the transition from childhood to adult-
hood for Cyrus, and also the transition in the narrative from
the serenity of royal court life to the war against the Assyr-
ians. The Assyrian king's son desires to hunt in Media to
catch game for his wedding day (1.4.17). This leads him into
an expedition across the frontier that brings Astyages' army,
his son Cyaxares, and finally Cyrus himself into battle. In
fiction Xenophon thus makes happen what he elsewhere ar-
gued should ideally happen: the games of youth lead
straight into the grown-up business of war.[13]

> I charge the young not to despise hunting or any other
> schooling. For these are the means by which men become
> good in war and in all things out of which must come ex-
> cellence in thought and word and deed. (*On Hunting*, 1.18)

In his first encounter with battle, Cyrus proves he is coura-
geous and a gifted tactician, if an impetuous one. In a work
filled with his political and military successes from end to
end, this first battle between the Medes and their Assyrian
invaders offers the reader of the *Cyropaedia* a rare glimpse
of an imperfect Cyrus. His conduct also elicits a rare simile
from Xenophon, one of striking banality: "As a well-bred
but untrained hound rushes recklessly upon a boar . . ."
(1.4.21).[14] This first exposure to actual battle works a kind

of magic on Cyrus, making him a little crazy and daring
(*mainomenos . . . têi tolmêi*).

As the rest made their way homeward, Cyrus did nothing
but ride around alone and gloat upon the slain, and only
with difficulty did those who were detained to do so suc-
ceed in dragging him away and taking him to Astyages. As
he came, he sent his escort well before him, for he saw that
his grandfather's face was angry because of his gloating
upon them. (1.4.24)

But Cyrus learns to repress this kind of revealing conduct:
it does not become the young man who has done so well as
the grandson of Astyages. This lesson in discretion is the
last thing he learns from his grandfather. He is soon sum-
moned home to complete his education in those things that
are particular to the Persians (1.4.25). The laws and cus-
toms of his own country will pose no challenge to the
grandson of Astyages. As a child and a youth he has gov-
erned others with a character and an intelligence typical of
maturity, or even old age. As a grown man, he breaks the
same rules of conduct. He will acquire power in no small
part because he retains that instinct for generosity that is
characteristic of the young rather than the old. The times of
life are like the laws and customs by which life is lived;
Cyrus bends and refashions them to his own advantage,
conforming and not conforming as the occasion demands.

FOES

The Envy of Uncle Cyaxares

Do whatever you please, since it now seems it is you who
are king.

Cyaxares, to the boy Cyrus

Kinship also knows how to envy.

Aeschylus, quoted in Aristotle, Rhetoric

THE POPULATION of the *Cyropaedia* is never what we expect it to be. Family, foes, and friends are basic categories of social and familial relationships in the *Cyropaedia*, but like the *nomoi* of the Persians and the Medes, they are there for Cyrus to observe or to ignore as the occasion seems to dictate. All things that custom says determine character and social standing become objects of his designing intelligence. To observe these distinctions of family, foes, and friends is only to begin to learn how Cyrus plays with each of them to his own advantage.[1]

In this regard there is one enemy who may seem conspicuous by his absence. The son of the Assyrian king is surely Cyrus's worst enemy. He causes the war. But that is all he is, a *casus belli*; he plays no role in the dialectic of character that is the education of Cyrus, because he is not someone Cyrus meets or deals with in any but the most distant, detached way. He is the negative pole of the *Cyropaedia*, the Other whose marginal status as an opponent enables Cyrus and his reign to be so simply and purely good. Once you have said that the Assyrian prince is wicked and cruel, you have said all there is to say about him. The logic of classifying Uncle Cyaxares as one of Cyrus's enemies runs along the same lines. In order for this romantic world to be instructive about every sphere of human activity, a certain amount of education needs to come from home. Reference to the *Hellenica* and the first book of the *Anabasis* reminds us that family quarrels will do very nicely for disturbing the peace.[2] Family strife is as much a potential problem for the ideal ruler of men as the resistance of the most determined enemy. So far as Xenophon is concerned, the instability of the household (*oikos*) is analogous to discord at the public, political level. To provide against this kind of instability on both the private and public scale is the aim of the *Oeconomicus*. A pervasive pattern of disruption in public and private government is our point of departure in the *Cyropaedia*. As we shall eventually discover, fraternal strife will also be the undoing of even Cyrus's empire, once he is dead.[3]

For these reasons it is important for Cyrus and his readers to gain an education in the dangers that members of one's own family can pose. But it would be entirely inappropriate for there to be a conflict between Cyrus and his mother or father. It is largely because such a conflict does not arise that the romantic world of the *Cyropaedia* exists in the first place. Cambyses determines both its basic ethical pattern and the structure of its narrative.[4] How then to teach Cyrus and us about the potentially disastrous consequences of family strife, when the possibility of using either his mother or father has been so effectively foreclosed?

Xenophon resolved his pedagogical and authorial dilemma by locating all serious familial strife in just one person: Cyrus's uncle Cyaxares. As Mandane's brother, he is Cyrus's maternal uncle. A patrilineal structure of kinship is the basis of both the narrative and ethical pattern of the *Cyropaedia*. And in this pattern, a paternal uncle could pose very serious problems for a nephew. From an anthropological point of view, one might say that Cyaxares is temporarily playing the wrong role.⁵ Malign and suspicious when he should be a friend, he acts for a time as if he were a paternal rather than a maternal uncle.⁶ He is envious of Cyrus from the moment he first appears, and this envy turns slowly into the most challenging crisis of Cyrus's career. From that same viewpoint of kinship structures, all Cyrus need do is persuade Cyaxares to return to the role he should play, which is to be a benign—but powerless—mother's brother.

I

No one is more annoying to Cyrus than his uncle Cyaxares. He is difficult not because of his intelligence or cunning, but because of the role he plays in the royal families of Media and Persia. One of the least talented persons Cyrus ever meets, he wins a certain kind of distinction in one respect. He is the first person in the *Cyropaedia* to become aware of Cyrus's imperial designs. He is also the first and most distinguished victim of his nephew's rise to power.

This portrait of envy is finely drawn. It begins early, in the childhood of Cyrus, when he displaced Cyaxares in Astyages' affections. When the two were together on Cyrus's first hunt outside Astyages' park (1.4.7–9), Cyaxares tried to dissuade Cyrus from presenting all their game to the court, because he feared his father's anger.

> If he finds out that you have been giving chase, he will discipline not only you, but me also for letting you do so. (1.4.9)

The characterization of Cyaxares is a tour de force in the psychology of the ruler and the ruled. The person who loses the most power and prestige because of Cyrus's rise to power is first reconciled to that unavoidable fact, then moved to offer his own daughter in marriage. In all this adroit manipulation, the contrast between their characters is obvious. Cyaxares is Cyrus's inferior in every way that matters. He is vain, hedonistic, quick-tempered, impatient, incapable of thinking through diplomatic or military strategy. He enjoys the pomp and ceremony of his royal position, but never sees beyond whatever he has inherited. He takes everything in life as it comes, whether it be the traditional court dress of the Medes, a message from the Indian king, or an enemy army drawn up in attack formation. Because he is nominally Cyrus's elder and his fellow commander, he can interfere in Cyrus's designs in ways no one else can. If it were not for Cyrus's prompt intervention, he would have tried disastrous strategies for battle, for the organization of the army and their new allies. It is symptomatic of his limited imagination that he can think of no better way to deal with the rebellious Armenians than to treat them "as father would" (2.4.16).

Yet Xenophon offers us more than a portrait of a weak man. Cyaxares' would-be kingship runs in elaborate counterpoint to the education of Cyrus. He exemplifies what a political career can be when it is pursued without design. While Cyrus everywhere looks to an end, in Solon's sense of the word, Cyaxares never looks to any end whatever. Although he is aware of his nephew's designing intelligence, he has neither the imagination nor the stamina to do anything but look to the present. He envies the ascendancy of Cyrus and realizes what it will mean for his own prestige. But envy is an intensely private emotion. It is one thing for Cyaxares to be petulant about the boy Cyrus and his privileged status with his grandfather (1.4.9), quite another for him to make the same kind of complaint when they are older and in higher office. Then Cyrus will capitalize on his uncle's private dilemma by conducting all their business in settings as open and public as he can arrange. By showing him every possible courtesy in public, by deferring to his judgment—or rather, by seeming to defer—Cyrus eventually isolates Cyaxares and strips him of every power that distinguishes a king from a subject.

Xenophon spent much care on his portrait of the envy of Cyaxares. All the opposition that tends to make for tragic conflicts within a family is displaced onto a single, comic figure who is ultimately at the periphery of power. Save for Cyrus himself, this is the most sustained characterization in the *Cyropaedia*.

2

From the beginning of the Assyrian war Cyrus perceives his uncle's capacity for mischief. As soon they join their armies together in Media, the differences between them start to mount up. Although Cyrus has brought a considerable force with him, Cyaxares thinks they still do not have enough men (2.1.17). Like General George McClellan, he is the kind of commander who never has his fill of preparations.[7] But Cyrus points out that preparations are not the key; if both sides employ the same tactics, the side with the greater number will win. And since the Assyrians cannot be surpassed in the number of men they can put into the field, the better tactic would be to devise a different strategy and new armaments to counter their superiority. This suggestion itself is no mean exercise in tactics: "If I were you, I would have armor made as quickly as possible for all the Persians who are coming here . . ." (2.1.9). Cyaxares thinks this is well spoken (2.1.10).

Cyaxares' limitations as a diplomat become plain just as quickly. When the ambassadors from the king of India come to determine which side to support in the war, Cyaxares assumes that the way to impress them is by displaying a magnificent court and royal dress. He summons Cyrus to appear in beautiful robes, as his messenger says, "for he wishes that you appear as brilliant and splendid as possible so the Indians will see how you come into his presence" (2.4.1). Cyrus does go to Cyaxares, but in the company of his Persian soldiers, who are perfectly drilled. While the men complete their drill, he appears in a simple Persian uniform. Cyaxares is pleased at his promptness, but angered at his dress.

> How is this, Cyrus? What do you mean by appearing this way before the Indians? I wanted you to appear as brilliant as possible, for it would have been to my credit to have my sister's son appear in as much grandeur as possible. (2.4.5)

Cyrus's reply is to show that his disobedience was in fact more flattering to Cyaxares than obedience would have been.

Should I be showing you more respect, Cyaxares, if I
dressed myself in purple and put on bracelets and a neck-
lace and at my leisure obeyed your order, than I have in
obeying you with such speed and come with a large and ef-
ficient army? or come myself adorned with sweat and
marks of haste to honor you and present others also obedi-
ent to you? (2.4.6)

Cyaxares again must agree. The Indian envoys want to
know who has been wronged in this war between the As-
syrians and the Medes and Persians; they will join the side
of the one wronged. All Cyaxares can think of to say is,

Well, then, let me tell you that we are *not* guilty of doing
any wrong to the Assyrian. If you need to, go to him now
and learn from him what he has to say. (2.4.8)

This response is innocent of all calculation. Cyaxares' mat-
ter-of-fact reply, while doubtless true, leaves the issue wide
open to the Assyrian king. If this is all the Medes and Per-
sians have to say on the question, the Assyrian will be able
to do at least as well, and probably better; he could, for ex-
ample, invent a more compelling argument that he has been
wronged. The Indian king expects each side to say it is right
and the other wrong. Cyaxares is acting not so much out of
strategic thought as out of reflex. Any calculation, however
brief, will give the enemy a better advantage with the Indi-
ans than what he has devised.

Cyrus intervenes at once, and at many different levels,
instructing the envoys, his uncle, and most of all, us. He
realizes first that the Indian king must make a decision. It
is equally clear that the Assyrian will claim that he has
been wronged. How else could he justify an invasion of Per-
sian and Median territory? And the Indian king will also ex-
pect a counterclaim from Cyrus and Cyaxares. Since the In-
dian has already set himself up as an implicit judge of the
matter, Cyrus makes him explicitly the judge, flattering
him by making him think Cyrus trusts his judgment. This
complicated scenario is played out in Cyrus's deceptively
simple instruction to the messenger:

"May I also tell them what I think?" Cyrus asked.

Cyaxares told him to do so.

"Well then," he said, "tell the king of the Indians this—
that is, if Cyaxares has no objection: Say that we say that if
the Assyrian says he has been wronged by us in any way,
we propose to choose the king of the Indians himself as our
judge." (2.4.8)

Cyaxares thinks this is a fine idea. And it is: the wooing of
the Indian king does not stop here. Cyaxares has also lost
all initiative in the war and he will never regain it.

While his uncle marches off at once to collect his cav-
alry and infantry, Cyrus takes care as always to offer sacri-
fices for the success of his expedition (2.4.16–18). He asks
his uncle for some of his horsemen, and many volunteer to
go. Although Xenophon does not say as much, Cyaxares'
jealousy is already at work; he allows only a few men to
follow Cyrus. He has everywhere assented to Cyrus's cor-
rections and revisions of his strategies—such as they are—
and Cyrus has taken great care to make it seem that his un-
cle is his equal or even his superior in all matters. Thus
Cyaxares strikes back the only way he knows, by denying
Cyrus the cavalrymen he asks for.

The fighting against the Assyrian king begins in earnest
in Book 3, and so does Cyrus's campaign to control his un-
cle. He marshalls all his staff officers and brings them to
Cyaxares' tent. This visible show of his power and disci-
pline speaks more eloquently to what he is about than any
number of deferential speeches to his uncle. His words are
as tactful as ever.

> I am sure, Cyaxares, that you have this long time been
> thinking no less than we of the proposition that I am going
> to lay before you. But perhaps you hesitate to broach the
> subject for fear it should be thought that you speak of an
> expedition from here because you are embarrassed at hav-
> ing to maintain us. Therefore, since you do not say any-
> thing, I will speak both for you and for us. (3.3.13–14)

This is disingenuous. Cyaxares was not silent because he
was embarrassed or because he had already thought of what

Cyrus proposes. He was silent because he did not have a thought in his head about any of the matters Cyrus then enumerates: for example, the desirability of waging war in the enemy's territory rather than his own (3.3.16), the burden of supporting Cyrus and his army (3.3.17), and the valuable boost going on the offensive would give to the army's morale (3.3.18). Cyrus's concluding argument clinches the matter.

> And my father always says, and so do you, and all the rest agree, that battles are decided more by men's souls than by the strength of their bodies. (3.3.19)

Naturally Cyaxares can only protest that he has not been embarrassed by having to support his nephew's army. He thinks that this, too, is a fine idea (3.3.20).

When Cyaxares finally shows some initiative, the results are predictable. It is clear that the enemy will not attack first:

> I propose, men, just as we are now drawn up, so to go up to the breastworks of the enemy and make it clear that we want to fight. Then, if they do not march out in reply, our men will withdraw more full of courage. But when the enemy see our daring they will be more frightened. (3.3.30)

"This," adds Xenophon drily, "is what he proposed." The tactic is characteristically bold but not thought through. Cyrus is not so circumspect as before.

> No, by the gods, Cyaxares, let us not do that! Never! If we march out and show ourselves as you suggest, the enemy will see us marching up but will not fear us, because they know they are secure against any injury. When we withdraw without having accomplished anything, they will also see that our numbers are less than theirs and despise us. And then tomorrow they will come out more encouraged than ever. (3.3.31)

Although Cyaxares must agree with Cyrus—along with everyone else in this public meeting—he cannot resist one more attempt at original thought. He sends a messenger to Cyrus proposing to attack anyway, since the enemy's forces

are not yet up to full strength (3.3.46). Cyrus replies by
pointing out that if less than half of the enemy forces are
involved, nothing will be proved and another battle will be
required (3.3.47). This argument is plausible, but Cyrus's es-
timation of his uncle's newest proposal is at best specula-
tive.

For by now it is apparent that it is as important for Cyrus
to disagree with his uncle's initiatives, as it is for him to
have sound strategic reasons for doing so. In this instance
Cyaxares presses his point with uncharacteristic vigor.
After learning of the Assyrian king's exhortation to his
troops, he argues that it would be a serious mistake to delay
and not proceed against him at once (3.3.56). And on this
point Cyaxares may well be right, for the attack does suc-
ceed. Cyrus's response suggests more clearly than ever that
he has two campaigns underway, only one of them being
against the Assyrian king.

> Make it clear to him that there are not yet as many men
> outside as there ought to be, and give him this message in
> the presence of everyone there. But of course, since he pro-
> poses this, I shall lead an attack at once. (3.3.56)

Cyrus distances himself from his uncle and his policy, mak-
ing it possible to evade responsibility for any defeat even
while sharing in any success.

From this point onwards Cyrus moves to isolate his un-
cle completely. He makes every private communication be-
tween them treat matters of little consequence, and every
major proposal, a matter intensely public. After he and
Cyaxares congratulate one another on their first victory, he
asks if there is anything he could do, and then rides back to
his own army (4.1.7). Formulaically, Cyaxares replies that
he needs nothing. The ensuing sequence shows how Cyrus
externalizes his uncle's challenge. First he thinks out loud
before his own army, regretting that the enemy has escaped.
A series of rhetorical questions whets his men's appetite for
pursuit (4.1.10). Why not go after the enemy, someone asks?
Because we do not have enough horses, Cyrus replies. All
the men then say, Why not tell Cyaxares about this? Cyrus

asks them all to follow him, "so that he may know that we are all in agreement about this" (4.1.11–12). Cyaxares is caught off guard. He is jealous at hearing any proposal from them; at the same time, Xenophon adds, he did not care to risk another engagement. He wished to stay where he was, for it happened that he was busily engaged in a party and saw many of the other Medes were doing the same (4.1.13). He is ambivalent about both himself and the war in which he is engaged. His mixture of what might be termed down-home thinking and military strategy is not a bad one. His limitation is that he cannot see beyond the immediate situation. I quote his speech at length because it is a brilliantly conceived lesson in how not to think like Cyrus the Great.

> Well, Cyrus, I know from what I see and hear that you Persians are more careful than other people not to incline to the least intemperance in any kind of pleasure. But it seems to me that it is much better to be moderate in the greatest pleasure, than to be moderate in lesser pleasures. What brings to man greater pleasure than the kind of success that has now been granted to us?
>
> If we then follow up our success with moderation, we might perhaps, be able to grow old in happiness unalloyed with danger. But if we enjoy it intemperately and try to pursue first one success and then another, beware that we do not share the same fate others say many have suffered upon the sea. Because of their success they have not been willing to give up seafaring, and so they have been lost. Many others, when they have gained a victory, have aimed at another and so have lost even what they gained by the first.
>
> And that is the way with us. For if it were because they were inferior to us in numbers that the enemy are fleeing from us, perhaps it might be safe for us actually to pursue this lesser army. But as it is, reflect with what a mere fraction of their numbers we, with all our forces, have fought and won, while the rest of theirs have not tasted of battle. And if we do not compel them to fight, they will remain unacquainted with our strength and with their own, and they will go away because of their ignorance and coward-

ice. But if they discover that they are in no less danger if they go away than if they remain in the field, beware lest we compel them to be valiant even against their will.

Let me assure you also that you are no more eager to capture their women and children, than they are to save them. Consider the case of wild swine. They flee with their young when they are discovered, no matter how great their numbers may be; but if anyone tries to catch one of the young, the mother does not think of flight, even if she happens to be the only one, but rushes upon the man who is trying to effect the capture.

Now, when they had shut themselves up in their fortifications, our enemy allow us to manage things so as to fight as many at a time as we please. But if we go against them in an open plain and they learn to meet us in separate detachments, some in front of us as now, some on either flank, and some in our rear, take care that we do not each one of us stand in need of many hands and many eyes. Besides, now that I see the Medes having such a good time, I should not like to rout them out and compel them to go into danger. (4.1.14–17)

Cyaxares is a strategist of the day, and, what is more striking still, a hedonist in his strategic thinking. An abiding desire for pleasure and personal comfort determines everything he says. As always, Cyrus makes no effort to disabuse someone so misguided, but picks up only the last point: no man should be compelled to go on this mission unless he wishes to do so. He asks only for volunteers. Cyaxares does not see the trap and allows Cyrus to take whomever he wishes (4.1.21).

Cyaxares has made his last mistake, and it is fatal. Cyrus, the Persians, and all the Medes who joined him pass their time in virtuous ways, having only bread and water for rations, watching for deserters from the enemy. Their frugality contrasts with Cyaxares and the Medes, who eat and drink the whole night through (4.5.1–7). The next morning Cyaxares awakes to discover that his entire army has gone off in Cyrus's service. Only his party-goers remain, with hangovers. Cyaxares sends an impromptu message:

Cyrus, I should think that even you would not have shown so little consideration towards me. And if Cyrus was so minded, I should think that at least you Medes would not have consented to leave me deserted like this. Well, if Cyrus wants to, let him come with you; but if he doesn't, you at least return to me as quickly as possible. (4.5.10)

But Cyaxares has not yet learned the whole story. The messenger asks how he shall find Cyrus, and Cyaxares asks him in turn to find the enemy he was pursuing. Hyrcanian deserters had gone with Cyrus as guides, he says. Cyaxares is angrier than ever for not having been told about this. Now he realizes that Cyrus's expedition was not at all the casual outing he had made it out to be.

The messenger leaves with an even sharper message—and vexed that he himself cannot join Cyrus, too. When he is at last able to deliver it, all the Medes are silent; they are well acquainted with Cyaxares' savage temper.[8] With his audience already in place, Cyrus now needs only the other actor in the drama to resolve the quarrel with his uncle. Cyaxares has presented him with a crisis for which he is already prepared.

3

The resolution of this conflict is complex, because Cyrus aims not only to effect a reconciliation with his uncle but also to make him useful to Cyrus in the future. To these ends he first gives a speech to the Medes which opens with a careful misreading of Cyaxares' irate message:

You, messenger, and Medes, I am not at all surprised if Cyaxares sees so many enemy and does not know what we are doing, and then is worried for us and for himself. When he discovers that many of the enemy have been slain, all of them driven off in a rout, first of all he will cease to be afraid, and then he will realize that he is not now deserted, when his friends are busily destroying his enemies. (4.5.20)

This model of calm and reasonableness reduces Cyaxares' rage to mere "worry." But what is it that Cyaxares has to fear? He had said nothing about fear in his message. Cyrus has not even begun. When he asks why Cyaxares should blame "us," Cyrus links himself with the Medes as fellow victims of Cyaxares' anger. All the initial shock of Cyaxares' message is deflected and made to seem merely an expression of fear for Cyaxares himself. Cyrus predicts a cheerful end, then goes on to deal with other matters. He refuses to become fixated on the anger of Cyaxares or give any impression to the Medes that it is his uppermost concern. Only after attending to other business with the Hyrcanian messengers does Cyrus compose the reply that Cyaxares will hear.[9] He is even more detached, and the reply is as much as ever a matter of public record. He sends a messenger to the Persians to let them know what has been happening with their Median allies, and orders his letter carried to Cyaxares, with this additional provision to the Medes and the messenger.

> I want now to read my message to you also, so that you
> may understand its contents and confirm the facts, if he
> asks you anything in reference to them. (4.5.26)

Reading his letter aloud to the Medes is more than a thoughtful anticipation of possible difficulties. It automatically turns a private communication into a matter of public record, as much for the benefit of the Medes who are present at this moment, as for the absent Cyaxares.

After indicating clearly that he is sensitive to the pathos of Cyaxares' situation—thereby suggesting that this situation is entirely one of Cyaxares' own making—Cyrus follows this up with irrefutable arguments, and more than a hint of justified irritation. He is more direct than he has ever permitted himself to be with his uncle. In adopting this manner he enrages his uncle all the more. But Cyrus's purpose is not to effect a reconciliation through correspondence—quite the opposite, in fact. He wants to show the Medes and everyone else that Cyaxares is in every respect his inferior as a person and a commander. Thus, Cyaxares is not in danger (he says); on the contrary, he is safer than ever. The further away friends and enemies are, the safer anyone is (4.5.27–28). Cyaxares must have forgotten all of Cyrus's past benefactions, especially his winning of the allies: "you are acting so as to force me to leave you out of consideration and to try to devote all my gratitude to those who have followed me" (4.5.30). In other words, it is Cyaxares himself who is guilty of ingratitude. But Cyrus will send to Persia for reinforcements—in short, he is now doing what his uncle wanted him to do in the first place. We are all the more confident that Cyrus's earlier reluctance to accede to his uncle's request for reinforcements had a hidden motive. Then the gloves come off:

> Furthermore, although I am a younger man than you, let me advise you not to take back what you have once given, if you don't want bad will to be your due instead of gratitude. And do not summon with threats those whom you want to come to you quickly. And let me also advise you not to employ threats against large numbers, when at the same time you declare that you are deserted, for fear you teach them to pay no attention to you. (4.5.32)

The reduction of Cyaxares to a caricature of a king is completed by this lecture. As a *coup de grâce*, Cyrus orders his Hyrcanian allies to set aside first what the magi direct; then he adds, thoughtfully, "Whatever they think Cyaxares would find most pleasing" (4.5.51).

> They laughed aloud and said that they would have to choose women for him.
> "Choose women then," he said, "and whatever else you please. And when you have made your choice for him, then you Hyrcanians do all you can to see that all those who volunteered to follow me have no cause to complain."
> (4.5.52)

The demolition of Cyaxares is complete. Cyrus can turn to the more pressing problems of his new allies Gadatas and Gobryas, as well as the care and protection of Panthea.[10] Only when he has moved further against the enemy and has his campaign advanced well beyond anything he had consulted Cyaxares about does he turn back to the annoying jealousies of his uncle.

Cyrus sends a messenger inviting Cyaxares to come for a council of war about the captured fortifications of the enemy, the review of the army, and advice on the next move in the war; and he adds, "If he orders me, tell him that I would come to him and join camps with him" (4.5.31). He knows very well that Cyaxares will come to him; as soon as the first messenger is off, he gives orders to bring out the tent captured from the Assyrian king. It is the prize the Medes have chosen for him, and he fills it with the women and the music girls that have been selected for Cyaxares' pleasure. When Cyaxares arrives, Xenophon adds, Cyrus sees to it that he is at the head of a large force of Persian cavalry, together with the Median horsemen and the Hyrcanians and other allies. All of these he displays to Cyaxares (5.5.1–5).

> And when Cyaxares saw the many fine and brave men in the company of Cyrus, while his own escort was small and of little worth, he thought it a thing dishonorable, and he was greatly ashamed. So when Cyrus dismounted from his horse and came up to him, intending to kiss him according to their customs, Cyaxares dismounted from his horse and turned away. He refused to kiss him and could not conceal his tears. (5.5.6)

With this attempt at a public show of affection out of the way, Cyrus abruptly changes course. He becomes an intimate and confidant, ordering all his men to draw back and wait. He takes Cyaxares by the hand, orders Median rugs to be spread out, and seats him in the shade of palm trees beside the road (5.5.7). By this show, Cyrus seems to be honoring his uncle. As we shall see, it is mainly for the benefit of the spectators, not Cyaxares.

Cyaxares loses no time letting Cyrus know why he is so angry and humiliated. Although Cyaxares is a king, he has a puny entourage. This would be hard enough to take from an enemy, but it is even harder from Cyrus. He feels humiliated and laughed at by his own men. He breaks down and weeps even more, and Cyrus joins him (5.5.8–10). Is Cyrus sincere? Or is it embarrassment or calculation that makes him weep? Whatever the reason, he turns crisply to logic as a way of getting at the truth of the matter. Like any angry person, Cyaxares is very far from being ready to submit to cool cross-examination. Cyrus knows this. First he repeats an earlier warning about not being angry at the Medes for following him rather than their own king.

> To me, it seems a serious error for a ruler to be angry with all his subjects at the same time. For as a matter of course, threatening many makes many enemies, and being angry with everyone at the same time inspires everybody with a common sense of wrong. It was for this reason, let me assure you, that I did not let them come back without me. I was afraid that in consequence of your anger something might happen for which we should all be sorry. (5.5.10–11)

Cyrus then proposes that whoever has done the wrong thing should be the one to admit his error. If Cyrus is wrong, he will say so; if he has done no harm and intended none, Cyaxares will confess that he has suffered no wrong at his nephew's hands. Cyaxares has no choice but accept this reasonable proposal, though he has no hope of withstanding Cyrus's cross-examination.

> Come then, let us consider all I have done, all my acts one by one. Then we will see most clearly what is good and what is bad. (5.5.15)

The aim of this is not to get at the truth, but to reduce Cyaxares to frustrated silence as quickly as possible. When Cyrus came to assume command with his uncle, he came with the Persians? Yes. This was a benefit to Cyaxares? Yes. Did Cyrus shrink from battle? No. When Cyrus defeated the enemy, he asked his uncle to join in the pursuit and in reaping the fruits of victory. Was there anything selfish in that? To this Cyaxares says nothing (5.5.16–19). Silence becomes his only possible response. Cyrus persists. Was Cyaxares wronged when Cyrus asked for the loan of cavalry to pursue the enemy? Again, Cyaxares says nothing in reply. The questions come faster, with no time even for pouting silence. Cyrus lists one victory after another. He concludes by

asking how any of these things could give Cyaxares grounds
for complaint.

Cyaxares replies with a speech (5.5.25–34). He cannot
possibly fight Cyrus on the terms Cyrus established, but he
can speak from the heart. All his resentment comes pouring
out. He is bewildered by the turn of events and has no way
of knowing how it happened, but the fact is that these "ser-
vices" of Cyrus are such that the more numerous they ap-
pear to be, the more of a burden they become (5.5.26). It is
a reasonable point. The others that follow are no less co-
gent. For all his anger, Cyaxares does not lose his head. He
would far rather have extended Cyrus's territories by his
power than see his increased by Cyrus's. He would feel bet-
ter enriching Cyrus, than being made richer; Cyrus's gifts
only make him feel all the poorer. What would Cyrus feel
like if he were in the same position? What if someone alien-
ated the affections of a man's dogs, or his attendant guards,
or even his wife? Should a person who did all these things
earn any gratitude? If someone made the Persians following
Cyrus more grateful and willing to follow him rather than
Cyrus, would Cyrus be pleased? Cyrus's treatment of Cya-
xares has been like this, or something very much like it.
The analogies are to the point and dangerously compelling.
The further he goes, the closer he gets to a true description
of the matter. He has not been able to turn aside any of Cy-
rus's stratagems, but he can describe the results of them
with increasing vigor and accuracy.[11] His last remarks are
his most eloquent.

> And now what you have taken with my forces you bring to
> me, and with my own strength you increase my realm.
> And I, it seems, having no share in securing this good for-
> tune, must submit like a mere woman to receive favors.
> You are a hero in the eyes of the world, especially of my
> subjects here, while I am not considered worthy of my
> crown. Do you think that these are deeds of kindness, Cy-
> rus? Let me tell you that if you had any regard for me,
> there is nothing of which you would be so careful not to
> rob me as my reputation and my honor. For what do I gain,
> if I have my realm extended wide and lose my own honor?

For I was not made king of the Medes because I was more
powerful than they, but rather because they themselves ac-
counted me to be in all things better than themselves.
(5.5.33–34)

These complaints have the ring of truth to them and must
be stopped at once. Cyaxares is coming dangerously close to
articulating Cyrus's strategies by exposing their effect, if
not their artifice.

"By the gods, uncle," said Cyrus, interrupting him before
he had finished speaking, "if I have ever done you any fa-
vor before, please do me now the favor that I beg of you.
Stop blaming me for the present, and when you have proof
from us how we feel toward you, if it then appears that
what I have done was done for your benefit, return my
greeting when I greet you and consider me your benefactor.
But if it seems the other way, then you can blame me."
(5.5.35)

Pleas work better with angry people than any argument ever
could. This allows Cyaxares a graceful way to back down.
He does so at once, relaxing into the role he most enjoys:
the elder statesman who enjoys deferential treatment from
Cyrus and everyone else. Either he is not aware that he is
playing an empty role, or he is content to play it.

Just how theatrical an occasion this really is becomes
clear as soon the royal actors leave their stage. The assem-
bled audience cannot hear Cyaxares' long speech and its in-
creasingly accurate description of Cyrus's strategies. All
they can see is uncle and nephew shaking hands in apparent
concord. As Cyrus and Cyaxares ride away, the Medes fol-
low after Cyaxares, Xenophon adds, "since Cyrus gave them
a nod to do so" (5.5.37). And this is how Cyrus fulfills his
promise not to alienate the Medes from their king:

And when they came to the camp and had lodged Cyaxares
in the tent that had been made ready for him, they who
had been detailed to do so supplied him with what he
needed. And as long as he had leisure before dinner, Cya-
xares received calls from the Medes. Some of them came of
their own accord, but most of them went at the suggestion

of Cyrus, taking presents with them—the one a handsome cup-bearer, another a fine book, another a baker, another a musician, another a cup, another a fine raiment. Every one of them as a rule presented him with at least one of the things that he had himself taken. So Cyaxares changed his mind and realized that Cyrus was not alienating their affections from him and that the Medes were no less attentive to him than before. (5.5.38–40)

The irony of Cyaxares' final "recognition" is not subtle. He enjoys the role of an elder statesman for the rest of the work.[12] In his last speech, he is completely benign, the very model of what a maternal uncle should be. He gives his daughter to Cyrus in marriage, and declares that Cyrus will inherit his kingdom at his death. For the purpose of learning how to rule others and create a world empire, however, Cyaxares had already given Cyrus everything he wanted when he agreed to sit happily in his tent, receiving the homage of subjects who came to him only because Cyrus had told them to. The story of Cyaxares is instructive to those princes who would like to know how to manipulate recalcitrant relatives to their advantage, rather than exterminate them.

CHAPTER SIX

Dialectical Imperialism: Tigranes and the Sophist of Armenia

It is necessary to know well how to disguise this nature and be a great pretender and dissembler. Men are so simple and obedient to present necessities that he who deceives will always find someone who will let himself be deceived.

Machiavelli, *The Prince*

For as I detest the doorways of Death I detest that man
Who hides one thing in his heart and says another.

Achilles to the false counselor Odysseus, *Iliad*

For as I detest the doorways of Death I detest that man
Who under constraint of poverty babbles beguiling falsehoods.

Odysseus in disguise, lying to the swineherd Eumaeus,
Odyssey

Cᴏᴏᴏᴏ YAXARES shows us one way the people of this romantic world may try to resist being ruled by Cyrus. Others are more resourceful than he in devising strategies of attack by which they hope to manipulate Cyrus. But though he always has it at his disposal, sheer force is never his response to these kinds of opponents. He beats them at their own game, whatever it may be, in order to turn them into useful subjects. In these encounters, his discourse is strategic in the original sense of the word: the calculated language of a *stratêgos* (general) who has mas-

tered the strategic arts of words as well as of war.¹ He is
what Cambyses terms the *poietês mechanêmaton*, the fash-
ioner of strategies. The same terms describe a playwright
like Menander who fashions contrived plots, but for the
comic stage.²

You are eager to learn all the arts of tricking the enemy,
but you must use not only what you learn from others; you
must be a fashioner of strategies as well, just like the musi-
cians who perform both the compositions they have
learned and try to compose others that are new. And just as
whatever is new in music earns applause, so new strategies
in war win greater praise. These new things can deceive
your opponents even more. (1.6.38)

One of the most familiar of Machiavelli's precepts is thus
first articulated as a crucial part of Cyrus's repertoire.³ The
blending of the artistic and the political is a basic attribute
of great leaders: they are politicians, but they are also poets,
in Cambyses' sense of the word.⁴

I

Tigranes is the first of two opponents who attempt to chal-
lenge Cyrus and bend him to their own designs. Croesus of
Lydia is the other. Given the project of this romance, nei-
ther could possibly succeed, but the reasons for their fail-
ures are interestingly different. We turn first to Tigranes,
who is drawn into a debate with Cyrus to defend his father.

The Armenian king had deserted from the service of Cy-
rus's uncle Cyaxares, and his son attempts to save his father
by dialectic. To counter him, Cyrus for a time adopts the
role of a philosopher. He speaks a philosopher's language,
but in a ruler's setting. The results will be distinctly
unphilosophical and entirely satisfactory, so far as Cyrus is
concerned.

The Armenian king himself is not a commanding pres-
ence. Cyrus orders him to come back voluntarily. Cyrus can
be quite direct when he wants to be.

Armenian, Cyrus orders you to bring as quickly as you can
both your army and your tribute. (2.4.31)

The Armenian does not obey. Cyrus's forces chase him and
his retinue to the top of a hill and surround them. He does
not launch a final assault, because he has other uses for
them in mind. In his treatise on sophistical refutation Aristotle ob-
serves that a shrewd or piercing argument is one which
causes embarrassment or helplessness (aporia) in one's op-
ponent, because it is the argument that bites the deepest.[5]
Cyrus employs just such an argument to deal first with the
king of Armenia (3.1.4–13). Tigranes then attempts to turn
the same strategy against Cyrus, with amusing results. Of
course the whole scene takes place in a world supposedly
innocent of such Greek subtleties as sophistry and dialectic.

Tigranes' father is a vague soul who seems to know
nothing in particular about how to be a king. His keenest
expression is a desire for liberty, which is his excuse for re-
volting from Cyaxares and the Medes. At the moment we
first meet him, he is aporetic or helpless in fact, because
Cyrus has trapped him on a mountain top. By way of a mes-
senger, Cyrus gives him three choices: to fight against hun-
ger, against thirst, or against Cyrus. The king replies that he
does not know what to do; he is, literally, an aporôn, a man
who is at a loss. Cyrus advises him to come down and face
trial. When the king enquires about who his judge will be,
Cyrus replies, "He to whom god gives the power to deal
with you as he wants to, even without a trial" (3.1.5–6).
This ambiguity naturally makes the king imagine all kinds
of punishments. The Armenian descends to face his trial.

Briskly, Cyrus leads his victim into a dialectical di-
lemma as inescapable as the army encircling his position.
From the very beginning, however, Cyrus's ultimate aim
has nothing to do with establishing the king's guilt or in-
nocence; as he earlier tells Cyaxares, he intends to make the
Armenian and his son Tigranes more loyal allies than they
were before their attempted revolt (2.4.14). His strategy for
achieving this is to aim for the same result through strategic

discourse that he has just achieved through military tactics: to reduce the Armenian to *aporia*. He masks his real intentions as much out of a sense of theater (3.1.9–13) as from a desire to see what Tigranes has learned.

First Cyrus compels the Armenian to answer his questions truthfully by warning that any lie discovered will lead to instant conviction: a man who lies here will receive no mercy (3.1.9). He then makes the Armenian admit that his revolt from the Medes was disloyal and wrong. The only excuse is that the Armenian longed for freedom. Implicit in this statement is the sense that the Armenian considered himself a slave, for those who are not free are slaves (3.1.10). Cyrus seizes on the terms of this excuse:

> "Yes, it is noble to fight to keep from being a slave," said Cyrus. "But when one is a slave, either as a result of being defeated in war or in any other way, and is then caught attempting to rob his master of himself, are you the first one to reward him as a good man who does what is right, or do you punish him as a wrongdoer, if you catch him?"
>
> "I punish him," said the Armenian, "for you will not allow me to lie." (3.1.11)

Cyrus now turns this easy moralizing about master and slave against the Armenian himself. He offers the Armenian a choice between a punishment he knows he deserves, and a reward he hopes for but knows he may not get.

> "Answer each of these questions clearly, then," said Cyrus. "If any one happens to be an officer of yours and does wrong, do you let him stay in office or do you put another in his place?"
>
> "I put another in his place."
>
> "And if he is wealthy, do you let him remain rich, or do you make him poor?"
>
> "I confiscate everything he owns," he said.
>
> "And if you find he is trying to desert to the enemy, what do you do?"
>
> "I put him to death," he said. "Why should I convict myself of lying and be put to death for that, instead of telling the truth?" (3.1.12)

At this point, his son Tigranes tears off his crown, rends his clothes, and all the family join in a lament as if the king were already dead (3.1.13). Cyrus does all he can to prolong this moment of high theater. He orders everyone to be quiet, then delivers what in philosophy is the conclusion to the argument, and in American vaudeville, the punch line:

> Well then, Armenian. So this is your idea of justice. What in consequence do you advise me to do? (3.1.13)

The Armenian is silent, because he is helplessly caught (*aporôn*) between recommending his own execution and proposing something the very opposite of what he himself has said he would do. Tigranes at last intervenes with a statement of the obvious.

> "Tell me, Cyrus," he said, "since father seems to be like a man caught in a dilemma [*aporounti eoiken*], may I advise you what I think is the best course for you to follow with him?" (3.1.14)

Cyrus has mainly a literary curiosity about Tigranes' newly acquired skills. He knows he has studied with "a certain sophist" whom Tigranes admired very much, and he is eager to hear whatever he has to say (3.1.14). Although Tigranes is none the wiser, we know that Cyrus has no intention of changing the decision he made before this interview began. He is assuming the role of *dikastês* not to punish the Armenians, but to recover them as useful allies.

In his role of a judge dispensing justice, Cyrus has made it seem that he has one course open to him: to execute the Armenian for his crime. The only other would be to suggest that he magnanimously pardon him, either for reasons of humanity, or for his own self-interest. But a sudden shift from stern judge to mild patron might seem weak, or irresolute. What he needs is someone who can provide him with an argument that will change him from that first role to the forgiving prince who pardons former enemies, for whatever reason. After a shaky beginning, this is what Tigranes accomplishes. Cyrus allows himself to seem persuaded to follow a course of action which it was his intention to follow from the first. Whether Tigranes is ever aware that he is being so used is unclear. Certainly his father the Armenian king will be none the wiser. As he exclaims when this exercise concludes:

> Cyrus, how little are we men able to foresee of the future, yet how much do we attempt to accomplish! Why, just now, when I was a slave striving to gain my freedom, I became more a slave than ever. Then when we were taken prisoner, we thought our destruction certain. Now we find we are saved as never before! (3.2.15)

The Armenian is not the only opponent of Cyrus who deals with failure by taking refuge in banality.[6] Tigranes is a worthier adversary. He is a favorite type of Socratic literature, the bright young man armed with a little learning from study with a sophist.[7]

2

Since there is nothing logically that Tigranes can say to free his father from the aporetic dilemma Cyrus has trapped him in, his first move is to try to change the role Cyrus is playing; Cyrus must not be allowed to remain a judge with the power of rendering a verdict (3.1.15). Such a role is essentially Socratic; it is characteristic of Socrates to argue that we should follow an example only if we think it is a good one. What the Armenian and Tigranes do not know is that it is also characteristic of Socrates to resist the idea of retributive punishment; one punishes wrongdoers only if it will improve them. The Armenian king has established the terms of his own punishment, and Tigranes has to do something to change that. His first tactic is to confuse these Socratic arguments by an appeal to self-interest.

> "Well then," said Tigranes, "if you approve of all the decisions and actions of my father, I strongly urge you to follow his example [mimeisthai]. But if you find that he has been mistaken all along, then I advise you not to follow his example [mimeisthai]." (3.1.15)

This is not a bad gambit. It is not Socratic to accept the judgment of another unless that person is expert. To be a truly good judge of the Armenian, Cyrus should thus determine first if what the Armenian says he would do to his hypothetical slave would be a good example for Cyrus to follow. What Tigranes wants to do here is to change Cyrus from a judge to an interpreter. He also wants to shift the burden of rendering a verdict from his father, where Cyrus has just placed it, back to Cyrus. And the action he now asks of Cyrus is not what Cyrus should do, which is a legal and moral question, but what example he ought to follow. This is a fundamental attack, and Cyrus gives it the back of his hand.

> "Well then," said Cyrus, "if I do what is right, then I should not follow the example of one who does wrong."
> "That," he said, "is true."
> "Then according to your reasoning, your father must be punished if it is just [dikaion] that one who does wrong be punished." (3.1.15)

Cyrus follows Tigranes' second alternative: if the Armenian rightly punished wrongdoers, then he rightly deserves to die. But he also introduces the issue of the justice of punishing a wrongdoer, thereby convicting the Armenian all over again, and on his own terms. Now the Armenian king is as guilty from the ethical perspective of just punishment for the wrongdoer, as he was by the terms of the original judgment.

Tigranes does not miss a beat, but shifts at once to another tack, ignoring the obvious fact that Cyrus is driving him toward the same aporetic position from which he vainly attempted to snatch his father. He sidesteps the embarrassing topic of justice and appeals to Cyrus's self-interest:

> "Which do you think is better for *you*, Cyrus, punishing others for your benefit, or for your injury?" (3.1.15)

This is shameless—and an entirely conventional move in sophistic argument. Cyrus is more than equal to it, since it is the direction he has aimed at from the first. He retains control of the line of questioning Tigranes thinks he is developing. At every turn, when Tigranes tries to force him to admit something that will make him spare the king for his own interest, Cyrus reponds with devastating common-sense judgments (3.1.15–28). In reply to this question, he says, "In that case I would be punishing myself." Tigranes is not able to advance a single argument without having it pushed out of shape with effortless ease. His strategy is to persuade Cyrus that disloyal allies can be transformed into useful friends by kindness. Cyrus subjects every part of this notion to rigorous examination. How can wrongdoers be friends? How can an unreliable person (*aphrôn* also suggests "mindless" or "witless") suddenly acquire discretion (*sophrosynê*)? How can we expect a man who was disloyal and arrogant before he was defeated to remain loyal once he has regained power? How can those who have wronged us be better friends to us than those who have never wronged us? Cyrus enjoys himself at Tigranes' expense. Tigranes finally senses this, for he abandons dialectic and resorts to a speech pleading the advantages of keeping the Armenian royal family in power (3.1.24–25). The length and floridity of the speech reveal how fresh he is from the schoolroom. It is also a characteristic response of those unskilled in dialectic to abandon questions and answers and turn to rhetoric instead. But note how Cyrus refuses to allow even this speech to get off the ground:

> "You mean to say," asked Cyrus, "that fear is a heavier punishment to men than actual punishment?"
> "You know that I am right," he said. "For you know that those who fear exile from their native land, those who fear defeat when they are about to go into the battle, and those who fear slavery and bondage, all such persons cannot sleep or eat because of fear. But those already in exile or defeated or enslaved can sometimes eat and sleep better than happier people.
> "Here is still more proof of what a burden fear is. Some who fear they will be caught and put to death kill themselves out of fear by jumping off a cliff, others by hanging themselves, others by cutting their throats. Thus fear crushes the soul more than all other terrors. What state of

soul," he said, "do you think my father is in? For he fears
not only for himself, but also for me and his wife and all
his children." (3.1.24–25)

Cyrus passes over the purple prose of Tigranes' many ex-
amples to concentrate on the weak link in his chain of anal-
ogies:

Well, it is not unlikely that he is in that state of mind. But
it seems to me that we can expect a man who is arrogant
in success and abject in failure to grow arrogant again and
cause trouble once he is restored to power. (3.1.26)

The rhapsody on the power of fear has completely lost its
effect. Tigranes lamely resumes by conceding that point.

"Well, by Zeus, Cyrus," he said, "no doubt our wrongdoing
does give you some cause to distrust us. But you can build
forts here and occupy strongholds and do whatever else you
think fit, and yes," he said, "you won't find us complain-
ing. We shall remember that only we are to blame. But if
you hand over our government to someone who has not
wronged you, and yet show that you don't trust them, they
will not regard you as a friend, no matter how well you
treat them. If again, you are on your guard against incur-
ring their hatred, you fail to watch them carefully, you
may have to give them even more lessons in self-knowl-
edge and restraint [sophrosynê] than you have given us just
now."

"No, by the gods," he said, "I would not like to employ
servants who served me only by compulsion. I would
rather have servants who worked for me out of gratitude
and friendship, even when they did wrong, than servants
who disliked me but worked faithfully under compulsion."

And to this Tigranes replied, "From whom could you
get such friendship as you can now from us?"

"From those, I presume, who have never been my ene-
mies, if I treated them as well as you are asking me to treat
you."

"But Cyrus," he said, "at this moment whom could you
find to whom you could do as great favors as you can to
my father? For example," he said, "if you grant life to one
who has done you no wrong, what gratitude do you think
he will feel for that? And again, who will love you more for
not depriving him of his wife and children than the man

who thinks he deserves to lose them? Who do you think would be unhappier than we to lose the throne of Armenia? It is obvious," he said, "that the man who would be most unhappy not to be king would also be the most grateful to have the kingdom.

"If you want to leave this country in as little confusion as possible," he said, "consider whether it would be more tranquil under a new administration than the one we are used to. And if you want to have as large an army as possible, who do you think would be better able to organize the troops than the man who has often employed them? And if you need money, who do you think could supply it better than the man who knows where it is and how to get it? My dear Cyrus," he said, "take care that in throwing us away you don't do yourself a greater injury than any harm my father has been able to do to you." (3.1.27–30)

At last Tigranes discovers the persuasive argument Cyrus himself had first thought of. In other respects, Tigranes' efforts to ensnare Cyrus in a dialectical refutation of his position have been a pedagogical nightmare. He may yet not see the reality of the situation, but we can: the case for pardoning the Armenian king became persuasive the moment Tigranes was able to spell out the practical benefits of a stable Armenian kingdom.

Tigranes' appeal to Cyrus's self-interest was the only argument he had. He attempted to expound a garbled version of the Socratic theory that punishment is just only insofar as it educates the criminal, but the theory could never emerge clearly because it was obscured by the sophistic appeal to self-interest. This is Socratic conversation under arrest, a dialogue halted in mid-course. For it is uncharacteristic of Socrates to refrain from at least attempting to clarify an argument. Cyrus's interests are very nicely served by leaving the matter in confusion.

3

At dinner afterwards Cyrus asks the whereabouts of the sophist whom Tigranes so much admired. Tigranes' reply narrows down the range of the possible identity of his *soph-*

istês to only one person. Doesn't Cyrus know that his father had had the man executed?

Father said that he was corrupting me [*diaphtheirein eme*]. And yet, Cyrus, he was so noble and so good that when he was about to be put to death, he called me to him and said: "Do not be angry with your father, Tigranes, for putting me to death; for he does it, not from any malice, but from ignorance. When men do wrong from ignorance, I believe that they do it against their will." (3.1.38)

This "sophist" is obviously Socrates, both because of the bewitching charm he exerted on his pupil and because of his attitude toward an enemy like Tigranes' father. He has precisely the correct Socratic position on ignorance and punishment.

Of course it is all a grim joke at the expense of actual history. Both Plato and Xenophon go to some trouble to show that to call Socrates a sophist is to misapprehend him entirely. This "Socrates" is being looked at from the outside, as if in innocence of the philosophical works that preserved him and his teaching, but with total awareness of the charges that convicted him. Corruption of the young is the charge made against Socrates as reported by both Plato and Xenophon, and the Armenian king justifies his conduct by claiming that he feared the sophist would alienate his own son from him. The perception that Socrates was in the business of alienating sons from fathers appeared as early as Aristophanes' *Clouds* in 423, and was then repeated, without Aristophanic humor, at the trial of Socrates in 399.

For a character created by the author of the *Memorabilia*, Cyrus's response is astonishing. "Ah, the poor fellow," he says upon hearing the news that Tigranes' father had had the sophist executed (3.1.39). After the Armenian's explanation, he dismisses the whole affair with a move to reconciliation of father and son.

But by the gods, Armenian, your error seems to me only human [*anthropina moi dokeis hamartein*]. As for you, Tigranes, you must pardon your father. (3.1.40)

The meeting concludes on a cheery note. Having had their dialogue (*dialechthentes*) and being now well disposed to one another (*philophronêthentes*), as is natural in a reconciliation, the Armenians go home with their wives, quite happy (*euphrainomenoi*) (3.1.40). Such good feelings are in notoriously short supply at the end of encounters with Socrates. But that philosopher is dead, if philosophy is not. The anonymity of the Armenian sophist adds insult to the injury, making a bitter joke more bitter still.

The whole encounter with Tigranes and his father might be summed up as everything the *Memorabilia* is not. Yet if we recall the ultimate aim of Cyrus's education, the reason for his neutral response is easy to discern. So is the purpose of Xenophon's burlesque of a figure he elsewhere admires so much. While it is clear that Cyrus has the intellectual power to challenge Tigranes, he prefers to have the Armenian and his son as grateful allies for the future, rather than to punish them for any misdeeds in the past. When confronted with an injustice identical to the one done Socrates, he need do nothing about it. As Machiavelli would later observe, a ruler like Cyrus cannot afford to do anything about it.

> This has to be understood: that a prince, and especially a new prince, cannot observe all those things for which men are held good, since he is often under a necessity, to maintain his state, of acting against faith, against charity, against humanity, against religion. And so he needs to have a spirit disposed to change as the winds of fortune and variations of things command him, and as I said above, not depart from good, when possible, but know how to enter into evil, when forced by necessity. (*Prince*, 18)[8]

CHAPTER SEVEN

In the Face of the Enemy:
A Meeting with Croesus of Lydia

The one who is able to acquire the most honestly and use
the most in a fine way is the one I regard as the happiest.

Cyrus to Croesus

I care not for the wealth of golden Gyges, nor have I ever
envied him.

Archilochus

EVERY KIND of human rela-
tionship and every kind of discourse contributes to the ed-
ucation of Cyrus. There is no meeting in the work that does
not lead to this purpose. There is the surface meaning of
what Cyrus and others say, and then there is the deeper
level where his intentions lie; these intentions may be con-
cealed entirely from those about him. In this respect there
is no essential difference between the way he treats an ob-
structive member of his own family like Cyaxares and
someone as gifted as Tigranes. Cyrus makes his moves with
an acute sensitivity to the character and the intelligence of
those he deals with. This kind of calculation is at its most
overt when he finally meets face to face the only person in
the *Cyropaedia* who is actually an enemy fighting against
him. He never sees the Assyrian king, but he does confront
the king's most resourceful ally, Croesus of Lydia.

On the face of it, Cyrus's interview with Croesus seems
an unexceptionable contribution to a long-standing ques-

tion about what constitutes the happiest or best kind of life. Unexceptionable, because the search for the *bios eudaimôn* is a matter treated with the utmost seriousness elsewhere in Xenophon's writings, as it had already been treated by Herodotus in Book 1 of the *Histories*.[1] The constitution of the best life is also a legitimate concern of Cyrus, and near the end of the story he will declare his own views on the subject (8.2.13–23). Here it is discussed, but in a way that is at once evasive and inconclusive. The meeting of Cyrus and Croesus in Book 7 (7.2.9–29) is actually an occasion on which both characters use this important question as a pretext for an entirely different kind of game. Croesus is the single most dangerous opponent Cyrus ever encounters in the course of his education. Croesus attempts to turn their conversation about the best life to his own advantage, betraying at every point that he is at once morally obtuse and self-serving.

I

Both Xenophon's characters and the scenes in which they appear are thoroughgoing revisions of Herodotus' account of the same persons and events.[2] In Herodotus, the meeting between Cyrus and Croesus (1.86ff.) is just one of several episodes devoted to Croesus. He is treated in such detail and his life displays such dramatic reversals that his story typifies the whole range of fortune that can befall human beings. He makes wealth the central fact of his life, and he recommends the same course to others. He measures happiness by it, and at first seems justified by his success. He becomes king of Lydia (1.26–28), and at that point, when his prosperity is at its zenith, Solon of Athens pays a visit (1.29).[3]

Appetitive as he is, Croesus is characteristically eager to acquire the answer to the question, Who is the happiest person (*olbiotatos*)? He expects Solon to flatter him by naming him, but instead Solon names the hero Tellus of Athens, and then the young men Cleobis and Biton (1.30, 1.32); in both instances, Solon measures happiness as a good life unspoiled by disappointment and rounded off by death at the moment of greatest success. When Croesus persists, obviously hoping to win at least third prize, Solon's words are even less welcome: every human being is altogether an accidental thing (*pan esti anthrôpos symphorê*), and there is a distinction to be made between the wealthy man (*olbios*) and the lucky man (*eutuchês*). The one who is lucky or happy is much better off than the rich man, but until one dies he is not truly blessed (*olbios*), only lucky (*eutuchês*). Croesus angrily dismisses Solon, but later suffers a great retribution because he thought he was the happiest of men (1.33).

The sequel is typical of Herodotus: those who rise very high can fall very low. Croesus' son Atys is accidentally killed on a boar hunt by the suppliant Adrastus (1.34–35). Croesus asks the advice of the oracle at Delphi, and misreads the ambiguous reply, that if he attacks Persia a great empire will be destroyed (1.71). The empire that is destroyed is of course his own. He becomes a slave and adviser to Cyrus (1.85–89). His spectacular reversals of fortune and loss of self-delusion combine to make him a mediating figure in the first book of the *Histories*; while Solon is innately wise and shrewd in his observations of others, Cyrus has his limits of understanding, and is not always capable of learning from Croesus. Thus Cyrus's sense of his own mortality and of the limits of human fortune makes him save Croesus from death (1.86), yet such an awareness deserts him at a crucial moment. Between these positive and negative polarities of wise and unwise men, Herodotus' Croesus emerges as the one who experiences the greatest range of fortune and misfortune. His experiences are replicated in an ironic way by the man he tries most to help. As a wise counselor whose life exemplifies the truth of Solon's words, he nonetheless cannot save Cyrus from a disastrous defeat by Tomyris and the Massagetae (1.207–214).

It is plain that this *paideia* of Croesus cannot be repeated in the *Cyropaedia*. Xenophon's Cyrus exemplifies every virtue that the Herodotean Solon knows, Croesus learns, and Cyrus lacks. As we have already observed, Xen-

ophon's Cyrus already knows to look to the end of every-
thing that touches on his life. A perfect ruler, he is the dis-
tillation of the wisdom acquired early or late in the *logoi* of
Solon, Croesus, and Cyrus. This single encounter with
Croesus illustrates Cyrus's superior moral and intellectual
virtues as well as any number of scenes could.

At first it seems to allow only this reading. Xenophon
has compressed, if not indeed suppressed, so much of He-
rodotus that not much more seems left than an urbane con-
versation between two civilized men.[4] The roles of Cyrus
and Croesus in Herodotus have been reversed. And we
could go further. There is not only a reversal in roles, there
is a reversion in character, with Croesus demoted to his
original benighted state. All the dynamics in Croesus' and
Cyrus's Herodotean careers are gone. All the *logoi* of Croe-
sus, Solon, and Cyrus are gathered into one scene, and those
narratives are now represented by one comparatively brief
dialogue. Whereas in Herodotus Croesus learned from ex-
perience the wisdom of the gods (1.91.6), it is now Cyrus, a
man who has become like a god, who teaches him. Or so he
says. In Croesus' eyes, the authority of Apollo's oracle has
devolved onto Cyrus; so far as he is concerned, Cyrus is now
the grantor of the happiest life. Hence he even addresses Cy-
rus as if he were a god.[5]

Naturally we might say that Croesus is Cyrus's moral
and intellectual inferior; it would be contrary to the roman-
tic portrait of an ideal ruler for an enemy like this one to be
otherwise.[6] But it is unlikely that Xenophon intends so easy
a catechism here. Moral and intellectual superiority do not
in themselves confer world empire on anyone. Two men he
considered preeminent remind us of that fact: Socrates and
Agesilaus embody most of the qualities he admires and
seeks to preserve in his writing, and neither of them
achieved what Cyrus achieved. In what sense then is this
encounter educational for Cyrus, or for the reader? Unless
Xenophon has momentarily lost his way in what is plainly
a radical revision of Herodotus, there is bound to be an aim
more in line with his theme of showing how Cyrus came to
supreme rule.

We may observe first of all that Croesus' philosophy of life is not merely inferior to what Cyrus believes in and lives by; for the author of the *Memorabilia*, it is philosophically absurd. Croesus thinks his wife leads the happiest of all lives because she shares all his wealth and happiness, but not his worries or misfortunes (7.2.27–28). This improbable claim is identical to the choice that Socrates says Evil (*Kakia*) offers Heracles at the crossroads (*Memorabilia*, 2.1.21–34). There Heracles must choose between Evil and Virtue (*Aretê*). Evil tempts Heracles by pretending to be Happiness (*Eudaimonia*).

> I see, Heracles, that you are in doubt as to which road to take in life. Make me your friend and I shall lead you along the easiest and most pleasant road. No delight will go untested. You will live a life without hardship. First of all, you will take no thought of wars or troubles. Instead, your concern will be what choice of food or drink you should find; what you should see or hear or touch or smell to delight you; what youths you would most enjoy associating with; how you may have the sweetest sleep; and how to get all this with the least labor. Should the suspicion ever arise that you lack the power to get this, don't be afraid that I will lead you through miserable discomforts of soul and body to win them! No! You will reap the fruits of other men's work. You will keep from nothing which you could have of gain. My friends call me Happiness, but those who hate me disparage me with the name of Evil. (*Memorabilia*, 2.1.23–26)

Heracles chooses the path of virtue, and so does Cyrus. The Greeks often drew parallels between the characters of Cyrus and Heracles.[7] The contrast between Croesus' and Cyrus's views of life is egregious. Even more pointed is the contrast between what Croesus says here and the heroic conduct of Panthea which is to follow. Within a few pages, she will provide a devastating counter-example to Croesus' easygoing praise of his wife.[8] Yet Croesus claims now that his wife enjoyed the best kind of life because she shared only in his good luck and never in his misfortunes. Now he himself will enjoy the same kind of happiness, thanks to a similar

generosity from Cyrus (7.2.27–28). There is a bizarre impli-
cation here about Croesus' present status. By comparing his
former relationship with his wife to Cyrus's relationship
with him now, Croesus unknowingly likens himself to a
woman.[9] So much for the moral lessons of the meeting with
Croesus.

Cyrus's response to Croesus is interestingly complex. It
suggests that he sees more in Croesus of Lydia than merely
a moral and intellectual inferior of himself. For as soon as
Croesus has finished his account of the blissful life he will
now lead under Cyrus's aegis, Xenophon adds:

> When he had heard these words Cyrus marveled at his
> good spirits, and after that he used to take Croesus with
> him wherever he went, either because he thought he would
> be useful to him in some way, or because he considered
> that this would be the safer course. (7.2.29)

Enlightened self-interest might explain the first reason Xen-
ophon offers; only a sense of potential danger can account
for the second. What would Cyrus have to fear from a man
of demonstrably inferior character, one whose bizarre no-
tions about life run so deeply counter to his own? He must
see something more than moral weakness in Croesus. Ami-
able and urbane as the interview seems to be, Croesus is
evidently not a man before whom he cares to let his guard
down; indeed, he does not even let him out of his sight.
This precaution is unique in the *Cyropaedia*. Elsewhere Cy-
rus flourishes by delegating authority to others.

The readiest explanation for Cyrus's caution is to be
found in Croesus' past conduct. When the Assyrians
brought on the war, their commanding general opposite Cy-
rus was Croesus of Lydia. He joined the king's alliance, he
says, because he was persuaded that Cyrus posed a real dan-
ger; it is even more likely, given his character, that he did
so because he was bribed by the Assyrian king's gifts (1.5.3).
According to Cyaxares, he added a substantial force to the
Assyrian army, bringing cavalry and infantry with him
(2.1.5). He was chosen both field commander and com-
mander-in-chief of all the enemy's forces (6.2.9). Of all Cy-

rus's enemies he showed the greatest initiatives in foreign policy; he compelled all the Ionian Greeks to join his alliance, and even sent to Lacedaemon to negotiate an alliance (6.2.10).

Scrupulously courteous in this meeting, Cyrus is elsewhere less guarded in his opinion of Croesus. In a speech to his army before the battle, he describes him in what for Cyrus are the most scathing terms. When the Syrians were routed in an earlier battle, Croesus and other allies broke ranks, too (4.1.8). But Croesus was "more cowardly than the Syrians. They fled because they had been beaten in a battle, but instead of standing by his allies, Croesus took off in flight when he saw they were defeated" (6.2.19). As commander-in-chief of the enemy forces, Croesus also had a battle plan that might well have worked if it had not been for his Egyptian allies. They insisted on fighting in deep ranks at the center of his line, just as they were accustomed to do at home (6.3.20). According to one of Cyrus's spies, Croesus consented to the Egyptians' plan, but reluctantly. His strategy was to outflank Cyrus's army as much as possible. It might have worked. To this news Cyrus responded sardonically: the "ones surrounding may be themselves surrounded (kukloumenoi kuklôtheien)" (6.3.20). This reply neatly summarizes the tactics of Croesus both on the battlefield and in his meeting with Cyrus after the surrender of Sardis. He does not succeed in encircling Cyrus with his army, but this does not discourage him from attempting to encircle Cyrus in another way. We shall now reread their meeting, leaving its surface discussion of the good life to one side.[10]

2

To judge from what Croesus himself says, the only mistake he made in the Assyrian war was not to win it. For all their politeness, neither Cyrus nor his captive is unaware of what Croesus has attempted to do in the past. When Cyrus's troops take the citadel of Sardis, for example, the Lydians flee to any part of the city they can. Croesus shuts himself up in his palace and calls out for Cyrus (7.2.5). Even in defeat he attempts the imperious gesture.[11] Cyrus's response is to leave a guard on Croesus and attend to the more pressing matters of subduing a conquered city. His Persian troops remain in perfect order, but the Chaldean allies break ranks and start to plunder (7.2.5–8). When that minor problem is resolved he turns back to his fabulous captive.

Not before. If Cyrus had come at Croesus' bidding, he would have encountered him on home ground, presumably in a magnificent setting which would have emphasized in none too subtle ways the wealth and nobility of his host. Cyrus would have been the one summoned, rather than the summoner. Instead, he demonstrates his control over Croesus by putting him under guard with ordinary soldiers, and he makes it clear that there are more important matters to attend to than Croesus of Lydia. The first round has gone in Cyrus's favor.

But their match has just begun. As soon as Croesus comes before Cyrus, he tries once again to seize control of the situation, this time by defining the roles each will play during their meeting.

> I salute you, my sovereign lord. For fortune has granted that you hereafter have this title, and granted to me that I address you by it. (7.2.9)

This clever opening masks in terms of the utmost servility a double snare: Croesus invites his conqueror to assume the role of sovereign lord, with Croesus implicitly his slave. This is calculated to appeal to Cyrus's vanity. In effect it would also imply that Cyrus has now stepped into the role of the Assyrian king, so far as Croesus is concerned, for the Assyrian king refers to himself as a *despotês* (master) in a letter to Gobryas[12]. At the same time, the explanation Croesus gives for using these titles is not one Cyrus should be eager to accept. Croesus claims that fortune (*tychê*) is the reason Cyrus has his new title of *despotês*, and that it is fortune that makes him use this word. But can good luck be the reason Croesus is in his present predicament? If this were true, it would imply that what has happened to Croesus is merely bad luck. Even worse is what it implies about Cyrus's victory: that also would be a matter of mere luck. Whatever we may think of the truth of the matter outside the romantic world of the *Cyropaedia*, within it there is no question that these notions are all quite false. Cyrus is a supremely lucky person, but because he is the hero of this fiction—not because of what Croesus says.[13]

Cyrus's reply adroitly neutralizes both the appeal to his vanity implied in the relationship of *despotês* and *doulos* (slave), and also the idea that fortune rather than competence and hard work was somehow responsible for his victory: "And I salute you, too, Croesus. For we are both human beings."[14] This thrust and parry owes much to the first meeting of the two in Herodotus (1.86–90). There Cyrus naturally does not object to being called king, because he already is one. But he decides to try to save Croesus because he realizes that he himself is a mortal man and is burning alive another once as prosperous as he. This thought, and the fear of retribution and the sense of how frail humanity is, all combine to make him change his mind (1.86.6). In this sense Cyrus has absorbed completely the lessons the Herodotean Croesus has to teach. His pleasantry silently disarms the trap Croesus laid for him, which was to pose as a slave hailing a master whose victory was won by good fortune. Thus, for Croesus "We are both men" means "We are both mortal"—and, for the reader, "I know my Herodotus as well as you do."

Now it is Cyrus's turn. He follows up his platitudinous reply with a question: would Croesus be willing to give him some advice? Croesus can only answer yes. In his self-serving way, he points out that if he did find some good for Cyrus, that would bring some good to him as well (7.2.10). Cyrus then turns to matters of substance: his army needs pay after so arduous a campaign; he will not be able to control them if they are not rewarded. Yet to plunder Sardis would destroy the city, and very likely give the worst men the largest share. What to do? (7.2.11). This proposition also reflects a thorough knowledge of the meeting of Croesus and Cyrus in Herodotus. There it is the wise counselor Croesus who points out that Cyrus's army will be robbing Cyrus if they plunder Sardis, for Sardis and all its wealth now belong to their conqueror (1.88). Herodotus' Cyrus sees the point. But Xenophon's Cyrus has given Croesus only one possible answer, and he phrases it to appeal to his conqueror's self-interest. He pledges that the Lydians themselves will bring in everything of value in the city. In this way, Sardis will survive intact, along with its crafts, so that it will be just as wealthy within a year as it is at present. Cyrus himself will then be able to judge what plunder is needed, after he has seen how much treasure Croesus can amass in one place. Of course Cyrus accepts.

The "dilemma" Cyrus outlined determined what Croesus could say.[15] To order the looting of the city would not be a good precedent, since it would frighten future enemies and make their surrender less likely later in the campaign. Instead of ordering the treasures brought forth, Cyrus makes himself the mediator between two highly desirable goals: a Sardis unplundered, and an army content and rewarded. Croesus cannot find fault with either aim. He has been denied the role of the child of misfortune, which is the role he wanted to play, and given instead the job of serving as Cyrus's tax-collector.

Even though he himself does not appear to know it, Croesus' present status has little to do with bad luck and everything to do with character. Accordingly Cyrus follows up the practical matters of Sardis and his army with a personal question: what has become of the responses Croesus received from Apollo's oracle? He is reputed to have served the god well and done everything his oracles suggested (7.2.15). Croesus' present situation implies either that there is something wrong with Apollo, or with Croesus. In this way he draws Croesus into telling his life story. First Croesus sought to test the oracle, to his regret.

> When the fine and noble [kaloikagathoi]—to say nothing of the gods—discover that they are mistrusted, they have no love for those who mistrust them. (7.2.17)

This unexceptionable sentiment is as devious as Croesus' greeting. It is an unsubtle reminder to Cyrus of the relationship that ought to exist between them. Cyrus had best be aware that if he mistrusts Croesus, Croesus will have no reason to be loyal. The first question to the oracle, however, was whether or not Croesus should have children. After many donations, the oracle said yes; then one was born dumb and the other was killed. Croesus had asked too specific a question. It then occurred to him to ask a more basic one: What should he do to pass the rest of his life most happily? The oracle's answer is, "If you know yourself, Croesus, you shall be happy." As Croesus observes, he lives a long way from Delphi. He may thus be excused from not knowing that he has paid a great deal of money for advice that tourists could read for themselves in the famous inscription at the entrance to Apollo's temple. For he completely misreads this Hellenic simplicity.

> When I heard this prophecy, I was pleased, for I thought that this was a very easy thing he was assigning me as the condition for happiness. For in the case of others it is possible to know some; and some, one cannot know; but I thought that everybody knows who and what he himself is. (7.2.21)

He does not grasp that "to know" (gignoskein) can mean knowing in the sense of self-awareness, even knowledge of one's mortality—not, as he evidently thinks, knowledge in the simple sense of personal acquaintance or identity.[16]

Subsequent events did not contradict the oracle. Since Croesus is altogether innocent of religious and moral scruples, he does not see the irony of discovering the meaning of his life in Cyrus.

> For the succeeding years, as long as I lived at peace, I had no complaint to make of my fortunes after the death of my son. But when I was persuaded by the Assyrian to take the field against you, I came into every kind of danger. However, I was saved without having suffered any harm. Here I have no fault to find with the god. For when I realized that I was not equal to you in battle, I got away in safety with his help, both I and my men. (7.2.21)

Thus he describes his abandonment of the Syrians, the same cowardly act Cyrus had earlier singled out for scorn in a speech to his men (6.2.19). Evidently Croesus has already forgotten what he had just said: when men and gods are mistrusted, they have no love for those who mistrust them (7.2.17). Cyrus offers not a word of correction in reply.

This Lydian Song of Myself concludes with breathless amalgam of confessions, flattery, and self-abnegation. Xenophon is fond of describing the folly of comic or contemptible characters like Jason of Pherae and Cyrus's lieutenant Araspas in one long sentence.[17] Here the honor is given to Croesus. There is no better way to expose hypocrisy than to let this actor reveal himself in his own words.

> And now again, spoiled by the wealth I had and by those who were begging me to become their leader, by the gifts they gave me and by the people who flattered me, saying that if I would consent to take command they would all obey me and I should be the greatest of men, puffed up by such words, when all the princes round about chose me to be their leader in the war, I accepted the command, deeming myself fit to be the greatest, but indeed not knowing myself, because I thought I was capable of carrying on war against you—but I was no match for you, since in the first place you are descended from the gods, and in the second place nurtured in an unbroken line of kings, and finally you have been practicing virtue from your childhood on, while the first of my ancestors to be a king was, I am told, at the same time a king and a freedman—*therefore* as I was without knowledge, I have paid the penalty justly.
>
> Now Cyrus, I do know myself. But do you think that Apollo was telling the truth, that if I knew myself I should be happy? I ask you this because under the present circumstances it seems to me that you can judge best; for you are also in a position to fulfill it. (7.2.23–25)

Whereas the long sentences for Jason and Araspas culminate with an intrusion of the reality principle into their deluded lives (Jason, the greatest man of his time; Araspas, the man who is immune to the dangers of Eros), Croesus' long sentence is just one more move in his campaign to ingratiate himself with Cyrus. This ironic technique is thus here at its richest (or at least at its most complex): Croesus thinks that by describing his life as a fall into grateful servitude to Cyrus he will earn his new master's favor. He rushes many ideas together in one sentence in the hope that Cyrus will be so beguiled by the flattery that he will not notice the obvious gaps in his reasoning. Croesus did not know himself in the sense that the gifts and flattery of others caused him to think he was the greatest of men, when he clearly was not; and he was fighting Cyrus, who was. This praise of Cyrus is a hyperbolic echo of the narrator's prologue, and his resumption of the story after the excursus on the *nomoi* of the Persians.[18]

Croesus's volubility does not conceal for a moment the incoherence of what he is saying. He excuses himself by measuring his lack of self-knowledge by the opponent he faces: if his opponent had not been such a man, and if Croesus had won, would he then have known himself? In his mind, the maxim from Delphi is turned from an exhortation to arduous self-scrutiny into a command to measure material success and failure. "Now I know myself" to him means he is a mere mortal in the presence of a god-like man. It is another way of saying, "Now I know that I am beaten." Since Croesus is thereby confessing nothing of importance, it is easy for him to say that he once knew nothing, and now does. Flattery is the entire aim of this admission. Cyrus makes no effort to unravel the illogic of his captive. Perhaps we should now follow his example.

Croesus' attempt to manipulate Cyrus is laughable, and instructive. It is precisely because Cyrus is dealing with a man who even in defeat is maneuvering and shifting around him like a wrestler—or an impecunious custom tailor—that he must be cautious about the future. Croesus can be useful. Who would not be, who is seeking at every turn to ingratiate himself and prove himself indispensable to the king? His capacity to be infinitely adaptable betrays an opportunist without moral conscience. Croesus' only discernible loyalty is to those who are more powerful than he. Everything said here is an expression of his flawed view of the world. He is at once dangerous and useful. As always, Cyrus is in the business of ruling others rather than educating them and does not disabuse Croesus of his notions about the happy life. He restores him to his wife, daughters, friends, servants, and the lavish table to which he is accustomed (7.2.26). He gives everything Croesus says he needs to be the happiest of all men. The question of how to lead the happiest kind of life is a serious one, but this meeting with Croesus of Lydia has not been a serious discussion of it.

FRIENDS

CHAPTER EIGHT

The Uses of Eros and the Hero

And Socrates said, "But Critobulus, with my skill it is impossible to force beautiful persons to submit to me by laying hands on them. I am sure men avoided Scylla just because she did this. Since the Sirens touch no one but sing to everyone from afar, men say that all people submit to them; by hearing them they are bewitched."

Memorabilia, 2.6.31

CYRUS'S STRATEGIES for empire require that he maintain a certain distance from other people. Even as we note a growing reputation for his solicitude for others, we cannot fail to sense this distance. Apart from his doting grandfather Astyages, his immediate family is unrelenting in the constant testing of their precocious prince and heir. His mother and father are severe teachers; there are few signs of love or affection anywhere from either of them. The spontaneous chatter of the boy Cyrus was charming but also something Xenophon was constrained at once to describe and excuse (1.4.1–2). In later life, Cyrus is admired by all and attracts every kind of person to his cause by the kinds of strategies we have been following. Never after childhood and adolescence is he depicted as the victim of any passion, whether love or hatred. In this austere world Cyrus himself does not suffer from the loneliness of power, nor in his farewell speech does he give the slightest hint of anything but complete satisfaction about his life and achievements. His dynastic marriage to Cyaxares' daughter confirms his widening empire. His sons are a mute and attentive audience for his deathbed speech. He fulfills all the obligations expected of one who heads an imperial household and an empire.[1]

This calculation about every kind of human affection can be applied to the most elemental forces. Xenophon did not have to write a love story for Cyrus, but he did need to show that Cyrus knows what a love story is. For this purpose he created one woman who could serve in many roles at once: the paradigm of a faithful wife, who could confirm or dissolve political alliances, as need be; above all, one who could inspire deep affection in other men.[2] The character Xenophon invented for this extravagant, all-purpose role became the heroine of Philostratus and the novelists: Panthea, the fairest woman in all of Asia. Save for Cyrus himself no one else in the *Cyropaedia* is so idealized. Her husband Abradatas of Susa is a brave but reluctant ally of the Assyrian king. To later poets and novelists she became the first of many heroines in Greek romance, a legendary beauty who is the paradigm of the faithful wife.[3] She fends off Cyrus's amorous lieutenant Araspas, then commits suicide rather than live after her husband has died in the battle of Thymbrara. She is the one character in the *Cyropaedia* anyone knows when they know nothing else about the education of Cyrus.

But Panthea is also something of a mystery for much of her story. In order to talk clearly about the episodes in which she appears, it is necessary to misrepresent Xenophon's artful paraphrase ("the fairest woman in Asia," "the wife of Abradatas"). He is playing a game with his readers. Save for Abradatas, the least complicated and least interesting of the players, everyone involved in her story is named casually, sometimes even as if by accident. Cyrus's two lieutenants Araspas and Artabazus first appear in Book 1, but they are not actually given names until they appear in Books 5 and 6.[4] The most egregious postponement of all is the naming of the heroine herself. We do not actually know her name until her story is half over.[5] This discretion is due in part to Greek custom, which was to refrain from naming women in public, but not entirely. There is as much artifice as custom in the delayed naming of the fairest woman in Asia.[6]

For Xenophon is not the only artist at work in this romantic world. As a fashioner of empire, Cyrus is no less skillful in his shaping of these events. He has an altogether different view of his famous captive. In what seem to be romantic episodes, he is as calculating about all kinds of human affections as he is about military strategy and dialectic. He is capable of using the most powerful human feelings for a very unfeeling purpose. Every character in the story, including Panthea, is drawn to him like iron filings to a magnet. He is the center of this romantic world, not she. On the contrary, the character in the *Cyropaedia* who inspired the heroines of later romance here plays a marginal role, precisely because she appears in this imperial context.

I

To begin with, there is Panthea's high reputation: she is said (*legetai*) to be the most beautiful woman in all of Asia (4.6.11). Since her beauty is a quality perceived entirely by the eyes of her male admirers, the first thing that has to happen is an episode of admiration in its literal sense. And the story of Panthea does focus from its very beginning on seeing and not seeing; at first, the debate about whether or not to look at her is the only issue raised by the fairest woman in all of Asia (5.1.2–18). Panthea herself does not appear but is the subject of an intense conversation between Cyrus and a boyhood friend. Xenophon reminds his reader of the Mede to whom Cyrus gave a princely robe when he returned from his grandfather's court to Persia (1.4.26). Araspas is that same person. Their conversation is a dialogue between one who has seen beauty and is unaware of the power of Eros, and another well aware of its power, who knows he can control it by refusing to look on the woman at all.

Araspas' first words are about his assignment, and they

go to the heart of the beginnings of romantic experience:
"Have you seen (heôrakas) the woman, Cyrus, whom you
order me to guard?" (5.1.4). If Cyrus has not, Araspas has,
and his account of first seeing her turns into more than a
report: it is what Philostratus would later imitate, an ec-
phrasis that reveals as much about Araspas' infatuation
with the woman as about the woman herself (5.1.4–7). His
aim is to make her as vivid in the mind's eye of his listener
as she already is to him. In this he succeeds only too well.
This is not the speech of a disinterested man. As befits a
heroine in romance, Panthea's innate nobility of soul shines
through her humble garments—at least, it shines through to
Araspas' eyes.[7] He concludes by saying that when the
woman learned she was the property of Cyrus,

> "she rent her outer garment from top to bottom, and wept
> aloud; and her servants also cried aloud with her. And then
> there appeared most of her face, and then there appeared
> her neck and arms. Let me tell you, Cyrus," he said, "it
> seemed to me and all the rest who saw her that there never
> was so beautiful a woman of mortal birth in Asia. But," he
> said, "you must by all means see her for yourself." (5.1.4–
> 7)

But Cyrus will have none of this, certainly not if the woman
is so beautiful as Araspas says she is:

> Because if now I have heard from you that she is beautiful
> and am inclined just by your account of her to go and gaze
> on her, when I have no time to spare, I am afraid that she
> will herself much more readily persuade me to come again
> to gaze on her. And as a consequence of that I might sit
> there, neglecting my duties, idly gazing upon her. (5.1.8)

Cyrus's caution about gazing on his captive is well-founded
from several perspectives. What Araspas wants him to do is
the prime inspiration for romance both as an experience and
as a literary and artistic form.[8]

    To take one example from a later novelist who knew the
Cyropaedia: the lovers' first gaze is the point of departure
for the hero and heroine in Chariton's *Chaereas and Callir-
hoe*. Callirhoe was so beautiful that her parents kept her in-

visible, rather like a secret weapon. Finally during a festival of Aphrodite, at her mother's command, her father allowed her out to worship the goddess.

> Just at that time Chaereas was walking home from the gymnasium; he was radiant as a star, the flush of exercise blooming on his bright countenance like gold on silver. Now, chance would have it that at the corner of a narrow street the two walked straight into each other; the god had contrived the meeting so that each should see the other. At once they were both smitten with love . . . beauty had met nobility.
>
> Chaereas, so stricken, could barely make his way home; he was like a hero mortally wounded in battle, too proud to fall but too weak to stand. The girl, for her part, fell at Aphrodite's feet and kissed them: "Mistress," she cried, "give me the man you showed me for my husband!"
>
> When night came it brought suffering to both, for the fire was raging in them. (Chaereas and Callirhoe, 1.1.6)

The mere sight (opsis) of Callirhoe is enough to inflame any man with a passion for her. Besides her future husband and Theron the bandit (1.13.3), more distinguished victims include the king of Persia and Dionysius, governor of Miletus. Dionysius in particular is an instructive example of the pathological condition Cyrus is determined to avoid.

> The night was far advanced when he dismissed the company. He was too preoccupied to sleep. In thought he was in Aphrodite's shrine, recalling every detail: her face, her hair, the way she turned, the way she looked at him, her voice, her appearance, her words; her very tears inflamed him. There was a visible conflict in him now, between reason and passion; desire was flooding over him, but his noble soul tried to bear up against it; as if rising above the waves he said to himself:
>
> "Dionysius, you ought to be ashamed of yourself! The most virtuous, the most distinguished man in Ionia, the admiration of satraps, kings, whole populations—and you behave like an adolescent! You fall in love at first sight— and while you're in mourning, at that, before you've even paid proper respect to your poor wife's departed spirit! Is that what you've come into the country for—to marry in

your mourning clothes? And to marry a *slave*? She may not even belong to you—you haven't got the registration deed for her."

This was good sense; but Eros, who took his restraint as an insult, set himself against Dionysius and fanned to greater heat the blaze in a heart that was trying to be rational about love. (*Chaereas and Callirhoe*, 2.4.4–5)

If Dionysius was a reader of the *Cyropaedia* it did not fortify him for the sight of Callirhoe. For Cyrus, the fairest woman in all of Asia is a momentary intrusion of the destabilizing power of Eros in the tightly controlled world of his evolving empire. The opposite is the case with Dionysius. He has the misfortune of trying to be a responsible officeholder in a world that is as masterfully run by Eros as Cyrus's world is run by him. Hence the charming inversion of ordinary values typical of Chariton and the Greek novelists: the god Eros regards Dionysius' efforts to maintain self-restraint (*sophrosynê*) as *hybris*, its very opposite. Dionysius has already lost the case he is trying to argue, and he knows it.

Araspas has already lost his case, too, and he does not know it. His speech about the fairest woman in all of Asia links him to the infatuated heroes of later romances and reveals a victim of Eros who does not realize Eros' powers. While Cyrus dismisses the idea of risking even one glance at the woman, Araspas is not so easily turned away. Thus he engages Cyrus in two dialogues about the nature of love.

Araspas is the same age as Tigranes, but has not had the benefit of an Armenian sophist's education. Without even the little learning of Tigranes, he leads with his chin from the very first. He argues that beauty does not compel anyone to love against his will; only the weak and cowardly do so. This self-serving thesis implies that Araspas himself is one fair and noble youth (*kaloskagathos*) who can resist this temptation, rather than being the weakling Cyrus might suppose (5.1.9–11). The analogy that he reaches for to support this proposition leads ultimately to the discovery that love is a flame. To begin with, Araspas is thinking of flames in a literal sense.

> "Don't you see," he said, "how fire burns everyone the
> same way? That is its nature. But of the beautiful we love
> some, and some we do not; and one loves one and another;
> for it is a matter of free will and each one loves what he
> pleases." (5.1.10)

After other, even less persuasive analogies about brothers
not loving sisters and thirsty people not being legislated
into being cured of thirst, he concludes that love is like a
pair of shoes, or a change of clothing. You can put it on or
not as you please (5.1.11).

Cyrus does his best to counter with common sense, with
the well-known metaphor of love as a wasting disease
(5.1.12). None of this makes any impression on Araspas.
Anyone who succumbs to love is a weakling; he is no weak-
ling, and he will not. He has seen the woman and thought
her surpassingly beautiful; nonetheless, here he is, he says,
still doing his duty for Cyrus (5.1.13–15). Cyrus finally
sums up their entire conversation with the cliché we have
been waiting for.

> "For you know it is possible for a man to put his finger in
> the fire and not be burned at once, and wood does not burst
> at once into flame. Even so, I do not put my hand in fire or
> look on the beautiful, if I can help it. And I advise you, too,
> Araspas," he said, "not to let your eyes linger upon the
> beautiful; for fire, to be sure, burns only those who touch
> it, but beauty insidiously kindles a fire even in those who
> gaze upon it from afar, so that they are inflamed with
> Eros." (5.1.16)

But now even when Cyrus has appropriated Araspas' own
imagery, his lieutenant is none the wiser. His self-assurance
and Cyrus's neutral response create a delicious Socratic
irony.

> "Never fear, Cyrus," he said, "even if I never cease to look
> upon her, I shall never be so overcome as to do anything
> that I ought not to."
>   "What you say," he said, "is most excellent. Keep her
> then, as I order you, and take good care of her. For this

woman may perhaps be of very great service to us when
the time comes." (5.1.17)

More precisely, this is another instance of Socratic irony
under arrest, productive for the reader but not at all for
Araspas. Cyrus exposes Araspas' folly for our benefit alone.
As he dealt earlier with Tigranes, so now he deals with
Araspas; it is not his business to draw others out of their
self-delusion. The future uses of the woman are far more on
his mind than the present disputation with his boyhood
friend. Like Jason of Pherae or Croesus, Araspas declines
and falls (from guardian to lover) in one breathless sentence.

> And as the young man found the lady so beautiful and at
> the same time came to know her goodness and nobility of
> character, as he attended her and thought he pleased her,
> and then also as he saw that she was not ungrateful but al-
> ways took care by the hands of her own servants not only
> that he should find whatever he needed when he came in,
> but that, if he ever fell sick, he should suffer no lack of at-
> tention; in consequence of all this, he fell desperately in
> love with her; and what happened to him was perhaps not
> at all surprising. (5.1.18)

Araspas is a good lieutenant and a loyal servant, and noth-
ing more. Cyrus has already explained, to a person who
would not listen to him, what one might risk by seeing the
woman Araspas describes. He does not spell out what
would be lost by any harm coming to her. He could take
advantage of the situation in one of two ways: either risk
ruining himself as the leader he intends to be by earning the
hatred of a dedicated enemy, or reunite husband and wife
and win them as his grateful allies. Of course he prefers the
second course to the first. The vehemence with which he
resists Araspas' invitations is not due merely to moral cour-
age, but to an ever-present instinct to do what is in his own
best interest.[9]

2

The fall of Araspas strikes a familiar chord. In this dialogue
on love, all the wisdom is on one side, in Cyrus, all the folly

in Araspas, on the other. This imbalance of virtues creates the same situation as Cyrus's meeting with Croesus of Lydia, where Xenophon gives Cyrus all the accumulated wisdom of Solon and Croesus in Herodotus, and leaves little but cleverness and hypocrisy for Croesus.[10] The lesson that Eros may subvert empire is not an original discovery of either Cyrus or the author who created him, nor is the awareness of the danger of seeing the beautiful, nor the need for the repression of our desires to do so. The brief story of Gyges and Candaules in Herodotus (1.8–13) illustrates the point very well. There everything turns on the connection between political power and its gain or loss, through the visibility or invisibility of the characters.[11] A sentimental reading of the Panthea story has so long dominated the scene that it will not be out of place here to stress its essentially political purpose. That purpose can be brought out by reference to the similar story in Herodotus.

Candaules the king of Lydia falls in love with his own wife. He is not content with praising her beauty to his favorite servant Gyges. Herodotus tells us from the beginning that Candaules is destined to come to a bad end. He forces Gyges to hide and observe her naked. Gyges carries out Candaules' plot, though he is not himself in love with the queen. She sees him slip from her bedroom and forces him to choose between killing Candaules and assuming the throne, or being executed for his crime. Gyges eventually follows her advice and kills Candaules, and takes the wife and the throne.

This is a terse summary of a story that exemplifies the political dimensions that may underly certain kinds of romance. To be as concise in spelling out some of its meaning: Candaules loses both his empire and his life by falling in love. Eros impels him to insist on making his wife's body, which should be a thing invisible to Gyges, visible. Candaules achieved this by making the person who should always be visible, namely his favorite servant, invisible. His wife's counter-strategy is to adopt the same tactic, by making the servant Gyges, who should be visible and controllable, an invisible assassin.

In the conversation between Cyrus and Araspas, the cast

of characters is larger and they play reversed roles. Instead of a wife who is a powerful consort to a king, Panthea is a captive entirely at the mercy of Cyrus and his lieutenants, with an absent husband capable of returning to his wife and taking revenge for anything that happens to her. There is a similar division of roles with Cyrus and Araspas. Whereas Candaules' misfortune was that he combined the power of a king with the weakness of a lover, that power and Eros are now located not in one person, but two. Xenophon makes this conflict external to Cyrus so that it can be an affliction for him to observe, rather than one he has to experience. Araspas is the lover, but he is also Cyrus's servant and he can at most attempt to persuade Cyrus to see the loveliest woman in all of Asia. Since Cyrus already knows what Eros can do to political power, and since he has not seen the woman that so transformed his friend, he eludes romantic entanglements altogether. This is the story of Gyges and Candaules, but with a happy ending.

The hot and cold responses of Araspas and Cyrus show how an empire may be gained as well as lost. By dividing the roles of wise king and foolish lover between Cyrus and Araspas, Xenophon creates a dialectical examination of the problem raised by the exchanges between Gyges and Candaules, and Gyges and Candaules' wife. The interior monologue of the hapless Dionysius of Miletus in Chariton is closer to the pathological condition of Candaules, where the one who possesses power is himself possessed by the power of Eros. Naturally, the later novelists created worlds where Eros the destabilizer would be the center of all power.[12] There, for example in Chariton, Cyrus would be an aberration. But here in the *Cyropaedia*, he gets an education about Eros and politics, as it were, free of charge.[13]

3

After parting from Araspas, Cyrus is concerned with a great many problems, not the least of them Uncle Cyaxares. Only when he decides that a spying mission should be undertaken does he think once again of the man he left in charge of the most beautiful woman in all of Asia (6.1.31). When Cyrus finds out about his lieutenant's love affair, he laughs outright at the man who had claimed to be superior to Eros. Araspas' pathology is conventional in every respect.[14] Cyrus sends Artabazus to him with an order not to attempt to take the woman by force. He adds the proviso that if Araspas can persuade her, he himself will have no objection (6.1.34). Cyrus is neither outraged by his friend's conduct, nor worried that Araspas will persuade his captive to do something Cyrus knows she will not likely do. His messenger Artabazus is not so benign:

> When Artabazus came to Araspas, he rebuked him severely, saying that the woman had been given to him in trust; and he dwelt upon his ungodliness, sinfulness, and sensuality, until Araspas shed bitter tears of contrition and was overwhelmed with shame and frightened to death that Cyrus might punish him. (6.1.35)

The message is puritanical in its severity, more like the invective of an orator than the language of a messenger.

This is not the message Cyrus asked to be delivered. The reason for the discrepancy lies in his choice of messengers. If Artabazus is not neutral on the subject of Araspas' misdeeds, that is in part due to his loyalty to Cyrus, but even more to the particular character of that loyalty. His ties to Cyrus are distinctly different from the feelings of Cyrus's other boyhood friend, Araspas. Artabazus appeared much earlier in Cyrus's life, at the time Cyrus was leaving the Medes and returning to Persia. This was on the same occasion that Cyrus gave a splendid Median gown presented by his grandfather to a friend he took most delight in; this friend was Araspas, but we also learn his name only much later, in Book 5 (1.4.26, 5.1.2).

Although he was not named in Book 1, Artabazus was the subject of a peculiar tale apologetically introduced as a story of boy-love (*paidikos logos*). When Persian men parted from one another, Xenophon says, they had the custom of kissing one another farewell. A certain kinsman at this point described simply as a Median gentleman (*kaloskaga-*

thos) had for some time been struck by Cyrus's beauty. When the rest of Cyrus's kinsmen had gone, he asked Cyrus whether or not he was the only relation Cyrus did not recognize. Cyrus is not surprised.

> "That is the reason," they say that Cyrus said, "why it seems that you used to stare at me. For I think that I have often noticed you doing so." (1.4.27)

The kinsman wanted to but was too bashful, he says.

> "But you ought not to have been," they say Cyrus said, "if you really are my kinsman." And at once he went up to him and kissed him, according to them. (1.4.28)

Xenophon the narrator goes to great lengths to distance himself from this erotic tale: "If then one ought also to report a story of boy-love, it is said . . ." (*ei de dei kai paidikou logou epimnêsthênai, legetai*) (1.4.27). The prudishness is understandable, perhaps; the alleged kinship of Artabazus is nothing but a pretext to allow him to indulge in the most direct kind of courtship of Cyrus. All the symptoms of the courtly art of Greek homoeroticism are in evidence: the passion for an unattainable beauty, the bashfulness in the face of witnesses, and perhaps most telling of all, Cyrus's sharp eye for the gaze of his admirer. Cyrus has evidently known for some time that he was an *erômenos* of Artabazus the *erastês*.[15] He also knows very well that Artabazus is no kinsman. Like a Milesian tale in Petronius or Apuleius or, for that matter, Xenophon's own *Symposium*, the *paidikos logos* abounds in jokes and punch lines:

> And when he had been given one kiss, the Mede asked: "Really, is it a custom in Persia to kiss one's kinsfolk?"
> "Certainly," they say Cyrus said, "at least, when they see one another after a time of separation, or when they part from one another."
> "It may be time then," said the Mede, "for you to kiss me." (1.4.28)

This badinage continues for some time, with the same result.[16]

Thus, while Cyrus can afford to be amused at Araspas'

misconduct, it is no wonder Artabazus goes on a rampage. What better envoy could Cyrus have chosen for reining in his erring lieutenant than a man who, to judge from his past conduct, was far more interested in Cyrus than in any woman? If he were looking for the most unsympathetic kind of messenger, the one who would least understand the sufferings of young Araspas, he could not choose one better than the protagonist of that tale about another kind of eros. We note also that Artabazus and Araspas are named at the moment each begins to play a role in the romance of Panthea, which we assume is their proper role.

Because his frustrated suitor Artabazus instructs Araspas in so gratifyingly severe a manner, Cyrus can remain in his customary moderate role. He admits that he himself would have done no better if he had been the guardian of the fairest woman in Asia (6.1.36). It does not greatly matter that he had said precisely the same thing about Eros' power before Araspas got into his difficulties. The effect of this reasonableness on Araspas is profound: he is eager to do anything he can to redeem himself, and becomes the ideal candidate for a spying mission. Cyrus suggests he pretend to desert to the enemy. The affair with his captive will make the desertion credible (6.1.37–40).

And then Cyrus puts an end to the romance of the fairest woman in all of Asia. It is a romance that exists in the overheated imagination of Araspas, or in the mind of later sentimental readers of Xenophon like Georges de Scudéry (Illustration 5), but not in the mind of Cyrus. "Will you also be able to give up the beautiful *Panthea*?" (6.1.41). The fairest woman of Asia is here named for the first time, in Cyrus's question to Araspas. He gives her a name at the point when she has been freed from the romantic fantasies of her guardian, when she is someone to be left alone (*apolipein . . . Pantheian*), safely removed from Araspas and of great use to Cyrus; for so he intended her to be from the moment he first heard about her (5.1.17). And in a sense, Panthea is only half a name, a proper adjective made into a substantive. In this Hellenized world of Greek-speaking Persians, "Panthea" is Greek and eloquent of her character.[17] She is

5. An Image of Panthea. From *Les Femmes illustres*
(1664).

as divine in name as she is in appearance. She is the person-
ification of an abstraction, "she who is altogether divine,"
panthea, halfway between a goddess (Araspas' conception of
her) and a human being (her actual status as the wife of
Abradatas). Her name is a typical romance name, an elo-
quent name, an outward embodiment of an inner truth.[18]

In the matter of naming and not naming, the arts of the
monarch and the novelist of the *Cyropaedia* coincide. Xen-
ophon the narrator does the same thing to his characters
that Cyrus the commander does to his men:

At this point the men went to their tents, and as they
went, they remarked to one another what a good memory
Cyrus had and how he called everyone by name as he as-
signed them their places and gave them their instruction.
In fact Cyrus had made a study of this. He thought it very
strange that every craftsman knows the names of the tools
of his trade and that the physician knows the names of all

the instruments and medicines he uses, but that a general should be so foolish as not to know the names of the officers under him. For he must use them as his instruments not only whenever he wishes to capture a place or defend one, but also whenever he wishes to inspire courage or fear. And whenever Cyrus wished to honor any one, it seemed to him proper to address him by name. Furthermore, it seemed to him that those who were conscious of being personally known to their general exerted themselves more to be seen doing something good and were more ready to abstain from doing anything bad. And when he wanted a thing done, he thought it foolish to give orders as some masters do in their homes: "Someone go get water," "Someone split wood." For when orders are given that way, he thought, everyone looked at one another and no one carried out the order. All were to blame, but no one felt shame or fear as he should, because he shared the blame with many. It was for this reason then that he himself spoke to everyone by name to whom he had any command to give. Such at least was Cyrus's thought about this matter. (5.3.46–51)

This talent of Cyrus is a useful commentary on Xenophon's activities as a writer. That is, there is some interplay between the way Xenophon thinks an ideal leader should conduct himself and the way Xenophon himself goes about creating a narrative. When he chooses to name or not to name, he confers narrative importance on a character, or alternatively narrative anonymity.

Araspas is merely a character in the story and in no position to notice such niceties. He shifts the conversation as quickly as he can to a brief philosophical discourse designed to explain his unfortunate experience.

Clearly I have two souls, Cyrus. I worked out this philosophical doctrine in the school of that unjust sophist, Eros. For if the soul is one, it is not both good and bad at the same time. Neither can it at the same time desire the right and the wrong, nor at the same time both will and not will to do the same things. But it is obvious that there are two souls, and that when the good one prevails, what is right is done; but when the bad one gains ascendency, what is wrong is attempted. And now, since she has taken you to be her ally, it is the good soul that reigns. (6.1.41)

This is a facile condensation of speculations about the nature of the soul that can be found in more serious discussions in Xenophon and Plato.[19] The last sentence completely undercuts Araspas' philosophizing by revealing his real state of mind: he has not been so much educated out of his passion for Panthea, as chased out of it. His "good soul" prevails because Panthea is Cyrus's ally, rather than his captive. To this latest revelation Cyrus is as impassive as ever, moving without reply to the next matter at hand ("If you are also ready to set out, then . . . ," 6.1.42). With Araspas safely out of the way, Panthea does what Cyrus expected her to do. Abradatas praises Cyrus's piety, self-restraint, and compassion, and wonders how he can repay him. "How else," replies Panthea, "than by trying to be to him what he has been to you?" (6.1.47). Abradatas complies and the romance of the fairest woman in all of Asia seems to end happily.

Cyrus has been guarded about Eros, but is far from innocent of his powers. He manipulates Artabazus' love as surely as he redirects the erotic energies of Araspas' comic passion for Panthea. He realizes from the first that the bond between Panthea and her husband is of an altogether different order from anything either Araspas or Artabazus understands.

In this love story, each person has fallen into his or her place around Cyrus, the ruler as *eromenos*: Artabazus, forever at a distance, yearning for an intimacy with Cyrus, who is forever in sight, but just beyond having; Araspas, frightened away from wanting to look at the most beautiful woman in all of Asia, still obviously interested, but relieved and only too grateful to serve Cyrus more loyally than ever before; and, not the least of his attainments, Panthea and her husband, happily reunited and firmly won over to their savior's service. Cyrus has made all of them serve him to the maximum that their identities as lover, friend, husband or wife will allow. In the most practical sense, the only Eros in the *Cyropaedia* is Cyrus himself.

4

The transformation of romantic hero and heroine into tragic victims of the Assyrian war is not directly Cyrus's doing, but it is a possibility he clearly foresees. The use of Abradatas on the battlefield will call for different kinds of strategy. Cyrus channels the heroic energy in those who fight for him, but avoids being swept up in the fortunes of war—and swept away by them. Panthea and Abradatas are not so lucky. This is the one part of Cyrus's education that comes close to the vicissitudes that are the stuff of genuine history and tragedy. These episodes are also the one part of the *Cyropaedia* that has been reckoned to be of the greatest literary interest. In the evolving empire that Cyrus is fashioning, however, the deaths of Panthea and Abradatas acquire their most important meaning in relation to the imperial theme. Cyrus greatly regrets their loss, but the pathos of these scenes must not distract us from realizing a basic fact: however sincerely he may mourn Abradatas and Panthea, he is as responsible as anyone for their deaths.

Probably because the *Cyropaedia* has now temporarily acquired a pair of tragic figures, Xenophon adapts the narrative technique and language of epic and tragic poets. Like his rare effort at making a simile (1.4.21), these poetic touches are awkward and naive in their effect. More than once they are introduced so abruptly that they seem more a garnish than anything integral to the plot. The substance of the narrative is powerful enough. Abradatas' doom is foreshadowed from the moment he asks for the lead position at the most dangerous point in the line of battle. Cyrus reluctantly assigns him this post after a democratic vote by the other commanders (6.3.35–37). The parting of Panthea and Abradatas (6.4.2–11) has been compared to the parting of Hector and Andromache in the *Iliad*.[20] Thus, Panthea swears that she will die rather than live with any other man, and she also thinks once again of how much both of them owe to Cyrus (6.4.5–8). As before, Abradatas allows his wife's words to shape his thoughts. To the extent that it is an adaptation of Hector's prayer in the *Iliad*, however, his prayer reveals a significant contraction of the heroic imagination. Hector's prayer is tragically ironic, since it is the perfect expression of a Homeric warrior's code. It invokes in prayer the same ethic which will cause both Hector and his son to die, and Andromache to survive in slavery.

> Zeus and you other immortals, grant that this boy, who is my son, may be as I am pre-eminent among the Trojans, great in strength, as am I, and rule strongly over Ilion: and some day let them say of him: "He is better by far than his father," as he comes in from the fighting; and let him kill his enemy and bring home the bloodied spoils, and delight the heart of his mother. [*Iliad*, 6.476–481]
>
> And Abradatas, touched by her words, laid his hand upon her head and lifting up his eyes toward heaven prayed, saying, "Grant me, I pray, almighty Zeus, that I may show myself a husband worthy of Panthea and a friend worthy of Cyrus, who has shown us honor." (6.4.9)

Instead of the prayer of a heroic warrior, Abradatas hopes he will be worthy of two ideals: one is his wife, and Cyrus is the other. The tragic consequences of this heroism are not surprising. Before Abradatas goes to battle, Cyrus gives him his final instructions (7.1.15–18), but Abradatas is disappointed because his position may turn out to be the safest one after all. This is but one more anticipation of the ironic reversal of the coming battle (7.1.16), as is Cyrus's careful warning:

> "And do not hurl yourself upon the opposing ranks, I beg of you, until you see in flight those whom you now fear." Cyrus boasted like this only when he went to battle; otherwise he never boasted—"but when you see them in flight, then be sure that I am already at hand and then charge on them. For at that moment you will find your opponents most cowardly and your men most brave." (7.1.17)[21]

Naturally Abradatas does the very thing Cyrus has ordered him not to do at the battle of Thymbrara.

Abradatas also lost no more time, but shouting, "Now
friends, follow me," he swept forward, showing no mercy
to his horses but drawing blood from them in streams with
every stroke of the lash. (7.1.29)

Xenophon had seen the face of battle and knew as well as
anyone how to describe it. But the death of Abradatas is
based on more than general experience; it is a variation of
the death of Cyrus the Younger at Cunaxa as Xenophon de-
scribes it in the *Anabasis*.[22]

Left with a few table-companions, he caught sight of the
King and the closely formed ranks around him. Without a
moment's hesitation he cried out "I see the man," charged
down on him, and struck him a blow on the breast which
wounded him through the breastplate, as Ctesias the doc-
tor says, saying also that he dressed the wound himself.
But while he was in the very act of striking the blow,
someone hit him hard under the eye with a javelin. (*Ana-
basis*, 1.8.24–27)

Both Abradatas and Cyrus shout one last, brief cry (*andres
philoi, hepesthe; ton andra horô*), both plunge into the cen-
ter of the enemy line, both are killed at the moment their
attack turns the tide of battle, and both are followed by
loyal companions. In a counterattack on the enemy, Cyrus
himself survives an equally dangerous moment as if by
magic. When his horse is wounded and throws him in the
battle, his men rally at once and save him: "Then one might
have realized how much it is worth to an officer to be loved
by his men" (7.1.38).

In one sense, the connection between Abradatas and Cy-
rus the Younger is a matter of literary opportunism; Xeno-
phon had to write a battle scene, and he had something
ready-made at hand in the *Anabasis* (1.8), so he used it. But
we need not rest with only that reading. The episode of
Cunaxa revisited can also be related to the imperial designs
of the monarch and the novelist of the *Cyropaedia*. Abra-
datas is an ideal warrior for a monarch like Cyrus because
he is willing to fight and die for his leader. And he is not
much more than an embodiment of that virtue. He dies like

Cyrus the Younger because Xenophon wishes to place Cyrus the Younger and the grand scheme which ended at Cunaxa into the place they belong, so far as the *Cyropaedia* is concerned: heroic adventure and bravery must be subordinate to the imperial designs of the new ruler. Cyrus must be able to attract men like Abradatas to his cause, but he must not make the mistake of dying with them. However many similarities we care to draw between the fictive Cyrus and the Cyrus of history, there comes a point where the two of them must part company. Cyrus in the *Cyropaedia* must rise above the tragic paradigm that history and Cyrus the Younger offer.

The death of Abradatas is thus a critical stage in Cyrus's evolution as a ruler. Abradatas' unfortunate death shows precisely the difference between the Cyrus of the *Cyropaedia* and the Cyrus whom Xenophon knew. It is not simply the difference between romance and history, that opposition of fiction and fact that has so long detained readers of the *Cyropaedia*. It is the difference between an admirable but dead hero, and an equally admirable but untragic survivor. When Cyrus goes to Panthea and views Abradatas' mangled body (7.3.3), it is as if the Cyrus of the *Cyropaedia* were looking down on the remains of the Cyrus of the *Anabasis* (1.8.26–28).

5

Ortega y Gasset observes that tragedy cannot be produced on the ground level.[23] One must rise up from the real to the unreal, to the larger than life. For this reason Napoleon wanted no comedies performed before conquered sovereigns. Laughter might give them dangerously liberating ideas about changing the carefully wrought tragedy which his imperial genius had imposed on them. The ruler of men must be forever vigilant about the possible effects of a change in tone. So must those who write about him. The *Cyropaedia* already occupies a stage considerably above ground level. In order for the tragedy of history to intrude on Cyrus's education, even for a brief time, there would

have to be a fairly sharp divergence in tone. Whether Orte-
ga's metaphor of high or low applies is not so important as
that there be a recognizable difference, at least for a time.
Panthea has to die, and her death has to matter, and then
Cyrus's education has to go on.

As we have just seen, the first of these two death scenes
was relatively easy for Xenophon. To create a convincing
account of the death of Abradatas in battle, and to suggest
how an ideal leader might be able to rewrite actual history,
he had only to turn to his own *Anabasis* and personal ex-
perience. But when he faced the death scene of Panthea, his
repertoire was more limited. His representation of the last
moments of Panthea is awkward and conventional in its
characters and design. Familiarity with Homer and Athe-
nian tragedy seems to have been helpful; if Panthea parts
from her husband like Andromache in the *Iliad*, she dies
like a heroine on the tragic stage. However, we shall try to
steer toward the way Cyrus's conduct in this scene con-
forms to his imperial design. From that political point of
view Xenophon is very original.

When Cyrus hears the news of Abradatas' death, he slaps
his thigh like a warrior in Homer and rushes off to console
Panthea (7.3.6). His thigh-slapping is also appropriate to the
present Homeric context, and typical of Homeric warriors
in similar moments of distress (*Iliad*, 12.162, 15.113). Not
at all typical of Homeric warriors is his ready forgiveness of
the enemy responsible for Abradatas' death. The Egyptians
fighting in the center of the enemy line were the only ones
who distinguished themselves in the battle by their bravery
and their fierce resistance to the Persian attack (7.1.46). Cy-
rus thinks it pitiful that men as brave as they should be
slain. He draws back, negotiates a truce, and wins them as
firm allies for the future (7.1.41–44). Panthea's view of the
world is necessarily less strategic.

> When he saw the woman sitting upon the ground and the
> corpse lying there, he wept at this suffering and said,
> "Alas, O brave and faithful soul, have you then gone and
> left us?" As he said this, he clasped his hand, and the dead

man's hand came away in his grasp. (The wrist had been severed by the sword of an Egyptian.) And Cyrus was still more deeply pained at seeing this. And the wife wept aloud. But taking the hand from Cyrus, she kissed it and fitted it on again, as well as she could. (7.3.8)

There is a harsh clash between Cyrus's words of comfort and Panthea's loving reassembly of a husband who has become something of a jigsaw puzzle. The scene aims for the kind of shocking effect familiar from the finale of tragedies like the *Hippolytus* or *Bacchae*. In this way Xenophon turns the *erôtika pathêmata* or love sickness of romance into the *pathos* of tragedy. Once again Cyrus witnesses but is not harmed by the sad fate of others. Panthea is transformed from a heroine of romance to a heroine of tragedy. Tragic also is the moment of recognition (*anagnôrisis*) that comes to her: she understands clearly but too late the consequences of Cyrus's respect for her. What she has to say to Cyrus has as little effect on him as Cyaxares' long complaint in Book 5 (5.5.25-34).[24] Like Cyaxares, however, she also speaks the truth:

> The rest of his limbs you will also find in the same way, Cyrus. But why should you see this? I am well aware that not the least am I to blame that he has suffered so, and so also no less are you, Cyrus. For in my folly I urged him to be a friend to you. And as for him, I know he never had a thought of what might happen to him, but only of what he could do to please you. And so, he has indeed died a blameless death, while I who urged him to it sit here alive. (7.3.10)

Cyrus weeps for some time in silence. He cannot reply to this charge. When he finally does speak, he is once again intensely conventional:

> "Well, lady, he has indeed met the loveliest of all ends for he has died in the moment of his victory. But accept these gifts from me" (for Gobryas and Gadatas had come with many beautiful ornaments) "and deck him with them. And then, let me assure you that in other ways also he shall not want for honors, but many hands shall rear to him a monu-

ment worthy of us, and sacrifice shall be made over it,
such as will befit so brave a man." (7.3.11)

Cyrus cannot afford to answer what Panthea has said.
Hence his turn to the conventional consolations for the sur-
vivors of dead heroes. To compare his response with the la-
ments over Hector that end the *Iliad* is to see just how
much is not being said.[25]

Nor does Cyrus care to intervene in Panthea's obvious
determination to commit suicide. Some readers have al-
ready suspected that he knows what she intends to do.[26] He
does more than merely acquiesce; he may even supply Pan-
thea with her ambiguous metaphor of death and dying when
he says, generously,

> "You also shall not be deserted, but on account of both
> your goodness and all your virtue I shall show you all
> honor, and I shall deliver you to some one to escort you
> wherever you yourself desire to go." He then added, "Only
> let me know to whom you wish to be conducted." (7.3.12)

Panthea responds to this ambiguous offer with equal ambi-
guity:

> And Panthea said, "Ah, take heart," she said, "Cyrus. I
> shall not hide from you who it is to whom I wish to go."
> (7.3.13)

The placement of the second "she said" (*ephê*) delicately
emphasizes the pathos of her command to take heart (*thar-
rei*). Cyrus plays his role perfectly. Having uttered the nec-
essary pieties, he leaves Panthea to her fate. A nurse—is she
on loan from Euripides' *Hippolytus*?—suddenly appears to
play the role of the second actor in the tragic stage from
which Cyrus has just made his timely exit.

> But she told her nurse to stay with her, and ordered her to
> cover her and her husband when she was dead with the
> same cloak. The nurse, however, pleaded earnestly with
> her not to do so, but when the prayers proved of no avail
> and she saw her mistress becoming angered, she sat down
> and burst into tears. Panthea then drew out a dagger with
> which she had provided herself long before, and plunged it

into her heart; and laying her head upon her husband's
bosom she died. Then the nurse wailed aloud and covered
them both, just as Panthea directed. (6.3.14)

Cyrus returns to view the corpse. He performs a lament and
sees to it that husband and wife are buried in a large mon-
ument, with full honors. He does everything one could ex-
pect of him (7.3.16). He seems the model in this office, as in
every other. He has impressed many readers this way; for
example, this depiction of him as a pious Christian prince
accompanying the translation of Vasque de Lucène. (Illus-
tration 6.)

Compare also Sir Philip Sidney, who wrote an exquisite
tribute to the Panthea and Abradatas story in Book 3 of *The
Countess of Pembroke's Arcadia*, where Artabazus becomes
"Argalus," and Panthea, "Parthenia."

> His being was in her alone,
> And he not being, she was none.
> They joyed one joy, one grief they grieved;
> One love they loved; one life they lived.
> The hand was one; one was the sword
> That did his death, her death, afford.
> As all the rest, so now the stone
> That tombs the two is justly one.
> (*The Countess of Pembroke's Arcadia*, Book 3)[27]

But how relevant is Cyrus's piety? Panthea's critique re-
mains unchallenged. It is worth noting that Cyrus will have
a different way to measure his own life when his time
comes to die; he will reject the very kind of monument he
builds for Panthea and Abradatas:

> What is more blessed than to be united with the earth,
> which brings forth and nourishes all things beautiful and
> all things good? I have always been a friend to man, and I
> think I should gladly now become a part of that which does
> him so much good. (8.7.25)

At every stage in the affair of Panthea, each person who par-
ticipates in it says and does the conventional thing. What is
not at all conventional is Cyrus's manipulation of these

6. Cyrus at the Tomb of Panthea and Abradatas. From the *Traitté des faiz et haultes provesses de Cyrus* of Vasque de Lucène (1470).

conventions for his own advantage. So far as human affections are concerned, he has the power to attract the noblest kind of persons to his cause and make them work on his behalf. At the same time, he has an equal talent for avoiding any misfortunes that may befall them. So far as Abradatas and Panthea are concerned, Cyrus was not the Scylla, pulling others to him by sheer force, but rather the Siren who touched no one, only singing from afar. In this case it was a song of Cyrus's virtue. How irrelevant that virtue could be to Panthea and Abradatas can be summed up by repeating what she herself says to Cyrus:

> I am in no small degree to blame that he has suffered so, and you, Cyrus, perhaps not less than I. For it was I that in my folly urged him to do his best to show himself a worthy friend to you; and as for him, I know that he never had a thought of what might happen to him, but only of what he could do to please you. (7.3.10)

Rather than be detained by praise for the nobility of Cyrus's conduct—it is everywhere exemplary—let us look instead to this final outcome. It is harsh and instructive. Cyrus has learned an important lesson about acquiring an empire: a prince must be able to find good people willing to die in his service. The only persons who could object to this are dead. The thing people always forget is what happens to them, once they hear the Sirens and fall enchanted victims to their song.[28]

CHAPTER NINE

The Economy of Empire

It is not the consciousness of men that determines their
being; on the contrary, their social being determines their
consciousness.

Marx, *Toward a Critique of Political Economy*

$\mathbf{B}$UT IF THERE are any sinister
aspects to Cyrus's rise to power, they disappear with the
death of Panthea and Abradatas. From the moment Babylon
falls and the evil Assyrian is slain (7.5.30–36), the world of
the *Cyropaedia* is a radiant and happy place, with not a vil-
lain in sight. It is well for Cyrus that this happens. His con-
siderable skills at creating an imperial fiction and imposing
it on those about him would amount to very little if he did
not change the world for the better. He began the Assyrian
war knowing that it can be as difficult to maintain an em-
pire once it is won as it is to gain it in the first place. The
way Cyrus achieves this last of his imperial designs is the
culmination of his education. In Book 8 the calculation be-
comes more overt; commands replace polite indirection. Be-
cause he has absolute power, he can afford to dispense with
the involved strategies of earlier days. By the end of his ed-
ucation (8.6.23) he is the perfect monarch Xenophon de-
scribes in the prologue, issuing orders to the willing sub-
jects of an empire that embraces all the world worth living
in.

For Cyrus the new monarch, his father's instructions are

more relevant than ever before. If he does not take care, he may be undone by the very friends and wealth he has worked so hard to gather.[1] The postwar world of the *Cyropaedia* with its blessings of peace (7.5.37–8.6.23) has never attracted poets and novelists the way the heroism of Panthea did, and they may well prove less engaging even now. All the same, it is no less important. To readers like Augustus or Elizabeth I, the later pages of the *Cyropaedia* may well have been more relevant. When princes succeed in creating an empire, sooner or later they must pay as much attention to the organization of those who support them as they do to the suppression of those who oppose them. Willing subjects are indispensable to the kind of rule Cyrus aims to create; like Agesilaus, Teleutias, or Ischomachus' ideal Persian king, he aims to create a monarchy that will be the antithesis of tyranny.[2] Yet even willing subjects do not know how to serve Cyrus on their own initiative. They require as much strategic thought as the Assyrian king or a devious ally like Croesus.

Earlier strategies suggest the direction Cyrus will take. From his first appearance as a child in the court of his grandfather, he deals with anyone he meets with a sensitivity to who they are and who they expect him to be. It could be said of him, as of Socrates, that there are as many Cyruses as the sum of the people he meets. The Cyrus Astyages knows is not the Cyrus of Cyaxares, nor is Cambyses' dutiful pupil the same as Artabazus' *erômenos*. The honorable, discreet Cyrus whom Panthea and Abradatas so admire is different again. Now that he has supreme power over others, he has far more subjects than he can deal with individually, and he necessarily has at best a distant relationship with them. Hence the last challenge Xenophon poses to Cyrus the Persian as he becomes Cyrus the Great: how will he govern the empire he has created?

Cyrus does what Xenophon would have any ruler do: establish an economy for his empire. This is "economy" in Xenophon's expanded sense of *oikonomia*, the regulation of an *oikos* or political household, of which Cyrus is the center. The metaphoric connection between household management and the management of an empire conceived as *oikos* is fully developed in *Oeconomicus* 7–9, where the administration of the Persian empire serves as paradigm for the management of the household of Ischomachus and his wife. In Xenophon's view, *polis* and *oikos*, public and private life, can be organized according to the same principles. Recall the analogy drawn between public institutions and private households in the prologue of the *Cyropaedia*. To exploit the possible connections among all parts of life is also the aim of the ideal ruler described at the end of the *Oeconomicus*; the common denominator for successful gardening, politics, household management, and war, is successful rule (*Oeconomicus*, 21.2).

In the calculus of ruling an empire, ordinary ways of conducting life may all be turned to a ruler's advantage. What Cyrus desires, above all else, is to rule others, and in this world of imperial erotics, nothing is more valuable to him than his subjects. Naturally he can afford to scorn ordinary ideas about personal wealth; his riches are the new friends, allies, and subjects he can acquire. This disdain for wealth is commonly mentioned as a virtue of Cyrus the Great.[3] Shows of personal simplicity and austerity could be as useful as pagentry; both are different ways of suggesting the power always in reserve, always to be used if necessary. Cyrus's use of austerity as well as his public displays of wealth were not lost on later students of his education.[4] James I of England offers this Xenophontic precept in his own handbook of kingship, the *Basilikon Doron*. He advises his son that a monarch must not only pass good laws, but exemplify them "with his vertuous life in his owne person, and the person of his court and company; by good example alluring his subjects to the love of virtue, and hatred of vice. . . . Let your owne life be a law—book and a mirror to your people, that therein they may read the practise of their owne Lawes; and therein they may see, by your image, what life they should lead."[5]

Thus Cyrus need only find the role that will enable him to persuade his subjects to let him use the laws. The one he chooses to play is father to an empire conceived as the

Greek *oikos* (household) writ large.[6] The *Oeconomicus* states explicitly the goal of Cyrus's program:

> When you have inspired someone to desire you to have good things, and when you have inspired in the same person a diligence to secure them for you; when you also have seen to it that he knows how each kind of work is to be done to provide greater benefits; when you have also made him fit to rule, and when finally he is as pleased as you would be at exhibiting a rich harvest, I will no longer ask whether someone of this sort still needs something in addition; for it seems to me a steward [*epitropos*] of this sort would already be worth very much. (*Oeconomicus*, 15.1)

A highly skilled *epitropos* is well disposed toward his master and considers him a fit ruler, and a just one (ibid., 15.5). He is the same as the contented subject of Cyrus. His empire is an expanded version of Socrates' ideal, a realm in which the lieutenants who serve him will be the stewards who maintain the economy of his empire.

I

Cyrus's creation of a court and an empire is an exercise in persuasion, because his entire aim in both court and empire is to persuade others that he should be their king. In this sense his calculations can be viewed as a problem of rhetoric, and rhetoric not in a contemporary, attenuated sense of the word, but in the sense that Cicero, Aristotle, and Quintilian conceived it to have: the art of persuasion by the spoken word, the orator's means of changing or preserving a course of action. For them, language was a form of power.[7] Since rhetoric was completely bound up in the political processes of Xenophon's world, the most accomplished of all leaders of men would naturally be the most accomplished of all rhetoricians. As Cyrus's polished speech in Book 1 might suggest, however, he does not aim for technical perfection in the ordinary manner of orators. The entire *Cyropaedia*, and not only Cyrus's discourse in public and private, invites rhetorical study. His words and his rhetorical strategies were what proved transferable and adaptable in other times and places; the adroit manipulation of Cyaxares or the interview with Croesus could instruct Alexander and Machiavelli in ways profoundly more useful than the invention of the scythe-bearing chariot or the reorganization of the army.

Because moral and political suasion are achieved through the spoken word, Xenophon devotes much attention to the public utterances of Cyrus in both formal and informal meetings: not only speeches, but also messages, letters, and even the relaxed conversation of guests at his dinner table. And his rhetoric extends beyond this. His art of persuasion may be exemplified by the arts he uses to win over the king of the Indians.

Cyrus requires something more substantial from the Indian king than his neutrality. He needs him as an ally, yet he will never meet him in person. First he thinks out loud in the presence of the Armenian king and other allies about the money he will need to continue the war; he has troops coming from Persia who will need to be paid, but he does not want to impose on his new allies for the money (3.2.28). He sends a message to the Indian king, which is at the same time a message to his new allies:

> "Cyrus sends me, Indian, to you; he says he needs more funds, for he is awaiting another army from home in Persia"—and indeed I am awaiting them—"If therefore you will send him as much as is convenient for you, he says, if god should grant him success, that he will try to make you think that you were well advised in doing this favor for him." (3.2.29)

For their part, he adds, his allies may give whatever instructions they please to their own messengers to the Indian king. He appeals to the Indian king's self-interest by promising a future effort on his part, contingent on the king's granting his request. But he is deliberately vague about what that reward will be. Knowing that the Indian expects some kind of appeal to his self-interest, he leaves tantalizingly vague exactly how that interest will be served. The Indian king knows only that Cyrus is doing what he expected him to do; he does not know how Cyrus is going to do it. The king is left free to exercise his own imagination to fill in the details of the coming rewards of serving Cyrus. It is characteristic of Cyrus's art that the apparent issue at hand (the Indian king) is actually not the main target he has in mind. Although the Armenians and Chaldeans are already allies, he wants to confirm them in his service. Just as he organizes his army so that it will be like any good army, a sentient extension of his will, efficiently carrying out his commands, so now he turns his new allies into messengers who will be more effective spokesmen for him than any text he could write. He accomplishes this by supplementing his message to the Indian king with this candid analysis of the results of the embassy: if the Indian is generous, Cyrus and his allies will have the money they both need; if he is not, they will owe him nothing and can settle matters with him in the future as they please (3.2.20). Cyrus said this because

> he thought that those Armenians and Chaldeans who were going would say the kind of things he wanted all men both to say and to hear about him. (3.3.31)

This is an important thought to overhear. The number of persons whom Cyrus can meet is finite. No matter how persuasive he is in person, his imperial strategies cannot be directed to the number of persons he meets personally. He extends his powers by delegating the converted to speak on his behalf. Grateful, loyal messengers can be more effective in luring new subjects than any number of speeches, letters, or gifts could ever be.

It is thus essential to make those who serve Cyrus understand their proper roles and to encourage them to want to be as good at them as they can be. The more experience Cyrus gains, the more jejune his first speech in Book 1 (1.5.7–15) comes to seem. By allowing his lieutenants to orchestrate opinion he deflects attention from the obvious fact that he is actually the one in charge. Even when he does deliver a formal speech, he treats his army as a collection of soldiers who know as well as he does the proper role each one plays (3.3.34–39, 3.3.41–44). The orchestration of his army is an orchestration in literal fact; each man knows where he should stand better than the member of a chorus (3.3.44; cf. 1.6.18). The tradition of a general's exhortation before battle thus becomes a convention to be derided rather than observed.

> Do you really think that one word spoken could all at once fill with a sense of honor the souls of those who hear, or keep them from actions that would be wrong, and convince them that for the sake of praise they must undergo every toil and every danger? Could it impress the ideal indelibly upon their minds that it is better to die in battle than to save one's life by running away? (3.3.51)

This shifts the rhetorical burden from Cyrus himself to his men. Only when the battle is over does he deliver the kind of speech that commanders customarily give beforehand:

> you can best judge these matters now when you have experience of them and while the event is so recent an occurrence. (4.1.5)

Until he has absolute power, Cyrus prefers to seem to be guided by the views of others rather than simply by his own opinion. He chooses to stage a debate about continuing the war against the Assyrians, but only once the war is well underway. Rather than take the initiative himself, he sees that Cyaxares presides over a conference (Cyaxares by then being contented in his role as elder statesman), with comments from his allies, Artabazus, Gobryas, Gadatas, and Hystaspas (6.1.6–24). He himself speaks only at the end (6.1.12–18). By seeming to surrender authority voluntarily to a group of lieutenants and an army already fired up for war, by seeming to defer to the opinions of others, he becomes all the stronger because those who now follow him think that what they are doing is what they want to do. Cyrus never commands more effectively than when he makes himself seem to be commanded.

The economy of an empire requires that we look beyond particular persons and events, to a larger design. If there is a war to be waged, the war itself is not the end, but a means of strengthening an empire. If an army needs to be organized and trained, that army's organization and training are not ends in themselves, but the basis for the administration of the future empire. It is desirable to win loyalty and affection from others, but one learns to do this not only because of the pleasures and comforts of friendship; those sincere feelings will also provide the basis for the best kind of servants and lieutenants in other contexts. If banquets and symposia are to be held, these relaxing occasions can be simultaneously pleasant and instructive. The prince encourages his lieutenants to speak, not merely to vary the conversation, but to avoid dominating such gatherings himself. He engages as much in a manipulation of occasion as in a manipulation of discourse.[8]

2

Here there is a particular challenge to the imagination of the new prince. From the viewpoint of both a monarch's subjects and spectators of later times, the ceremonies of an empire seem proof of imperial power.[9] Less perceptive rulers may actually come to believe that these public shows are a reification of that power. They believe that they can legitimize and make permanent the reign they enjoy by transforming material wealth into impressive monuments.[10] The problem might be exemplified by the difference between Augustus and Nero: the first one built Rome as part of a comprehensive design to legitimize his regime; the second misread the means and took them to be the ends. Nero's reign and its greatest monument, the Domus Aurea, were abruptly terminated in mid-course.[11]

In the Cyropaedia Xenophon gives little space to portraying this tendency of new rulers to use the monumental and the ceremonial as a way of valorizing their regimes. Instead he shows how Cyrus redesigns the political world, both the one he has acquired and the one he inherits. He is as willing to discard old laws as he is ready to institute new ones:

We think that we have observed in Cyrus that he held the opinion that a ruler ought to excel his subjects not only in point of being actually better than they, but that he ought also to cast a sort of spell upon them. He chose to wear the Median dress himself and persuaded his associates also to adopt it; for he thought that if any one had any personal defect, that dress would help to conceal it, and that it made the wearer look very tall and very handsome. For they have shoes of such a form that without being detected the wearer can easily put something into the soles so as to make him look taller than he is. He encouraged also the fashion of pencilling the eyes, that they might seem more lustrous than they are, and of using cosmetics to make the complexion look better than nature made it. (8.1.40–41)

Cyrus has transformed himself into the image of his grand-father Astyages, the very person he marvelled at when we first saw him as a young boy (1.3.1–2), and he has made the shift from Persian to Median *nomoi* without hesitation or comment. When Alexander attempted the same strategy, he encountered more serious opposition from his Macedonian companions.[12]

Everything Cyrus does after his conquest of Assyria is directed to reordering the *nomoi* of the world to accommo-date to him. By means of this change he can most effec-tively control the opinion of those he rules. While it is im-portant for him to be remarkably demanding of himself in moral and intellectual matters, it is even more important that everyone know this (8.1.6–48). He treats others in ways calculated to induce changes in their attitude to him, by changing their social status and their personal fortunes, nearly always for the better. To effect this transition from war to peace, which is actually a transition to an empire with Cyrus at the center, he moves from what is established (his army), to what he is yet to establish (his empire). He adapts the *oikonomikai praxeis* or organization of the army to these peaceful, imperial conditions (8.1.14). His custom-ary sensitivity to the feelings of others is as strong as ever. He wants to establish a court fitting for a king, but he also wants to do this in a way that will not arouse the envy of

his subjects (7.5.37). To accomplish this he devises an in-
genious masque to persuade his Persians that a formal court
is not something he personally desires, but rather an insti-
tution imposed on him by necessity.

Cyrus holds court but requests that his Persian friends
wait until all other petitioners have been heard. The crowds
increase all day long, and the audience is over before Cyrus
can see the men he most wants to see. Their distress is un-
derscored by a comic touch reminiscent of the end of the
Symposium: Cyrus's old friends are kept waiting so long
that they must rush off at once "to attend to the call of na-
ture."[13] The next day promises much the same perform-
ance, but Cyrus first holds a private audience with his Per-
sian friends. What should he do? His lieutenants Artabazus
and Chrysantas deliver Cyrus's speech for him: ever the
comic character, it is Artabazus the *erastês* who most wants
to see Cyrus (7.5.48–54). This elicits polite laughter. Chry-
santas is then free to declare what needs to be done: Cyrus
must protect the time of his friends and himself by becom-
ing more remote, harder to impose on. Everyone agrees to
the logic of this proposal. No one notices that it was Cyrus's
staged chaos at the first day's reception that makes them
now think Chrysantas' notions of a splendid isolation so
reasonable (7.5.55–56). This first step in the making of a
court was the crucial one. Cyrus has changed the way his
Persians think about him and about themselves. They are
no longer a general and an army, but a king and members of
a court, and yet this fundamental change in status seems
imposed on Cyrus and his followers by the press of events,
rather than by any desire of his own.

At this point Xenophon writes more about what Cyrus
thinks than about what Cyrus does. He reasons that eu-
nuchs will make the best kind of guards for his new court,
because of the contempt other men hold them in. They will
be loyal, like gelded stallions, but not less strong than other
men (7.5.58–65). The analogy is detached, clinical, linking
the art of ruling human beings with the arts of animal hus-
bandry. At the end of the *Cyropaedia*, Cyrus and the narra-

tor of the prologue have the same tastes in analogy, and the same uses for it. As Xenophon once reasoned about his project of writing about Cyrus, so now Cyrus reasons about his own creation, the Persian empire. Narrator and character blend into a single voice as the story winds down to its end. Cyrus supplements his grateful geldings (7.5.71) with an ever-widening range of imperial forces to protect him and his court. He calculates that a show of *philanthropia* will make men loyal to a king they think is kind (8.2.1). At the same time, even as he binds others to him in one way, in another he establishes an ever greater distance between himself and those he governs. His state appearances are contrived to create as much awe and admiration in his subjects as possible (8.3.1ff.). In private he continues to be as intimate with his old lieutenants as ever, using generous presents to confirm their loyalty to him. Food, gifts, and wit are always in abundance (8.4). But the entire purpose of these shows of generosity is to make his new conquest, Babylon, secure. Once this is accomplished, he returns to Persia (8.5.1) and the careful instruction of his father Cambyses.

In order to become the ruler he desires to be, at once remote and responsive to those he rules, Cyrus uses allies and lieutenants as intermediaries between himself and the ever-widening empire he governs. In effect he creates a process which might be termed the imitation of Cyrus; his lieutenants do not simply carry out his orders, but become extensions of his imperial personality. Of course this is all a game, with rules that suit Cyrus and those who serve him. Its deadly seriousness can be measured by the fate of the few who are not willing to play it. Xenophon invented two characters who resist inclusion in the economy of Cyrus's empire: Aglaïtadas, "a rather astringent man" (*struphnoteros*) (2.2.11) and Daiphernes, "rather boorish in manner" (*soloikoteros*) (8.3.21). Their fate shows the limits of Cyrus's much-praised *philanthropia*. Their patently symmetrical personalities reveal yet again the way Xenophon conceived of most of the supporting cast of characters in the *Cyropaedia*.[14]

Cyrus likes to mix wit and seriousness to make even re-
laxed occasions like dinner parties entertaining and instruc-
tive (2.2.1; cf. 8.4). When Hystaspas and an unnamed cap-
tain tell moderately amusing stories of bad table manners
and literal-minded recruits by way of contributing to this
purpose (2.2.1–10), Aglaïtadas refuses to play by the rules
Cyrus has established and charges them with playing the
fool (alazon) (2.2.11). He is finally jollied into a smile by
this strategem:

> "What!" said Aglaïtadas. "Do you really think, Hystaspas,
> to get a laugh out of me?"
> "Well, by Zeus," said the other captain, "he is a very
> foolish fellow, let me tell you, if he does. For I believe one
> might rub fire out of you more easily than provoke a laugh
> from you."
> At this the rest laughed, for they knew his manner, and
> Aglaïtadas himself smiled at it. (2.2.15–16)

Cyrus shortly turns the conversation towards more earnest
matters. But the ill-tempered Aglaïtadas appears nowhere
else after this scene at Cyrus's table. He is dropped from the
narrative, and, we assume, from Cyrus's service. The other
grouch Daiphernes is incautious in a different way. He
makes the mistake of the Armenian king. He thinks he will
show himself to be more independent (eleutheroteros) than
others by not hurrying to Cyrus's presence when sum-
moned. Cyrus's meticulous attention to this slight shows
how seriously the prince must take the rules of court eti-
quette.

> Cyrus noticed this, and so before Daiphernes came and
> talked with him, he sent one of his sceptre-bearers to him
> privately to say that he no longer had need of him; and he
> did not send for him ever again. But when a man who was
> summoned later than Daiphernes rode up to him sooner
> than he, Cyrus gave him one of the horses that were being
> led in the procession and gave orders to one of his sceptre-
> bearers to have it led away for him wherever he should di-
> rect. And to those who saw it, this seemed to be a mark of

great honor, and as a consequence of that event many more people paid court to that man. (8.3.22–23)

The private message conceals from everyone else an act that might be construed as petty. The reward of the prompt man and the oblivion of Daiphernes convey the rule of the new court, which is to make Cyrus the center of one's life. And yet that rule is not uttered. Compare the slights, real or imagined, which the boy Cyrus complained of in the cup-bearer Sacas (1.3.8–11): Cyrus has refined his earliest experiences as a courtier. In retrospect, we realize that the child really is the father of the man in the *Cyropaedia*. The boy Cyrus was an embryonic anticipation of the adult we see at work in Book 8.

3

Malvolios like Aglaïtadas and Daiphernes are rare. Xenophon much prefers to invent characters who are happy to be ruled by Cyrus, rather than oppose him. The father-son bond seems to be the relationship he most enjoys portraying. To that end, his symmetrical conception of fathers and sons is nowhere more striking than in the two Assyrian suppliants who come to Cyrus because of atrocities committed by the degenerate son of the Assyrian king. Both king Gobryas and the eunuch prince Gadatas are victims, but in obviously different ways that are carefully worked out to allow them to be complementary to one another and Cyrus. The son of Gobryas was murdered by the Assyrian prince because his success on a hunt aroused the jealousy of the king's son. Gobryas' entire recital is a pathetic tale by a heartbroken father grieving for his son (4.6.2–7). Gobryas is childless—more precisely, son-less:

> I have come to you and fall a suppliant at your feet. I offer myself to be your slave and ally and ask that you will be my avenger. And so, in the only way I may, I make you my son, for I have no male children. (4.6.2)

After cautious exploration, Cyrus is convinced that his Assyrian suppliant is telling the truth (5.2.4–5). Gobryas' son was the victim of a fate Cyrus himself very nearly suffered.[15] Naturally Cyrus is moved to ask if there are any more suppliants where Gobryas came from (5.2.27).

There are. Gobryas tells Cyrus of the fate of a young prince who was seized and castrated, either because the son of the Assyrian king's concubine had merely praised him, or because he was suspected of having an affair with her (5.2.28). Cyrus commissions Gobryas to bring over the eunuch prince to his side, and he does so. Prince Gadatas' circumstance is remarkably similar to what we observe in Gobryas. The difference is that he is proleptically childless (*apais*):

> "These gifts, Cyrus, I now beg to offer you, and do accept them, if you have any use for them. And please consider that everything else I have is yours. For there is not and never can be a child of my own to whom I can leave my estates, but with my death our race and name must be altogether blotted out. Cyrus," he continued, "I swear this to you by the gods who see all and hear all: it is not for anything wrong or shameful that I have said or done that I suffer this affliction." As he uttered these words he burst into tears over his lot and could say no more. (5.4.30–31)

Cyrus accepts him readily; he is the victim of the worst of all the Assyrian prince's atrocities (5.2.28, 5.3.9–21). Since Gadatas has no prospect of having children, his life has acquired a certain simplicity about it that causes Cyrus to pity him as much as any person he meets in the *Cyropaedia* (5.4.32).[16] Gadatas is easily won over. Cyrus accomplishes this by declaring that he and his army will henceforth be the children whom Gadatas could otherwise not have.

> From you, Gadatas, the Assyrian has, it seems, taken away the power of begetting children, but at any rate he has not deprived you of the ability of acquiring friends. Let me assure you that by this deed you have made of us friends who will try, if we can, to stand by you and aid you no less efficiently than if we were your own children. (5.3.19)

Xenophon conceived of his suppliants Gobryas and Gadatas in his customary way. Symmetry is everywhere. They have the double satisfaction of leading the attack that captures Babylon, and of killing the unholy Assyrian king (*anosios basileus*) with their own hands (7.5.30–32). They continue to enjoy all the prestige of being kings and princes in their own right, with the added bond to Cyrus that in effect makes himself their "child" (*pais*).

Nonetheless there are limits to this kind of sentiment, and Cyrus eventually reaches them. While the affection and gratitude of Gobryas are especially strong, Cyrus does not care to make his relationship with his new "father" any stronger than metaphoric. When he returns Gobryas' presents to his new ally's daughter and "the man who will marry her" (5.2.8), Gobryas hopefully assumes that Cyrus is referring to himself. But Cyrus has no intention of marrying Gobryas' daughter. He aims for a dynastic marriage far higher, because he intends to lead an empire of which Gobryas and his kingdom will be only one part, and far from the most important. For this purpose only Cyaxares' daughter will do.[17]

In this way Cyrus plays the role of a son without really being a son at all. This strategy with human affections is paralleled by the opposite kind of role he plays with the troops he leads. Using essentially the same technique, he creates a metaphoric kinship with the men in his army, and later, the subjects of his empire. They regard him as their father when he is not really their father at all. As his alter ego Chrysantas puts it,

> Men, I have often noticed before now that a good ruler is not at all different from a good father. For as fathers provide for their children so that they may never be in want of the good things of life, so Cyrus seems to me now to be giving us counsel of how we may best continue in prosperity. (8.1.1)

Some of Cyrus's personal connections were formed so early in life that he has no choice but to play them out as best he can, as in his dealings with Cyaxares, Artabazus, or Araspas.

But as his rule of army and empire expands, he assumes the role Chrysantas describes. The son of Cambyses becomes the father to the children of his empire.

4

As Chrysantas' thoughtful words about "Father Cyrus" may suggest, there are also certain persons in the *Cyropaedia* who are not objects of Cyrus's strategies in either war or peace, but rather accomplices in his designs. Xenophon says nothing about the education of such men, but introduces them fully formed. They serve Cyrus as if by instinct. One is reminded of Harry Hopkins and Franklin D. Roosevelt, or Agrippa and Augustus. In the *Cyropaedia*, Chrysantas and Pheraulas first appear in a public discussion Cyrus conducts on rewarding merit during his reorganization of the Persian army (2.3). There, as always, symmetry prevails. They come from the top and the bottom of Persian society. Chrysantas is one of the peers (*homotimoi*) and therefore of the same class as Cyrus himself. As a counselor he recalls Menelaus' version of Odysseus in the *Odyssey*, a man neither large nor powerful to look at, but preeminent in understanding.[18] Pheraulas is a member of the Persian commoners (*dēmotai*), but like Eumaeus the swineherd, he is a man who resembles a nobleman in both body and spirit.[19]

Pheraulas and Chrysantas are equally useful to Cyrus precisely because they come from opposite ends of the Persian social classes. Toward the end of the organization of his empire, Cyrus spells out why he would choose Pheraulas to help him plan the grand procession in such a way that it will seem most splendid to those who are loyal to him, and most intimidating to those who are disaffected. Pheraulas the common man is intelligent, a lover of beauty, and well disposed to please him (8.3.5). He is a perfect instance of the way Cyrus restructures old laws and customs to create a new kingdom. Pheraulas flourishes in this new world in much the same way that rustics flourish in Aristophanes' comedies. This is not a temporary injection of democracy into Cyrus's monarchic world, however; Pheraulas the common man wins preferment because his rise through merit destabilizes the Persians' traditional hierarchy. Aristocratic excellence is redefined as excellence in service to Cyrus.

Since Cyrus has to defend Pheraulas, he also needs to justify his preferment of Chrysantas. Another boyhood friend, Hystaspas, is a member of the Persian *homotimoi* who proves himself useful to Cyrus in the relaxed atmosphere of Cyrus's symposium. He is a capable cavalry commander, but not the equal of Chrysantas in intelligence or ability. He grows jealous of Cyrus's preferment of Chrysantas, and after some hemming and hawing, asks: Why did Cyrus give Chrysantas a more honorable place than him (8.4.10)? Cyrus's answer is tactful to Hystaspas, but even more informative to us:

> In the first place Chrysantas did not wait to be sent for, but presented himself for our service even before he was called; and in the second place, he has always done not only what was ordered but all that he himself saw was better for us to have done. Again, whenever it was necessary to send some communication to the allies, he would give me advice as to what he thought proper for me to say. And whenever he saw that I wished the allies to know about something, but that I felt some hesitation in saying anything about myself, he would always make it known to them, giving it as his own opinion. And so, in these matters at least, what reason is there why he should not be of more use to me even than I am myself? And finally, he always insists that what he has is enough for him, while he is manifestly always on the lookout for some new acquisition that would be of advantage to me, and takes more pleasure and joy in my good fortune than I do myself. (8.4.11)

In his account of Chrysantas' virtues, Cyrus stresses the intellectual abilities of his alter ego.[20] He is entirely at Cyrus's disposal and works in a dialectical way complementary to his designs. Often it is difficult to distinguish between Cyrus and the lieutenant who fills out his speeches for him, sometimes even preempts them, and everywhere contributes to the general impression (quite a misleading one) that what Cyrus undertakes is not simply his personal invention, but an idea that arises spontaneously, as it were, from others about him. It is Chrysantas, for example, who introduces the notion of laws modifying the existing laws of the Persians in such a way as to make it possible for a common man like Pheraulas to have an equal share in the glory and rewards of war. He is worried (he says) that bad men would share equally with good men, simply because they are both present in the same army (2.3.5–6). Chrysantas gives Pheraulas all the pretext he needs to make his argument in favor of judging men by their merit, rather than by their class.

> Let me inform you then, Cyrus, that I for one shall not only enter this contest but shall also expect you to reward me according to my deserts, whatever I am, for better or worse. And you, fellow commoners, I recommend you to enter eagerly into the competition with these educated men [pepaideumenoi] in this sort of warfare. For they are now trapped in a common man's contest. (2.3.15)

Since he comes from a class less privileged in the *paideia* Cyrus shares with the *homotimoi*, Pheraulas brings his own innately good qualities to bear in Cyrus's service, and he can imitate Cyrus himself. This he does, on an impressive scale.

While Chrysantas comes from the same class as Cyrus and need do no more than be who he ought to be, Pheraulas must do more. He is at once the obedient lieutenant and Cyrus's first imitator. Cyrus stages a horse race which he and his lieutenants win, in order of nationality (8.3.24): Cyrus the first of the Persians, Artabazus first of the Medes, Gadatas first of the Assyrians, Tigranes first of the Armenians, and so on. A "certain Sacian" outruns his men by half the course. Cyrus asks King Richard's question: Would he take a kingdom for his horse? No, the Sacian answers, but he would like to make a brave man grateful to him (8.3.26).

> Cyrus pointed out the place where most of his friends were. And the other, shutting his eyes, let fly with the clod and hit Pheraulas as he was riding by. Pheraulas happened to be carrying some message under orders from Cyrus. But

though he was hit, he did not so much as turn around but
went on to attend to his commission. (8.3.28)

This perfect obedience earns Pheraulas the Sacian's horse.
They become friends and this enables Pheraulas to carry his
imitation of Cyrus one step further.
    Immediately after Cyrus has his second, brief conversa-
tion with Croesus about the uses of wealth (8.2.15–23),
Pheraulas replays the same scene (8.3.35–50), with the same
outcome. He likes nothing so much as to be liked by other
men and to serve them; hence his greatest pleasure is to in-
crease his new friend's affection and loyalty. He accom-
plishes this by giving the Sacian everything he owns. His
excuse is that he will be freed from the burden of having to
worry about his possessions, and the Sacian will in turn
have what most impresses him. This encounter replicates
the conversation of Croesus and Cyrus about wealth, not
simply to show Cyrus's moral superiority, but to show what
it means for a prince to be a paradigm for the moral life of
others. For this is what Cyrus resolves to do when he is rea-
soning out the organization of his court and his empire
(8.1.21–33):

> he believed he could in no way more effectively inspire a
> desire for beautiful and good things [ta kala k'agatha] than
> by trying as their ruler to set before his subjects a perfect
> model of virtue in his own person. (8.1.21)

Or, as Spenser puts it in his letter to Sir Walter Raleigh, "So
much more profitable and gratious is doctrine by ensample,
than by rule."[21] Thus Pheraulas is the first example of this
transference of virtue from the model king of the Persians
to the commoner lieutenant. This mimetic exchange
within the text signifies the utility of Cyrus's education: go
and do likewise.
    Nor does this exemplary tale exhaust the usefulness of
Pheraulas. Cyrus selects him to be the marshal of the grand
procession which is designed to impress Cyrus's friends and
terrify his enemies (8.3.1–18). By putting a demotês in the
lead position, he underscores the place which individual
merit and personal loyalty to the king will have in his new

empire. Giving Pheraulas pride of place sends a clear message to everyone who sees the procession: those will rise the highest in the new empire who will be most like Pheraulas, unquestioningly obedient, content with their status, inspired by the positive example the king sets for all his subjects to follow.

In this way, the norms of social standing and political status in Cyrus's new empire shift so that the new *nomoi* are observed and nurtured by those who stand to benefit the most from them. Cyrus could do nothing less. It would be a serious miscalculation for him to retain the old order of Persia, with the *homotimoi* still in place by virtue of birth and tradition, and at the same time attempt to institute the new laws of his empire. Revaluation of the culture he inherits from his father and the Persians begins with the reorganization of the army for the war with the Assyrian king (2.1–2); indeed, we might even say it begins the moment we first see him as a little boy, adroitly moving back and forth between the *nomoi* of the Medes and the Persians, in Book 1 (1.3.2). Now his royal procession makes visible the economy of the new empire, a reordering already underway as Cyrus conducts the war against the Assyrian king (8.3). The usefulness of cutting across inherited hierarchies and structures of command may be measured by what results.

Briefly, it is that the imitation of Cyrus becomes the central task of all those who will administer his empire. He chooses men like Pheraulas and Chrysantas, ones who will be loyal to him alone (8.6.1). The most important rule is that all of them follow his example in everything they see him do (*mimeisthai*) (8.6.10). The courts they set up will in turn become imitations of the court of Cyrus: each will follow his example so faithfully that each satrap will undergo his own version of the *Cyropaedia*. His lieutenants become extensions of his personality and will, the king's eyes and ears, linked by a courier service that resembles nothing so much as the American pony express (8.6.17–18). The text of the *Cyropaedia* dissolves in mimetic replication of Cyrus, with his lieutenants and satraps doing what Xenophon's readers may now do in turn: imitate Cyrus.

5

These precepts on the care and nurture of an imperial econ-
omy are the culmination of the imperial fiction Xenophon
wanted to write about Cyrus's education. They also signal
that he has nothing left to develop in the theme he outlines
in his prologue. His solution to the challenge of finding an
end for his romance was to leap at once from the perfection
we have just been surveying, to the death of the ideal ruler
of men. The abrupt telescoping of Cyrus's life in 8.7.1 is
thus an unnatural way of getting to the most natural of all
closures.[22]

Cyrus's final speech is famous and often mentioned in
the title pages of early editions and translations of the *Cy-
ropaedia* in and after the Renaissance.[23] It seems the perfect
summation of a life perfectly lived. Without diminishing its
nobility, I think we can expect more of Cyrus than simply
the deathbed speech of a good and noble man. He instructs
us in his particular way even as he dies. Although Xeno-
phon himself was not present in Athens in 399, Cyrus's re-
marks about death and the immortality of the soul resemble
Plato's account of the death of Socrates in the *Apology* and
Phaedo. He also seems to be drawing on tradition from an-
cient Iranian literature, in which the dying king instructs
his successors about the disposition of the kingdom.[24] For
example, the Greek description of the mysterious being
who announces Cyrus's impending death is curiously
vague: a *kreittôn tis ê kata anthrôpon* ("a certain one
greater than man") (8.7.2). This larger-than-life figure func-
tions very much like *Surush*, the semi-divine angel of the
Shahnameh. These creatures appear regularly to warn a
shah of some problem or obligation.[25] This *kreittôn tis* is
part of a world more typically Persian than Greek. Cyrus's
prayers to Zeus and Hestia and his careful attention to the
requirements of his *magoi* all reflect an intermingling of
correct public ceremony with the exercise of office that is
also typical of the shah in Ferdowsi's book of kings.[26] In the
Shahnameh the dying King Vishtasp instructs his sons:

Vahman will be king after me. Pishiyotan will be his confi-
dant. Do not hesitate to be obedient to the orders of Vah-
man; do not fail in the loyalty that you owe to him. Serve
him as his followers, for he is worthy of the throne and of
the crown.[27]

As for the Socratic flavor to Cyrus's death, it is Socrates'
death scene, but considerably rewritten. Cyrus is not so se-
rene and resigned as he may at first seem. Cicero, through
the character of Cato the Elder, adapted part of Cyrus's final
speech to a far different context in his dialogue on old age
(De Senectute). There Cato's purpose in quoting Xenophon
is to dispel his younger companions' fear of old age and
death. He draws on Cyrus's speculations about the nature
of the soul and its possible survival after death. The nature
of soul within the body of a living person is such that it
might well survive the death of the body. It might not, of
course, and in that case Cyrus's sons must keep him alive
as a sacred memory. So says Cato.[28]

Like other Romans translating Greek, Cicero can be
scrupulously close to his original when it suits his purpose.
But his purpose is rather different from Xenophon's. He is
writing about "the things that Cyrus said as he lay dying"
(23/81), and Cyrus's last words are addressed entirely to the
consoling possibility of an afterlife. The Roman Cyrus be-
gins:

> Do not think, my dearest sons, that when I have departed
> from you I will never exist or be nothing. Nor indeed,
> while I was with you, were you used to seeing my soul, but
> you knew that it was in this body from those deeds that I
> performed. (De Senectute, 22/79)

Xenophon's Cyrus leads into his thoughts about the soul
and the afterlife in a very different way. His discourse on the
immortality of the soul is not uttered to comfort his sons,
but to *warn* them.

> But by the gods of our fathers, sons, honor one another, if
> you care at all to give me pleasure. For you seem to me not
> to know this at all clearly: that I shall no longer be any-
> thing when I come to the end of this human life; for now

indeed you do not see my soul, but you have detected its existence by those things it accomplished. (8.7.17)

Cicero omits Cyrus's plea to his sons because it is not needed in a speech about the immortality of the soul and the possibility of an afterlife. In Xenophon these Socratic themes serve as much a political as a philosophical purpose. Cyrus's speech is the last word in the art of fashioning the economy of his empire. It is at once the summation of a lifetime's effort at creating power, and a hedge against a coming threat to the continuation of that power. He correctly perceives that the great threat to his empire will come from his own family. The means of his own education will become the source of his empire's instability. Thus he introduces the topic of the immortality of the soul in part because he is about to die, and in part as a way of keeping his disposition of the world intact. He may still somehow be present or aware of what his sons do; they cannot know otherwise. He concludes by coming back to himself, the happiest of men, and advises them finally to learn from him if they can; and if not, from those who have lived before: this is the best of all teachers (8.7.24). Throughout the scene, there is a declension of authority from the gods to Cyrus; from Cyrus's father to Cyrus; and finally, from Cyrus to his sons.

The speech is worthy of Cicero's admiration and imitation, but its eloquence should not distract us from realizing that it is also a presentiment of a failure which even the monarch of the *Cyropaedia* will not be able to avert. In the end the economy of his empire is subject to the dangers even a household of the most modest scale must face: however well-constituted the *oikos* may be, it cannot easily survive the death of the central figure who administers the *nomoi* or laws by which it is run. Succession turns out to be the Achilles' heel of the whole enterprise. For all of Cyrus's ingenuity in serving as a Lycurgus to these Persians, his empire's future economy will be no better than the sons who are about to inherit it. He has done everything he could to control the consciousness of those whom he rules by reordering their material existence. He has described the consequences of fraternal strife with the greatest clarity. And yet he ends with a warning about future turmoil that brings us back to history and actual experience, not the fictive world of romance, to a place where brothers do not behave perfectly towards one another, where empires are undone by the very kind of disharmony Cyrus so well describes.

III

LEAVING CYRUS

CHAPTER TEN

Revision

The final belief is to believe in a fiction, which you know
to be a fiction, there being nothing else; the exquisite trick
is to know that it is a fiction and that you believe in it
willingly.

Wallace Stevens, Opus Posthumous

Between ourselves these are two things I have always ob-
served to be in singular accord: supercelestial thoughts and
subterranean conduct.

Montaigne, Of Experience

Like cyrus and his empire,
Xenophon's achievement should ultimately be measured
not by what he created, but by how he created it. Kenneth
Burke has described the circumstances which obtain for
many kinds of writing; what he says is especially relevant
to readers of this imperial fiction:

> Critical and imaginative works are answers to questions
> posed by the situation in which they arose. They are not
> merely answers, they are *strategic* answers, *stylized* an-
> swers.[1]

The *Cyropaedia*'s romance of model fathers and obedient
sons ends with Cyrus's death (8.7.28), so that we may say
that all the questions posed by the prologue are answered by
then. These are the answers Burke means, answers whose

formulation and purpose are already determined by the
questions Xenophon first asked. The symmetry of 1.1 and
8.7 is obvious and satisfying—if you like symmetry.[2]
It seems that Xenophon did not. He disrupts the very
harmonies he had labored to create. The strategic and styl-
ized answer to the question he posed at the beginning of the
Cyropaedia becomes itself a question, but with this impor-
tant difference: through his invention of the romantic world
that is Cyrus's education, he creates yet another question
for himself, and it is one he does not so much answer, as
complain about. For the end of *The Education of Cyrus* is
neither strategic nor stylized in Burke's sense of those
words. It is a return to the questioning mode of the pro-
logue, and not a graceful one; it is filled with anger and ex-
asperation. History and experience intrude at the end of the
Cyropaedia, so that what was the inspiration of its fictions
becomes the negation of those fictions. This is the burden
of the last chapter of the *Cyropaedia*: it turns a work of
idealistic fiction into a narrative of disillusionment.

Xenophon's rival, Socratic Plato also saw this incoher-
ence, and his comments on it are very substantial. As al-
ways in Plato, they are indirect, appearing in the "divina-
tions" of a certain Athenian in Book 3 of *The Laws*. The
Athenian aims to discredit the example of Cyrus and his
paideia. I shall argue that he is aided in his task by the dis-
illusioned comments of Xenophon himself. The Athenian
spells out the implications of Xenophon's final chapter for
the rest of the *Cyropaedia*, in essence rewriting it so that
the exemplary education of Cyrus is perceived as altogether
inadequate, something that would naturally culminate in
the disillusionment of Xenophon's final chapter.

In the process of exposing the inadequacies of Cyrus as
a manager of his own household, however, Plato also offers
us a brilliant dissection of the poetics of the *Cyropaedia*, a
poetics which he proceeds to deconstruct with lethal effect.
For the account of the *oikos* of Cyrus in *The Laws* is a par-
ody of *The Education of Cyrus*. If you read what the Athe-
nian says and then reread the *Cyropaedia*, you will find all
the artistry that we have labored to discern very hard to take

seriously. Such may be the immediate effect of any parody. But in the process, Plato also points toward an issue larger than the integrity of just one text. He and Xenophon together—Xenophon by inventing these fictions, Plato by attacking them—bring into focus the crucial question of the artistic and political limitations of what Xenophon created.

To see how Xenophon himself perceived the limits of his own writing, we need to return for a moment to the last words of Cyrus.

I

For an instant, Xenophon's text and his hero Cyrus seem to be in perfect harmony. Cyrus has no more to say, Cyrus dies, and the text of the *Cyropaedia* looks as if it will expire with him:

> "Remember this last word of mine," he said. "If you do good to your friends, you will also be able to punish your enemies. And now, farewell, dear sons; say farewell to your mother as from me. And to all my friends both present and absent, farewell." With these words he shook hands with all of them, covered himself over, and so he died. (8.7.28)

Even as he dies Cyrus has managed to make the thoughtful gesture. It is not easy to envision what better alternative Xenophon could have devised for ending the project he conceived in Book 1. Yet harmony promptly turns into dissonance. The death of Cyrus was not enough to silence Xenophon after all. He says immediately afterwards:

> That Cyrus's empire was the fairest and the greatest of all kingdoms in Asia, it is its own witness. For it was bounded on the east by the Indian Ocean, on the north by the Black Sea, on the west by Cyprus and Egypt, and on the south by Ethiopia. And although it was of this magnitude, it was governed by the single will of Cyrus; and he honored his subjects and cared for them as if they were his own children, and for their part they revered Cyrus as a father. (8.8.1)

This description of Cyrus's empire repeats a recent passage in Book 8, with little variation:

> From that time on Cyrus bounded his empire on the east by the Indian Ocean, on the north by the Black Sea, on the west by Cyprus and Egypt, and on the south by Ethiopia. (8.6.21)

The sequel to Cyrus's death does more than echo this passage; it recalls the entire *Cyropaedia*, through a rapid and impressionistic overview. The description of Cyrus's empire, previously elaborated with some care (1.1, 8.6.21–23), is now reduced to a pair of superlative adjectives (*kallistê* and *megistê*, "the fairest" and "the biggest"). The complex art of government Cyrus devised is summed up by the phrase, "it was governed by the single will of Cyrus." This is not an inaccurate summary; Cyrus cared for those he ruled as if they were his *paides* (children), and they in turn regarded him as their *patêr* (father). But Xenophon is rushing through what was good about Cyrus's empire, only so that he may get to his real theme, which is to tell what was bad:

> As soon as Cyrus was dead, however, his children fell at once into dissension, states and nations began to revolt, and everything began to deteriorate. (8.8.2)

With this brief transition out of the way, Xenophon briskly advances his criticisms. They are crude and vigorous. Everything has gone from bad to worse after Cyrus's death. The principles of the Persians (*gnômai*) are all changed from those Cyrus knew. Now Persians are irreligious and no longer cultivate the gods, they are wicked to friends and relations alike, they are dishonest with anything that has to do with money (8.8.2–7). Nor are they any better in the care of their bodies or cultivation of their physical strength. They neglect everything that would make them good warriors and good citizens. They shun any kind of labor; they are greedy, they drink too much, they go on marches rarely and then not for long. They neglect hunting, both for its own sake and as a training for war; and they do not teach their children horsemanship (8.8.8–14). These are capital crimes for the author of treatises on hunting and horsemanship. There has also been a genetic regression, to the model of only one of the two national characters Cyrus united in his person; instead of old-fashioned Persian rigor (*karteria*), the present-day Persians exhibit only the softness of the Medes (*malakia*) (8.8.15). They have expensive bedding, extravagant tastes in food and dress, they load down their horses with rich trappings, and they no longer employ the scythe-bearing chariots Cyrus invented. These are the reasons why the Persians have made themselves unfit for war. They make soldiers out of everyone, and expect that men who have been raised in luxury will be fit for war. But they no longer fight at close range, either as footsoldiers or as charioteers. Instead they let mercenaries do their fighting for them, and Greek mercenaries at that (8.8.20–26).

This polemic runs straight through to the end of the *Cyropaedia*. What began as an ironic and convoluted reflection (*ennoia*) in Book 1 now ends like a Cynic diatribe, or a piece of invective from an Attic orator, or a Roman satire. Everything is fair game, even the Persians' habits of dining:

> In former times it was their custom also to eat but once so that they might devote the whole day to business and hard work. Now, to be sure, the custom of eating but once a day still prevails—but they begin to eat at the hour when those who breakfast earliest begin their morning meal, and they keep on eating and drinking until the hour when those who stay up latest go to bed. (8.8.9)

The decline and fall can be measured by their use of chamberpots:

> They once had the custom of not bringing pots into their banquets, obviously because they thought that if one did not drink to excess, both mind and body would be less uncertain. So even now the custom of not bringing in the pots still obtains, but they drink so much that, instead of carrying anything in, they are themselves carried out when they are no longer able to stand straight enough to walk out. (8.8.10)

The effectiveness of this palpable hit is enhanced by the wordplay of chamberpots not carried in (*eispheresthai*), as opposed to the bodies of Persians who are carried out dead drunk (*ekpherontai*): *tosouton de pinousin hôste anti tou eispherein autoi ekpherontai*. There is a Juvenalian touch to the education of the Persian young, where the *paideia* of Persian *paides* is reduced to learning the art of poisoning:

> The boys of that time used also to learn the properties of the products of the earth, so as to avail themselves of the useful ones and keep away from those that were harmful. But now it looks as if they learned them only in order to do as much harm as possible. At any rate, there is no place where more people die or lose their lives from poisons than there. (8.8.14)

To the extent that the *Cyropaedia* shows how an ideal prince may fashion an empire and then run it well, this attack could be said to be a criticism of it. But the focus here is really more on Cyrus's descendants and contemporary Persia than on the text of the *Cyropaedia*. And the decline of Persia should be no surprise to anyone who knows anything about the course of political institutions. In Greece there would be first and foremost the example of Athens itself, a decline clearly foreseen by Pericles at the end of the second book of Thucydides—to say nothing again here about Xenophon's own *Hellenica*.[3] The question of the rightness or wrongness of Xenophon's ending, if indeed there is such a question, is not one that would likely detain a politically engaged reader of *The Education of Cyrus* for very long. It was first raised as a more narrowly conceived problem in textual criticism.

2

For most of its history—say, from the time Xenophon published until the middle of the nineteenth century—the last chapter was read as a continuation of the *Cyropaedia* after Cyrus's death. It was not read as a recantation, but as a recital of an all too familiar theme in history. Its point was simple and, to anyone who knew the course of empires, unexceptionable. What Cyrus created was admirable, but it did not last. Thus the last chapter brings us back full circle, not so much to where we began, the program outlined in the prologue, as to the social and political conditions that inspired Xenophon to write the *Cyropaedia* in the first place: the uniformly unhappy experience of all kinds of government, including empires and monarchies. There is no such thing as an empire that lasts, and the one that Cyrus created was no exception. Only those innocent of this fact of political life could be surprised.[4]

Then came readers who were surprised, and they thought themselves far from innocent.[5] It is all very well to say that the epilogue faithfully reflects what eventually happens to any empire if it lasts long enough. Was this Xenophon's point, to say something obvious to anyone who knows Herodotus or Thucydides? It requires no elaborate learning, ancient or modern, to grasp the idea that empires fade away. German philology passed by that truism and focused on Xenophon's Greek text with a single-mindedness that no previous commentators or translators had been prepared or willing to give it. The end of the *Cyropaedia* became strictly a problem of philology: how does this epilogue fit with the text that precedes it? This was an abiding question as modern critical editions of Xenophon began to take shape, roughly by 1857 and the publication of Dindorf's Oxford edition of Xenophon. It was observed that the last chapter—styled variously an epilogue, palinode, or recantation—was in no way prepared for by either the prologue or the main narrative. While the last chapter did not challenge the *Cyropaedia* directly, its attack on the degeneracy of Xenophon's Persia (roughly of the 360s B.C.) does implicitly question the efficacy of the education of Cyrus.

Translators of the Renaissance like Poggio, Vasque de Lucène, or William Barker did not register this problem, but textual critics did. They had their own agenda, and it was one as particular as that of any tutor to any prince. With a strong if sometimes unexamined determination to achieve harmony of ideas and symmetry of design, they discerned many obstacles in the way of the unquestioning acceptance of the epilogue. Previous commentators and translators as well as ancient and medieval scribes now all seemed guilty of an inattentive reading of the last chapter of the *Cyropaedia*. Here in brief was their objection.

First, the epilogue rendered the entire purpose of Cyrus's exemplary education irrelevant. What was the efficacy of having written about such ideals if they culminated in such miserable results? Secondly, the epilogue shifts from the most positive view of Persia in Greek literature, to one of the most negative, anti-Persian diatribes Greek literature has to offer. It was not clear how so divergent a statement could be reconciled with the text that precedes it. Beyond these substantive issues, there was the scarcely less important consideration of the epilogue's language and style: the last chapter seemed childish in its polemic, different in every way from the placid narrative of the *Cyropaedia*, and most especially its prologue (1.1). Closely read, the epilogue became an enigma, with no good reason to be where it is. Since German philology was raising even sharper questions about Homer, it is not surprising the debate would turn on questions of authenticity. One was inclined to look for discrepancies, and if necessary, to invent them where none had existed before.

These skeptical readings led to radical conclusions about what to do with the last chapter. Every proposal was designed to distance it as much as possible from the rest of the *Cyropaedia*. The best that could be said in favor of its authenticity was that Xenophon changed his mind and dashed off these afterthoughts, with no effort to make them harmonize with his prior text. He does not say what it was in contemporary Persia that so excited him, except its vices. These are enumerated with vigor and in some detail, yet they remain vices in a generalized sense, the way vices often are portrayed in political satire and lampoon. Thus a more attractive solution was to conclude that a classic stylist like Xenophon had had nothing to do with the epilogue. Someone else added it later, for his own purposes. By attributing the epilogue to a nameless interpolator, we could close the hermeneutic circle, more or less, by making the end of the *Cyropaedia* coincide with its hero's death. As we have seen, while this ending is not predicted in the prologue, Cyrus's final speech is so moving that no one seemed to notice the temporal leaps at the end. Thus the Loeb editor William Miller's comment in 1914: "It spoils the perfect unity of the work up to this chapter. . . . The chapter is included here in accord with all the manuscripts and editions. But the reader is recommended to close the book and read no further."[6] Instead of the epilogue the Renaissance had read, the last chapter could be taken as merely a footnote to fourth-century history that had nothing to do with an otherwise perfected life of Cyrus. If the rest of the *Cyropaedia* were dull, so be it. At least one could say it was a dullness well composed.

Such was one consequence of the desire to have a finished text. If Xenophon's earlier readers had been guilty of overlooking the difficulties the nineteenth century would expose, however, these later disbelievers were themselves all too philological, too much in love with Xenophon's words to the exclusion of other considerations that are just as relevant.

An enduring characteristic of those of us engaged in philology and literary criticism is our ability to discover solutions to the problems we ourselves have invented. In an inaugural dissertation of 1880, Gustav Eichler demonstrated that the alternatives need not be conceived as a simple yes or no to the question of authenticity.[7] He was a scrupulous reader of Xenophon's text; using the same method as his analytical colleagues, he came to rather different conclusions. He exposed the hidden assumptions of his predecessors by referring to *Cyropaedia* 8.8 as the last chapter (*caput extremum*) of the *Cyropaedia*, rather than its "epilogue." He agreed that it did not fit well with the text that preceded it; it is for this reason that he resists dignifying the last chapter with the formal term "epilogue." This reasonableness was disarming enough. But then, in a detailed analysis of all aspects of its rhetoric (language, style, arguments), he also demonstrated that if Xenophon did not write the last

chapter, its author was someone who knew Xenophon's
style instinctively, often even by heart. No summary of
Eichler's analysis can do justice to what he demonstrated,
since the force of his argument depends on its accumulation
of detail. You will need to examine it for yourself to see if
you agree. To summarize, Xenophon's stylistic markers can
be traced at every level of the last chapter's Greek, from
choice of words, to use of particles, to characteristic ways of
introducing and concluding the points of an argument.[8]
Eichler ends by confessing that he can find no persuasive
reason why Xenophon was moved to add such a coda. He
urges that we refrain from speculating about why Xenophon
added the last chapter. He can find no single historical event
that would explain it. The wisdom of his restraint has been
confirmed by later attempts to do otherwise.[9] Analytical
criticism had its answer, and on its own terms.

In support of Eichler's analyses we might bring forward
again a point already implicit in Chapter 2. For Xenophon,
the gap between the political and historical world he lived
in and the romantically successful but fictional world of the
Cyropaedia finally outweighed his authorial desire to pre-
serve the integrity of the text he had created. Contradictory
strategies and mutually exclusive points of view exist side
by side at many places in his writings. The final sentence of
the *Cyropaedia* is characteristic of his tendency to revise:

> If anyone finds that he holds an opinion contrary to mine,
> let him examine their deeds and he will find that these tes-
> tify to the truth of what I say. (8.8.27)

Elsewhere he poses a similar rhetorical challenge to some-
one or other (*tis*) as a way of validating his argument or an-
ticipating a possible objection. It is not surprising for Xeno-
phon to conclude with some such twist as this.[10]

Sometimes cited, more often not, the work of Gustav
Eichler has had less effect than it should have on subse-
quent readers of the *Cyropaedia*. So far as I can tell, his ar-
gument has made no impression even on the conscientious
few who do cite him. But Eichler is important precisely be-
cause his conclusions leave us with more than a little am-

bivalence about the last chapter. This is where we should
be: not so very different in our view of the text from Xeno-
phon himself. What follows will amplify Eichler's point and
extend it beyond the philological debate over the end of the
Cyropaedia. The issue to address now is not its authentic-
ity, but what this ending reveals about the connections be-
tween what Xenophon had created and actual political ex-
perience, both in Xenophon's time, and more generally.

3

The unrelievedly negative conclusion to the *Cyropaedia*
puts down Xenophon's Persian contemporaries. This move
may have been a self-serving one on Xenophon's part, a rhe-
torical ploy calculated to make what he had written more
attractive to a Greek audience. By attacking contemporary
Persia for its abuse of the legacy and example of Cyrus the
Great, Xenophon is not only able to come down from uto-
pian ideals to historical reality; he is also able to come back
to present-day Greece itself. A return to the contemporary
world would enable a Greek audience to deal with this Per-
sian model for good government in a particular way. The
last chapter brings *The Education of Cyrus* to the here and
now, where it would be, surely, an irrelevant model for the
Persians, but where it might yet be a possible model for the
Greeks. In the main, however, Xenophon's personal reasons
for turning so sharply away from the fictions he had created
are now something we can only speculate about. The irony
of history is that no Athenian or Spartan was ever able to
exploit the model he had created nearly so well as Alex-
ander and his Macedonians.

Not quite so much a matter for speculation is what the
end of the *Cyropaedia* can teach us about the poetics of *The
Education of Cyrus*, which is the issue with which we have
been concerned from the beginning; namely, how it was
that Xenophon managed to intertwine the fictional and the
political in a single text. For this purpose Plato's critique of
the *Cyropaedia* is of critical importance. As we observed in
Chapter 2, the comment in passing by the Athenian in Book

3 of *The Laws* inspired the notion that there was a rivalry
between Plato and Xenophon. This comment, along with
Cicero's *imago iusti imperii* in his letter to his brother
Quintus, is an influential testimony that has been replayed
from Diogenes Laertius and Aulus Gellius to the present.

> Now I divine that Cyrus, though in other respects a good
> general and a friend to his city, failed completely to grasp
> what is a correct education [*orthê paideia*], and didn't di-
> rect his mind at all to household management [*oikonomia*].
> (*Laws*, 3.694c)

Recall that this sideswipe at the *paideia* of the *Cyropaedia*
was actually only a point of departure for Diogenes and Au-
lus Gellius, a way of introducing speculations about the *Cy-
ropaedia* as a response to the *Republic*. As we also saw, if
such a rivalry actually existed, it was a powerfully ineffi-
cient one. The *Cyropaedia* expounds views that Xenophon
professes everywhere in his work; Plato might have pro-
voked him to reply, but we cannot know this for certain.
Later readers like Sidney or Milton in the *Aereopagitica* per-
ceived such a rivalry, but mainly because they preferred the
example of Cyrus to what Milton calls the "airey burgomas-
ters" of the *Republic*. Xenophon seemed to them more prac-
tical about the problems of government; his ideal prince
was a natural mirror in which they could see a reflection of
their own concerns. The rivalry of the *Republic* and the *Cy-
ropaedia* was mainly a contest in the eye of later beholders.

  With this passage from *The Laws*, however, we have to
deal with an obvious response to the *Cyropaedia*, and it is
much more than a sideswipe. It is a fundamental critique of
The Education of Cyrus, because it goes far beyond the sim-
ple observation of this often quoted passage, that the *Kyrou
paideia* was not an *orthê paideia*.[11] The Athenian begins by
focusing on what Xenophon does not tell us about Cyrus:
his conduct as a father to his own sons, and the way he ne-
glected the *oikonomia* or household management of his
own family. Throughout this "divination" of the Athenian
(693e–696b), Plato writes with an extreme sensitivity to the
text of the *Cyropaedia*, and with no little regard for what

Cyrus and his descendants actually did in history as re-
ported in the first and third books of Herodotus.[12] The gap
between what Xenophon says about the education of Cyrus
and what he does not say about the education of Cyrus's
sons permits the opening wedge of a critique that turns the
poetics of the *Cyropaedia* against itself.

The Athenian's comments in *The Laws* are essentially a
dialectical response to all of the *Cyropaedia*. We should not
be surprised that Plato would reply to Xenophon; it is part
of his own program to explore possible answers to the ques-
tion, What is a correct education, an *orthê paideia*? The
Athenian is committed to defining what education is from
the beginning of *The Laws*, because education plays a criti-
cal role in the *nomoi* of the city he seeks to found.

> Athenian: What we mean by education [*paideia*] is not yet
> defined. When we at present blame or praise the upbring-
> ings [*trophai*] of different persons, we say that one of us is
> "educated" [*pepaideumenos*] and another is "uneducated"
> [*apaideutos*], sometimes applying the latter characteriza-
> tion to human beings who are very well educated [*mala pe
> paideumenoi*] in trade or merchant shipping or some other
> such things. So it's appropriate that in our present discus-
> sion we do not consider these sorts of things to be educa-
> tion; we mean rather the education from childhood [*ek pai-
> dôn paideia*] in virtue [*aretê*] that makes one desire and
> love to become a perfect citizen who knows how to rule
> and be ruled with justice [*archein te kai archesthai meta
> dikês*]. It is this upbringing alone, it appears to me, that
> this discussion would wish to isolate and to proclaim as
> education. (*Laws*, 643e–644a)

This passage should be as disturbing to a reader of the *Cy-
ropaedia* as the familiar tag about Cyrus's misunderstand-
ing of *orthê paideia* in Book 3. Xenophon does not examine
the basic theme of his own work in this way, either in the
prologue or anywhere later in the course of the education
into which that prologue leads. It might be objected that
this charge is not altogether fair. Xenophon starts with a
problem in history and actual experience, not in philoso-
phy; he turns to the specific example of Cyrus and his edu-

cation as a way of solving that problem.[13] Nevertheless, by comparison to this enquiry—and we must remember it is a preliminary consideration that comes in the first of twelve books of *The Laws*—the *Cyropaedia* seems to move blithely forward, examining none of the critical issues the Athenian argues must be examined before one undertakes to educate the young.

Furthermore, the Athenian conceives of education in terms identical to the project of the *Cyropaedia*. Xenophon narrates the deeds (*praxeis*) of Cyrus *apo paidos*, from childhood onwards, describing an ideal ruler who excelled all others in the art of ruling and being ruled, *archein te kai archesthai*. Cyrus draws a sharp distinction between the educated and the uneducated, but these are *pepaideumenoi* and *apaideutoi* in the comparatively narrow sense which the Athenian is most determined to avoid.[14] Training in the arts of war is an activity desirable in citizens, but it is also training on the same level as trade or merchant shipping or other such things, because it is not concerned with the formation of those virtues that make a good person. As the Athenian concludes,

> As for an upbringing [*trophê*] that aims at money, or some sort of strength, or some other sort of wisdom without intelligence and justice, the argument proclaims it to be vulgar, illiberal, and wholly unworthy to be called education. But let's not get into a dispute with each other over the name. Let's simply hold fast to the argument now being agreed to by us, the argument that states: "Those who are correctly educated [*orthôs pepaideumenoi*] usually become good [*agathoi*], and nowhere should education be dishonored, as it is first among the noblest things for the best men. If it ever goes astray, and if it is possible to set it right, everyone ought always to do so as much as he can, throughout the whole of life." (*Laws*, 644a–b)

By this reasoning, *The Education of Cyrus* may be said to create a romantic vision of *paideia* that is finally contradicted by actual experience, because it was an education prematurely conceived, one focused on the creation of political power by one individual before the true nature and purpose of such an education had been adequately examined. Such is the Athenian's general consideration of the question, well before he turns to the specific example of Cyrus and his successors.

Cyrus and his education are then taken up in Book 3, in the course of a discussion of the comparative virtues of the Athenian and Persian systems of government. Each nation best exemplifies, respectively, democracy and its antithesis, monarchy. The best kind of government is one that weaves together elements from both (693d–e). The good empire that Cyrus created enjoyed something like this mixture, yet it was destroyed under Cambyses his son and then almost restored by his grandson Darius. The Athenian offers to figure out how this happened by divination (manteia) (694c). The offer of a "divination" by the Athenian is a significant move, because by prophesizing (the denominative verb from mantis, "prophet," is manteuomai), he is not explaining what happened by an account from history, but by the art of prophecy which links him with the oldest tradition in Greece of wisdom and wisdom literature, beginning with the portrait of the mantis Calchas in the Iliad. It is an art that will enjoy an important place within the city which The Laws aims to found. Diviners of laws will there have the same status as the nomophylakes or guardians of the laws in the city to come (828a–b, 871d).[15]

But the mantis the Athenian describes is not merely a neutral intermediary revealing truths by divine inspiration. He could be like Calchas, whom Agamemnon calls a mantis kakôn, a prophet of evils, full of guile and trickery. For this reason the diviners of the city founded by The Laws will occupy a clearly defined place in the function of their office. The divination of the Athenian is in pointed contrast to the ennoia or reflection of the author of the Cyropaedia. Reflections or inner thoughts are the product of personal experience recollected and reexamined. Xenophon's reflections at the opening of the Cyropaedia were cast in general terms, as we observed, but at the same time these were general views that had clear resonance in actual political experience. While the source of the prologue's wisdom was history and reflection about the lessons it seemed to teach, the source of the Athenian's wisdom is fundamentally different. It is a revelation or a prophecy, not, he avers, anything to be represented as known fact.

Of course this is disingenuous, and the conclusion of the conversation about Cyrus and the Persians proves it. The Athenian is claiming less for himself than he could if he cared to.

> Clinias: These things are said to have happened, and it is likely that they happened more or less this way. (695c)

The Athenian "divines" that what he says was true, but his interlocutor Clinias concludes that it is *said* to have happened (*legetai*), and that it is *likely* that it happened (*eoiken . . . gegonênai*). This is the same realm of probability of knowledge about the past that Cyrus recommends his sons study, if they cannot learn from the example of Cyrus himself:

> then learn from the things that happened in the past; for these things are the best kind of instruction (*tôn progegenêmenôn manthanete; hautê gar aristê didaskalia*). (8.7.24)

What the Athenian says can be confirmed the same way Cyrus's teachings are confirmed. But the things that have happened, "history" in a general sense rather than in the original Herodotean meaning of "inquiries," are also the source of everything that will contradict the example set by Cyrus. Things that happen in history after Cyrus's death are what mark the limits of Xenophon's fiction.

4

For all but the final scene of the *Cyropaedia*, Cyrus is without children, and the education of his sons is perforce nothing the *Cyropaedia* could describe. But as Xenophon says in the last chapter, it was the rivalry between Cambyses his elder son and the younger Tanaoxares that caused the breakup of the empire Cyrus created (8.8.2). He passed over the education of Cyrus's sons, as he passed over most of Cyrus's life, because the romance he had conceived did not require such completeness. One writer's economy of design thereby becomes in another's view an oversight to be corrected. Xenophon had given Plato all the opening he needed. While Cyrus himself was a disciplined person, the Athenian says, he failed to give his own sons the same education he enjoyed. He neglected them because he probably "spent his whole life, from youth onwards [ek neou], preoccupied with military matters, and turned his children over to the women to be brought up" (694d). The result was that they were reared as if already blessed by fortune (eudaimones), in what the Athenian terms a gynuikeia trophê, a "feminine upbringing." They lacked nothing from the moment they were born, were opposed by no one about anything, and praised by everyone for whatever they did or said (694d–e). While Xenophon's Cyrus lacks none of these good things, much of his education depended on his success in resisting such temptations. The children of the Persian royal family led the bios kakos or evil life children of exceptionally rich and tyrannical men often lead (696a). They were nurtured by the very things The Education of Cyrus shows us Cyrus avoided.

Cyrus's alleged neglect of the education of his own sons thus undercuts a central metaphor of the Cyropaedia, which is that of the "father" (patêr) to the army and all the nations he governs. Cyrus appears to the Athenian to have achieved this status of father to nations by denying his own children what he readily offered everyone else. Nor is that all. The concept of oikonomia, in both its strict and its more expansive, Xenophontic sense, also comes under attack. As the father failed, so fails his household management: not the economy of his empire, but the economy of the household that was the model for the larger oikos of his empire. Cyrus clearly knew nothing about how his own house should be run.[16]

With the patêr and oikonomia of Xenophon's imperial fiction under this kind of review, it is not surprising that the paradigm of the shepherd of men (poimên) does not escape the Athenian's notice. Recall the prologue of the *Cyropae-dia* and its droll analogy between the arts of governing men and the arts of animal husbandry: as Xenophon moves back and forth, from successful herdsmen, shepherds, and cowherds and their obedient "subjects," to the less successful rulers of human beings, there is created the impression that the arts of an ideal ruler like Cyrus might be viewed as, in a sense, a variety of human husbandry; a ruler's subjects can be treated with the same detachment with which a herdsman and shepherd treat the flocks in their charge. The force of this analogy in the prologue extends forward to Cyrus's later conduct with his subjects; compare his detachment about such troublesome people as the sophist of Armenia, Panthea, or Cyaxares. Now that metaphor of the shepherd of the people, and its literal counterpart, the actual shepherd who tends flocks of sheep, are both subjected to this "divination" by Plato's deconstructionist Athenian:

> Their father, meanwhile, kept acquiring flocks and herds, including many droves of men along with many other animals, on their behalf; but he didn't know that they to whom he was going to give all this were not being educated in their father's art, which was Persian [*tên patrôian ou paideuomenous technên, ousan Persikên*], for the Persians are shepherds [*poimenes*] because of the rough country from which they originate. This art is a tough one, sufficient to make men very strong herdsmen, capable of living outdoors, able to keep watch without sleep, and ready to serve as soldiers whenever they have to. He failed to see that women and eunuchs had given his sons an education which had been corrupted by the so-called happiness of the Medes, and the sons turned out as one would expect, after having been brought up without any restraint. (694e–695b)

The Athenian flattens out the *Cyropaedia*'s analogy linking shepherds and rulers together, as well as the implied lesson that one learn to cultivate the same attitude towards one's subjects that a shepherd has towards his flock.[17] He puts Cyrus into the business of indiscriminately acquiring flocks and herds of animals and droves of men together (*poimnia, probata; agelai andrôn).* Sheer acquisition is the theme; there is nothing here about an epistemology of rule. Compared to the arts which Cyrus learned, education is here conceived in a much simpler way. The Persian art the Athenian speaks of is concerned with making men strong herdsmen who can be tough soldiers when they have to be. This was Cyrus's inheritance from his father, but he fails to teach even this much to his own children. The regression to the softness of the Medes *(malakia)* is precisely the same charge Xenophon levels against the Persians at 8.8.15.

Plato's version of Persian royal history is not at variance with Herodotus' account of the same persons and events, but the source of most of his "divination" about Cyrus and his successors is, evidently, the *Cyropaedia* itself. What the Athenian says is almost entirely a negative revision of Xenophon's positive project. Even so, he does not refrain from observing that those who do not remember the past are condemned to repeat it. Cambyses' son Darius fared much better, says the Athenian, because he was not the son of a king and was not brought up in this kind of luxurious education (695c). He was as good a ruler as his father was bad, and he reestablished the empire that Cambyses had done so much to undo. But then Darius made the same mistake as his grandfather had; he allowed his son Xerxes to have a royal and luxurious education, with the same enervating results.

> "O Darius," it is perhaps very just to say, "you have failed to learn from the vice [*kakon*, "evil"] of Cyrus and have brought up Xerxes in the same habits as Cyrus did Cambyses!" Since he was an offspring of the same sorts of education [*tôn autôn paideiôn genomenos ekgonos*], he wound up suffering just about the same things as Cambyses. (695d)

The whole import of Cyrus's education in *The Education of Cyrus* is that one learn from his positive example. If Cyrus's sons could not learn from him, he says, then they should learn from the example of those who have lived before him, the *progegenêmenoi* mentioned at 8.7.24. This principle of following a good example is inculcated in us from the prologue to the end of Cyrus's life. It is one widely shared in much of Greek literature, beginning in Homer and continuing through Plutarch to the lives of Christian saints. One problem about following it is the value of the life to be imitated; the quality of one's paradigms can vary a good deal. Another is that this principle is often hard to observe, even when there is a worthy model. And this is the *coup de grâce* of the Athenian's divinations about Cyrus and Persia. The whole notion of learning from unexamined examples is called into question. It is a very typical move for Plato to make. There is not only nothing to be learned from Cyrus and his education; there is not even anything instructive about the fate of his successors in the art of ruling an empire. From the perspective of the *Laws*, the disillusionment of the final chapter of the *Cyropaedia* can come as no surprise. With a faulty conception of such basic things as education, household management, and the role of the father, none of which Xenophon examined the way the Athenian has examined them, what else could you expect?

5

Plato's criticism of Xenophon could be directed against any kind of fiction, whether novel, poem, or romance. Particularly vulnerable would be that point where the original vision of the author falters or transforms itself into something contrary to what he began with, as here. Yet this deconstruction of the *Cyropaedia*, while devastating in its completeness, has had little impact on Xenophon's later readers. The nature of political experience may account for this. Moments in which the laws of the world can be created the way *The Laws* prescribe are rare; its world is as remote and unreal in its own way as is the world of Cyrus and his education. It is far more typical that princes of a future empire, authors as they are of their own kinds of fiction, take the *nomoi* or customs and laws of the world as they find them and transform them in their imaginations. This invention is

what links the kingdom of a poet's fancy with a prince's
actual realm.

Beyond later rulers' inclination to ignore inconvenient
or impractical analyses of the way to gain power, there re-
mains the question of this closure as a literary phenome-
non. Xenophon's discovery of the limits of fiction proved
powerfully prophetic of things to come. Consider Cer-
vantes' adroit solution to the problem of ending the first
part of *Don Quixote* (Chapter 52), where the story of "the
rest of Don Quixote's life" gets to be told only by a chance
discovery worthy of Apuleius or Plato himself. An aged doc-
tor is found with a lead box containing parchments of Cas-
tilian verses written in Gothic script. From these Cervantes
says he was able to transcribe various tantalizing epitaphs,
sonnets, and wills about the knight errant, Sancho Panza,
and Dulcinea.

> These were such verses as could be deciphered. The rest, as
> the characters were worm-eaten, were entrusted to a uni-
> versity scholar to guess out their meaning. We are in-
> formed that he has done so, at the cost of many nights of
> study and much labour, and that he intends to publish
> them, which gives us hope of a third expedition of Don
> Quixote.

Spenser's open-ended ending of *The Faerie Queene* comes
even closer to the experience of the author whom he
claimed as his model. Like the *Cyropaedia, The Faerie
Queene* changes course toward the end, becoming some-
thing other than what it first promised to be. Unlike Xeno-
phon, and much more like Cervantes, Spenser is able to
dramatize this shift in his poetry and give it voice. To begin
with he may have had in mind Xenophon's Cyrus for his
allegorical figure of Arthur, but his imitation of Xenophon
may have made him a truer follower of the *Cyropaedia* than
he expected to be. *The Faerie Queene* is incomplete, judged
at least by the description of the project Spenser gives in his
Letter of 23 January 1589 to Sir Walter Raleigh. It was to be
a long epic poem in twelve books corresponding to "the
twelve private morall vertues, as Aristotle hath devised."

And the power that rules over this later change and incompleteness is Mutabilitie, a goddess who can put even Jove himself in his place.

> To whom, thus Mutability: "The things
> Which we see not how they are moved and swayd,
> Ye may attribute to your selves as Kings,
> And say they by your secret powre are made:
> But what we see not, who shall us perswade?
> But were they so, as ye them faine to be,
> Moved by your might, and ordred by your ayde;
> Yet what if I can prove, that even yee
> Your selves are likewise changed, and subiect unto me?"
>   (Mutabilitie, 7.49)

Spenser's conclusion to the poem consists of two stanzas reflecting on Mutabilitie's speech and her powers. The power of mutability is a familiar theme in English Renaissance poetry and thought.[18] What I should like to stress here is simply the resonance this famous closure has with the problematic ending of The Education of Cyrus.

The final stanzas of The Faerie Queene comprehend our entire experience in reading the Cyropaedia: that ennoia or opening reflection that began the work (1.1), the speech of Cambyses about the all-seeing and all-powerful gods who may or may not take notice of human affairs (1.6), the final speech of Cyrus on the disposition of his soul and his empire (8.7), and the disillusionment of the last chapter, where everything Cyrus created seems to have come to naught (8.8).

> When I bethinke me on that speech whyleare [earlier],
> Of Mutability, and well it way [consider]:
> Me seemes, that though she all unworthy were
> Of the Heav'ns Rule; yet very sooth to say,
> In all things else she beares the greatest sway.
> Which makes me loath this state of life so tickle
>   [uncertain],
> And love of things so vaine to cast away;
> Whose flowring pride, so fading and so fickle,
> Short Time shall soon cut down with his consuming sickle.

Then gin I thinke on that which Nature sayd,
   Of that same time when no more Change shall be,
   But stedfast rest of all things firmely stayd
   Upon the pillours of Eternity,
   That is contrayr to Mutabilitie:
For, all that moveth, doth in Change delight:
   But thence-forth all shall rest eternally
   With Him that is the God of Sabbaoth hight:
O that great Sabbaoth God, graunt me that Sabaoths sight.
                                    The VIII. Canto, unperfite.

Mutabilitie imposes her own limits on a writer, no matter what the original project.[19] To put it in terms of the twentieth century rather than of Spenser, Xenophon's imperial fiction turned into Lukács's novel of disillusionment.

> Nature is alive inside man but, when it is lived as culture,
> it reduces man to the lowest, most mindless, most idea-
> forsaken conventionality. This is why the mood of the epi-
> logue to *War and Peace*, with its nursery atmosphere
> where all passion has been spent and all seeking ended, is
> more profoundly disconsolate than the endings of the most
> problematic novels of disillusionment. Nothing is left of
> what was there before; as the sand of the desert covers pyr-
> amids, so every spiritual thing has been swamped, annihi-
> lated, by animal nature.[20]

The final chapter of *The Education of Cyrus* is disappointing in one way; in another these second thoughts are a useful comment on the relationship between fiction and poetry and the world of the poets and writers who create them. This relationship is fundamentally different from the contract that is established between fictional realism and the reader of the realistic novel—a perspective alien to the kind of fiction Xenophon sought to create.[21]

6

Like Cyrus's achievements, Xenophon's text is therefore itself an artistic creation subject to revision, change and decline; it returns to history to confront the frustrations experience imposes on persons and institutions in actual history.[22] As we have seen, when Xenophon begins his prologue with a cyclical view of Greek political institutions, it is a matter of indifference which government men choose. They can undo any of them willingly. His essential point is the innate disposition of men to resist those who attempt to rule over them.[23] Now the grand vision and the transcendent theme of the art of *to archein anthrôpôn* have collapsed into particularity once again. This is the most basic response to the fictions of poetry and romance. The very pressures from the world that drew Xenophon toward writing fiction in the end impinge on the perfected world that he creates through Cyrus. The death of Cyrus the character brings about not only the end of the *Cyropaedia*, but a dissolution of the romantic world he created. The gap between the perfections of Cyrus and the imperfections of present-day Persia is so great the fantasy cannot continue.[24] The result is discordant; compared to Spenser, Cervantes, and Tolstoy, it is certainly not so beautifully done, or so artistic.

But Xenophon is not their kind of artist, nor is he a poet who can resist an ontologically privileged reality and counterpose his own supreme fiction.[25] For him, the problems the *Cyropaedia* addresses are inescapably privileged by reality. Therein he discovers another kind of irony. Just as he records how Cyrus, Agesilaus, Epaminondas, and even he himself embarked on one project in life and ended up in ways none of them could foresee, so now he discovers that even the writing of fiction can be as much subject to revision as any other kind of text.

The difficulty for Xenophon was that although he had invented the imperial fiction of the *Cyropaedia*, he was himself far from being a romantic. Inescapable proof of the wisdom of his revisionist thoughts about what he had created lay no more than a generation away, in the career of Cyrus's first imitator, Alexander. With Xenophon an important inspiration, he made an empire by imposing a romantic fiction on the world about him; in life and even more in death he was the inspiration for romance. Yet his empire also failed to survive his passing. You might say that Alexander the Great followed the *Cyropaedia* to the letter, its final chapter as well as its prologue. The same career can be observed in later artists and princes who were inspired by the example of Cyrus. As they turned to the creation of their own fictional worlds, they also discovered similar ironies about themselves and their creations. I do not think Xenophon would have found these later developments in literature and politics at all surprising.

All at once, not five yards off in the fog, there was the President's Ford with big Gus Gennerich, the President's bodyguard, asleep against the wheel. And there beside the car was the President. He was sitting on the trunk of a tree, his legs folded out in front of him, his hands over his face. And suddenly, before they could move, the hands came down and there were his eyes looking straight into their eyes just a few steps off and not seeing them at all, the way a man's face will look out at you not seeing you from a flash in the movies; there was a kind of drawn grimace over his mouth and over his forehead like a man trying to see something in his mind and suffering. And then all at once they could see his eyes focusing and it was like a shutter clicking down on a camera the way the smile came back over the look in his eyes and he called out: "Hello there, Billy. Picking flowers?" They turned and got out of there. They could hear his big laugh back of them in the spruce.

"Franklin Roosevelt," *Fortune*, December 1933

NOTES

NOTE: To key this book to translations currently available in English, I have used versions from the Loeb Classical Library, especially Walter Miller's of 1914. His is the most recent English translation of the *Cyropaedia*. There and elsewhere revisions were sometimes necessary to bring out a particular point in the original. Rex Warner's *Anabasis* and *Hellenica* (under the titles *The Persian Expedition* and *A History of My Times*), in the Penguin edition, offer a livelier source for quotations from those texts, as do Carnes Lord's version of the *Oeconomicus* in Leo Strauss's *Xenophon's Socratic Discourse* and Thomas Pangle's translation of Plato's *Laws* (both cited in the Bibliography). I am grateful to Bryan Reardon for advance copy of his translation of Chariton, soon to appear in his edition of all the Greek novels in translation for the University of California Press.

PREFACE

1. Hägg (1983), 108–24; Forcione (1972), 13–63; idem (1985), 45; Perry, 169–74. Cf. Heiserman, 11–29 for a discussion of Apollonius of Rhodes as a precursor of romance (without reference to Rohde, 11–178). For a recent study of the *Odyssey* that argues for its backward glances to the *Iliad* rather than its anticipation of romance or *Bildungsroman*, see Pucci, 13–30.

2. Mallowan, 404 and 412; cf. Olmstead (1948), 34–58, and the proclamation of 538 reported in the Hebrew of Ezra 1.3–5: "In the first year of King Cyrus, the king issued this decree concerning the house of God in Jerusalem: Let the house be rebuilt as a place

244 NOTES

where sacrifices are offered and fire-offerings brought. Its height shall be sixty cubits and its breadth sixty cubits, with three courses of massive stones and one course of timber, the cost to be defrayed from the royal treasury. Also the gold and silver vessels of the house of God, which Nebuchadnezzar took out of the temple in Jerusalem and brought to Babylon, shall be restored; they shall all be taken back to the temple in Jerusalem, and restored each to its place in the house of God." What the Jews regarded as the fulfillment of God's prophecy (Jeremiah 25.11–14) was for Cyrus an act of political expediency. This calculated show of tolerance is characteristic of the fictive empire that Cyrus creates in the *Cyropaedia*.

3. A "novella" with many interruptions (4.6.11–7.3.16.); cf. Trenkner, 26 and Perry, 357, note 14.

4. Mansfield (1985), xxi. See also Pocock (1975), 156–182; cf. idem (1981), 61.

5. It is not my aim to reposition the *Cyropaedia* in a revised canon by an appeal to first principles, but I must acknowledge that I have learned much from this approach. Strauss (1948), 5 was the first scholar to raise the issue of what has lately been termed the canonicity of Xenophon: "The neglect of the *Hiero* (as well as the *Education of Cyrus*) is no doubt partly due to the fashionable underestimation and even contempt of Xenophon's intellectual powers. Until the end of the eighteenth century, he was generally considered a wise man and a classic in the precise sense. In the nineteenth and twentieth centuries, he is compared as a philosopher to Plato, and found wanting; he is compared as a historian to Thucydides, and found wanting. One need not, as well one might, take issue with the views of philosophy and of history which are presupposed in the comparison. One merely has to raise the question whether Xenophon wanted to be understood primarily as a philosopher or as a historian." An important departure from this once prevailing norm is Higgins (cf. Higgins, xiii); for recent contributions to the larger theoretical issue, see Fiedler, 145–245; Eagleton (1983), 194–217 and 229–331; Renza, 19–20; and esp. James Cox, 129: "Teachers, students, and critics of literature have more and more retreated from the world of fact, leaving it to the historian or political scientist. If there is too much fact or idea in a piece of writing, it is under threat of abandonment. Look at how Ruskin, Mill, Carlyle, and Newman have faded from the field of undergraduate and graduate Carlyle, and Newman have faded from the field of undergraduate and graduate study. The novel has all

but routed the essay from the period course." What he says has its obvious analogue in American classicists' conception of literature. Xenophon is not regarded as a literary author in the same sense that Plato, Herodotus or Thucydides all are.

6. Possibly because few read Xenophon now, the earlier readership of the *Cyropaedia* is a familiar theme to the specialist; cf. Bizos, lii–liv; Anderson (1974), 1–8; Lesky, 8–9 and 695 ("Die Wirkung der *Kyrupädie* is grösser gewesen als ihr literarischer Wert"). The theoretical uses of reception are another matter; see Holub, 53–106 and Jauss, 3–45; for critiques of reception theory, and its limitations, Wellek (1973), and de Man, xv–xxv.

7. The best critic of reception theory is Stückrath; see esp. 116–27.

8. Cf. Jauss, 92–94; Bakhtin (1981), 39; Jameson, 148–52; McKeon, 151–52.

9. Bakhtin (1981), 28–31; cf. Lukács (1983), 70–93; Eagleton (1976), 27–28; Brownlee and Brownlee, 1–21; McKeon, 273ff.

10. Cf. Cohen, 266; Todorov (1976), 163; Jauss, 192; McKeon, 23–64; and esp. Jameson, 135–36: "Genres are essentially contracts between a writer and his reader."

11. This is the import of Chapter 2; in effect the prologue (1.1) creates the poetics of the *Cyropaedia*, instructing us at every turn how to begin to read it.

12. As I shall argue, this is not the same as reconstructing the biography of Xenophon from his works; for that approach, see Delebecque (1957), passim, and esp. 6–22; cf. also Anderson (1974). For criticisms of it, see Higgins, esp. xii–xiii; Hans R. Breitenbach, 1571–1578; Bizos, xlvi–lii.

13. Chapter 10, "Revision."

14. See Momigliano (1971), 55–56; Hägg (1983), 113, and idem (1987), 193; Bakhtin (1981), 28–29; Perry, 167; Hans R. Breitenbach, 1707–1708. This very multiplicity of generic terminology argues for the need to avoid the comical–tragical, pastoral–historical snare inherent in normative conceptions of genre.

15. Barthes (1976). Although Barthes' Gallic hedonism disturbs the Puritans among us—as well as their Marxist cousins (cf. Eagleton [1983], 83)—his is a sensibility about literature Cicero would have recognized; Cicero's pleasure in this particular text is well documented in Münscher, 74–75.

16. Recent exemplary studies of this kind are Winkler (1985) and Goldberg (1981).

CHAPTER ONE

1. Sterne, 366–369 and 642 (note to 366).
2. Hume, 332.
3. Gibbon, chapter 24, note 119.
4. Gibbon (1814), 122–148; cf. also note 49.
5. Gibbon (1814), 126; cf. Shackleton.
6. Plutarch, *Moralia*, 189d. The best discussion of the historical context of the *Cyropaedia* is Murray, 1–37. Xenophon addressed the *Cyropaedia* to whoever could use it; later treatises on kingship were addressed to specific rulers beginning with Philip II of Macedon. Their number increased rapidly after the accession of his son Alexander.
7. Patricia Cox, 3–44 and 146; Graham Anderson, 227–240; Hunger, 157–165, esp. 162.
8. On the *Institutio Cyri* of Poggio Bracciolini (1447), see Gallet-Guerne, 57–84. It is a graceful, Ciceronian version that recasts Xenophon's eight books into six. Poggio's enemy Filelfo attacked him for his liberties, and published a literal but pedestrian version in 1464.
9. Herodotus, 3.80–88, esp. 3.80.3; cf. Hadot.
10. Morrow (1962), 44–59; cf. Edelstein, esp. 39–56.
11. Lichtheim, 58–82, 134–192.
12. See Levy (1967) and Dankoff.
13. Hirsch, 85–91; cf. Christensen, 122–135, Momigliano (1975), 123–150 and idem (1977), 25–36.
14. The preface and dedication to Henry VIII of Elyot's *The Boke Named the Governour* (1531) echoes the opening reflection of the *Cyropaedia* (*ennoia poth hêmin egeneto*, "the thought once occurred to us"): "I late consideringe (moste excellente prince and myne onely redoughted soveraigne lorde) my dutie that I owe to my naturall countray with my faythe also of alliegeaunce and othe, more over thaccoampt that I have to rendre that one little talent delivered to me to employ (as I suppose) to the increase of vertue, I am (as god judge me) violently stered to devulgate or sette forthe some part of my studie, trustynge thereby tacquite me of my dueties to go, your hyghnesse, and this my country."
15. Cf. Strauss (1958), 83. In his translation Mansfield (1985) cites Xenophon or Cyrus in XIV(60), VI(22–23, 24), XIV(60), XVI(64), XXVI(102); but note the way that Machiavelli's discussion in XIX(71–82) on avoiding the contempt and hatred of one's subjects captures the essence of *Cyropaedia* 5.1 and following, without mention of either Cyrus or Xenophon by name.

16. Dhuoda, 33–37.

17. It plays no role in even so standard a work as Marrou; for its importance in the history of Greek education, see Jaeger, 162–171.

18. For the first translation of the *Cyropaedia* in the English Renaissance, see the preface to Barker.

19. Cicero, *Epistulae ad Quintum Fratrem*, 1.1.23. A similar but less influential opinion is in Dionysius of Halicarnassus' *Letter to Pompey* (4).

20. Various inspirations for this letter have been discerned; see Shackleton Bailey, 147–148.

21. It was Cicero's handbook when his own term came to serve in this office: "You little know what a commander-in-chief [*imperator*] you have to deal with. The *Cyropaedia* which I have well thumbed in the reading of it, I have exemplified in its entirety during my command here" (*Epistulae ad Familiares*, 9.2.5.1). Elsewhere he wonders whether the work he so admired was really fit for his own times (*Brutus*, 112); yet Julius Caesar read it (Suetonius, *Caesar*, 87).

22. Suetonius, *Augustus*, 94. Cf. Yavetz, esp. 26: "I suspect that Augustus would have gloated over the frustration of twentieth-century scholars, still at pains to understand his enigmatic personality, as finding him 'puzzling, elusive, baffling, and inscrutable'—like the Sphinx engraved upon his signet ring."

23. For a well documented list of parallels between Arrian's account of Alexander and Xenophon's portrait of Cyrus, see Stark, 203–210. She draws a distinction between common traits in Alexander and Cyrus that could be ascribed to good generalship at any age, and others that suggest a more direct connection between Alexander and the Cyrus of the *Cyropaedia*. Parallels between Books 7–8 of Xenophon and Alexander's career after his defeat of Darius also reflect Arrian's intense devotion to his literary model Xenophon; cf. Stadter, 60–88.

24. Gallet–Guerne, 98–102.

25. Bingham, 87: "Peter Young recorded that, 'Lisant en Xenophon . . . Que Gadate avoit este chastre [castrated] pour ce que la concubine du Roy l'avoit regarde de bon oeil, le Roy [James] dit que la femme devoit plustos estre chastree.' The remark is redolent of the attitude"; cf. McIlwain.

26. Frame, 883, s.v. "Xenophon."

27. Sidney, 102–158, esp. 99.

28. Hägg (1983), 192–213.

29. For a recent discussion, cf. Lewalski.

30. Tasso, 59 (a view inspired by Aristotle; cf. *Poetics* 51a 36–52a 16).

31. Figgis, 137–47.

32. Williams, 220–221; cf. Barker.

33. Matthiessen, 169–227.

34. Held, 281–287.

35. Held, 287 and fig. 54; cf. Summerson, 16–18.

36. Cf. Orgel, 77: "The danger of political myths lies in their tendency to exclude realities: the mirror of the king's mind allows him to know only himself."

37. See Reardon (1971), 323–324 and note 32; Julian's dismissed romances masquerading as history (literally, "under the form of history," *en historias eidei*; Letter 89 [Bidez], 301b).

38. Graham Anderson, 227–236.

39. Cf. Reardon (1971), 353, and Stadter, 27–28, 37, and 54.

40. *Bibliothèque* (December 1775), 5ff.

41. For the artistic tradition of the figures in Apuleius' story, see Schlam; for a critique of its allegedly folkloric origins, Fehling; and for a reading of the tale as it functions in its original context in the novel, Tatum (1979), 47–68.

42. Wieland, 6–88.

43. Cf. Graham Anderson, 259–277.

44. See Graham Anderson, 283–287, and cf. Bowie (1974), Bowersock, 1–16, and Kennedy, 556–565.

45. Plato, *Symposium*, 180c–185c, cf. Dover, ii.C.5 and Martha Nussbaum, 188. As she observes, this and other conventions may reflect the norms of ancient Greek society, rather than actual facts (468, note 45).

46. "The wounds, my boy, are such as swordsmen make—for it accords with this style of fighting so to cut down the foe—some of his pure blood stains his armor, some the man himself, and some is sprinkled on the crest which rises hyacinthine red from the golden helmet and sheds splendor on the gold itself" (*Word Pictures*, 2.9, 354K). Philostratus took the following description of Abradatas' armor before his death in *Cyropaedia* 6.4.2 and put it in a more pathetic context: "When he came to put on his linen corselet, such as they used in this country, Panthea brought him one of gold, also a helmet, armpieces, broad bracelets for his wrists—all of gold—and a purple tunic that hung down in folds to his feet, and a helmet-plume of hyacinth dye."

47. Scudéry (1664), 165–182. An engraving of Panthée as if from an ancient medallion is reproduced in Chapter 8.

48. McDougall, 75–132.

49. Showalter, 11–37.

50. *Le Grand Cyrus* has been mined as a sourcebook of seventeenth-century social history as it is filtered through the conversations of the *précieuses* and *précieux* of the Hôtel de Rambouillet; on the *déguisements* of *Le Grand Cyrus*, see Cousin, 1.334; Showalter, 124–191.

51. Boileau (1965) ridicules the *puerilité* and *grand excès* of *Le Grand Cyrus*: instead of a model of every kind of perfection in a prince, imitating the *roman* of Xenophon, Mlle de Scudéry had made up an Artamène sillier than all the Celadons and all the Sylvandres (typical characters of French pastoral romance). He worries about nothing else but his care for Mandane, knows how to do nothing but lament from morning to night, to moan and spin out professions of perfect love. Molière's *Les Précieuses ridicules* (1659) focuses on the household of a *bon bourgeois*, Gorgibus, whose niece and daughter are infected with the contagion. To both writers the style of the *précieuses* was as much an object of satire as their morals—indeed, because they were French, it was probably their bizarre style that critics found hardest to forgive. There is even a lexicon of this language; cf. the *léxique du vocabulaire précieux* in Cuenin, 177–193.

52. For the way(s) to read such a prologue, see Winkler, 180–203.

53. Dryden, 11: "*Cyrus* was written by a lady"; Pepys, 122 (12 May 1666).

54. Boileu, 30.

55. Lennox, book VI, chapter VII ("Containing an incident full as probable as any in Scudéry's romances"), 264–266. Fielding had used Cervantes in the same way to support his own project of writing fiction in the tradition of *Don Quixote*, rather than Richardson's *Pamela*.

56. Showalter, 129.

57. Parry, 188; cf. McDougall, 121–130.

58. There was a serious debate in the salon of the *précieuses* and *précieux* on the status of the male lover ("l'amant absent, l'amant non aimé, l'amant jaloux, et l'amant dont la maitresse est morte"). Mlle de Scudéry's version of the romance of Panthea and Abradatas (*Le Grand Cyrus*, v.1) inspired Dorothy Osborne to search for the perfect lover (McDougall, 111).

59. In later editions Ramsay attempted to revise his novel and answer the grave criticisms that had been leveled against it; cf. his

preface to the fourth edition in English (1730): "The most general
defect in the former editions is the inaction of Cyrus, who thro'
the whole course of his travels has too much of the indolent Phi-
losopher, and too little of the Hero, who was one day to be the
conqueror of Asia. The nature of this work not requiring the action
of an epic poem, this fault might have been excused; the Author
has nevertheless submitted to the judgment of the Public, and has
made Cyrus *act* in the several countries thro' which he passes, and
this without departing from the character of a young hero upon his
travels, or shocking the reader with tales and fictions that have no
foundation in antiquity. Besides this general defect there are others
peculiar to each book" (v, emphasis added).

60. *Bibliothèque* (December 1775), 63–82.
61. *Bibliothèque* (December 1775), 64.
62. *Bibliothèque*, 100.
63. *Bibliothèque*, 78.
64. Ashley, Preface; cf. Brett, 33–58.
65. Cf. 1.6.27–34 and *Prince* xviii ("In what Mode Faith Should
Be Kept by Princes").
66. Ashley, 33.
67. Grote, vol. 4, chapter 33; vol. 9, chapters 69–73.
68. Cf. Cawkwell, 47: "as far as Republican Rome was con-
cerned the popular book was not the *Anabasis*, but the *Education
of Cyrus*, to our taste surely one of the most tedious books to have
survived from the ancient world."
69. E.g., Verrall; for an account of the way school editions can
shape adult perceptions of familiar classics, see Johnson, 1–8.
70. Holden. Cf. Gleason, Preface: "After meeting in college en-
trance examinations passages taken from Xenophon's *Cyropaedia*,
pupils often ask, 'Why do we not read something from the *Cyro-
paedia*, as well as from the *Anabasis* and *Hellenica*?' " There is a
certain similarity between this rhetorical question and the fictive
world of *Tom Brown's School Days*; cf. Jenkyns, 213–16.

"Come, none of your irony, Brown," answers the master.
"I'm beginning to understand the game scientifically. What
a noble game it is, too."
"Isn't it? But it's more than a game. It's an institution,"
said Tom.
"Yes," said Arthur, "the birthright of British boys, old
and young, as habeas corpus and trial by jury are of British
men."

"The discipline and reliance on one another which it teaches is so valuable, I think," went on the master. "It ought to be such an unselfish game. It merges the individual in the eleven; he doesn't play that he may win, but that his side may."

"It's very true," said Tom, "and that's why football and cricket, now one comes to think of it, are so much better games than fives or hare-and-hounds, or any others where the object is to come in first or to win for oneself, and not that one's side may win."

71. For a list in English of major editions and commentaries, see pp. xv–xvi in vol. 1 of Miller's Loeb edition; more recently, *Xenophon, Cyropédie*, vol. 1, ed. Marcel Bizos, 54–60; and for the multiplicity of critical editions, a multiplicity not always appreciated by those who are not textual critics, see Hägg (1983), 228–234.

72. Marchant, v.

73. Bizos, *Cyropédie* 1 (Paris, 1971), lix and note 1.

74. E.g., 1.5.14. Marchant prints this sentence from Cyrus's first speech to his army in Book 1 (the reading of fifteenth-century manuscripts from Oxford and Erlangen): *alla mên kakeino oimai humâs tharrein* ("Moreover I think that this will encourage you"), then reports a consensus of other readings in his critical apparatus: *alla mên dia touto humâs ouch hêkista oimai tharrein* (a slight shift in the Greek, but much too slight to be worth registering in translation). Bizos, the Budé editor, reversed these readings, carefully noting the change in a (perforce) new critical apparatus. A comparison of the Loeb version with the Budé's French will show the practical results: "This, moreover, will, I think, strengthen your confidence: I have not neglected the gods as we embark upon this expedition"; "Je crois aussi que ce qui vous donne surtout confiance, c'est que je n'ai pas négligé les dieux avant de partir en campagne." It did not matter in the least that Marchant had predicted this would happen. "Quae vero huiusce editionis in apparatum criticum relegata sunt, saepe non minus videntur esse probabilia quam quae in textu leguntur: neque lege formulave ulla stabiliri potest utrum utri sit anteponendum" (ibid., v).

75. To confine the reference to the Roman world only, see Millar, 31–40 (on imperial journeys); 59–122 (on the entourage of an emperor); 133–158 (on an emperor's gifts and exactions); and esp. 203–272 (on the emperor at work: functions and their social setting).

76. Aron, xi.

77. Hans R. Breitenbach, 1707–1721 sorts out the relationship with ancient literary genres as lucidly as any scholar has: to a certain degree, it is a part of ancient *politeia* literature (1708).

78. Xenophon's popularity among the Romans (the practical man who was also a philosopher and historian) virtually assured that he would be a central figure in the Renaissance; cf. Münscher, 70–106.

79. Besides Orgel's seminal work, cf. Greenblatt, esp. his remarks on the power of a prince and the role of the knowing observer: "power, whose quintessential sign is the ability to impose one's fiction on the world; the more outrageous the fiction, the more impressive the manifestation of power" (13); "the initiated observer can always see beneath the surface and understand how appearances are manipulated by the cunning prince" (14).

80. There will be an instance of this in Chapter 10.

81. Forster, 43–47; 83–84.

82. Bowie (1985), 683; Reardon (1971), 309–403. The terms "novel" and "romance" are strictly a convention of English usage, of course; the first now denotes something true to life, the second, something not so true to life. As I observe in the Preface and Chapter 2, the key to reading Xenophon is not to be found in the precise use of either term; cf. Kern.

83. Hirsch, 67ff. offers a valuable corrective to the notion that the *Cyropaedia* is entirely Xenophon's fabrication. One need only add that novelists are as capable of using "sources" as historians; cf. McKeon's discussion of "stories of virtue" (McKeon, 212–270).

84. The shift from plural to singular becomes somewhat more significant in the so-called epilogue (8.8, discussed in Chapter 10).

85. The intertextuality of Herodotus and Xenophon is a major aspect of the *Cyropaedia*, and not only in Cyrus's meeting with Croesus in Book 7; we shall return to this point in Chapter 7.

86. Machiavelli defines, where Xenophon does not, the crucial role the reader plays in this kind of work: his book is easily capable of being misread, because it looks as if it treats the same theme so many other books have already discussed (*Prince*, xv).

CHAPTER TWO

1. The most influential ancient testimony has been Aulus Gellius, 14.3 (cf. Diogenes Laertius, 3.34 and Athenaeus, 11.112); cf. Hirsch, 97–100.

Notes

2. Delebecque (1957), 389; cf. *Oxford Classical Dictionary*, second edition (1970), 1142 ("a counterblast").

3. Murray, 17–29; cf. Dittmar, 68–76, 77–84; Hirsch, 170–172; Schwartz, 61–62; Hoïstad, 75; Momigliano (1971), 55.

4. E.g., *Republic*, 9.580 on monarchy as the best and tyranny the worst form of government; cf. Vatai, 99–129.

5. Guthrie, 323–354; cf. Thesleff, 79–84.

6. Cf. Murray, 29 and note 3; on other parallels, see Delebecque (1957), 388–389. Much more pointed is the Athenian's dismissal of Cyrus and his *paideia* in *Laws*, 694e–695b (discussed in detail in Chapter 10).

7. A chorus in Aeschylus celebrates this virtue of Cyrus in *Persians*, 768–772: "Cyrus the man blessed by a good destiny, by his rule he bestowed peace on all his friends" (*eudaimôn anêr, arxas ethêke pasin eirênên philois*), and subdued his enemies the Lydians and the Ionian Greeks.

8. *Republic*, 1.332a–b. The notion is also examined early in the *Meno* (71e).

9. Cyrus's cross-examination of the Armenians and his uncle Cyaxares are the subject of Chapters 5 and 6.

10. The prologue of the *Cyropaedia* confirms the synoptic approach of Xenophon's recent and not so recent readers (Delebecque, Higgins, Hirsch). If you reread the *Anabasis*, *Hellenica*, *Memorabilia*, and *Oeconomicus* from the perspective of the prologue, you will see that the opening of the *Cyropaedia* is as much an exasperated commentary on the activity of producing those texts, as on the themes of those texts.

11. A point best articulated by Higgins, 1–20.

12. For chronologies of Xenophon's career, see Delebecque (1957), 506–509; Hans R. Breitenbach 1569–1570; Bizos, xlii–xliv.

13. Holden, vol. 4, 196–197 (a list repeated often in later commentators on the point); cf. Hirsch, 72–76.

14. The noble but dead hero Abradatas is actually as much an incarnation of Cyrus the Younger as the present Cyrus is; the parallel between *Anabasis*, 1.8.26–28 and 7.1.29–32 will be discussed further in Chapter 8.

15. On the nature of the historian as narrator in Thucydides, see Connor (1984), 3–19.

16. For the *persona* of Caesar in the *Commentaries*, see von Albrecht, 80–89; for the representation of his *clementia*, cf. Treu.

17. "There was a certain Athenian in the army named Xenophon . . ." (*Anabasis*, 3.1.4); cf. earlier references to him, where he is treated as merely one other actor in the drama before and after

Cunaxa (1.8.15, 2.5.37, 2.5.41). While Xenophon is no one but Xenophon in the *Anabasis*, he says elsewhere that someone else was the author; see Hans R. Breitenbach, 1644–1649. Plutarch judged that the third-person narrative (in effect, never identifying the author Xenophon with Xenophon the character) made the *Anabasis* more believable (*Moralia*, 345e).

18. Arrian thought the opening effective enough to imitate in his own *Anabasis of Alexander*; after a brief prologue inviting his readers to make as many invidious comparisons as they please between Arrian and his predecessors, he launches *in medias res* with the death of Philip of Macedon and the accession of *Alexander* (1.1.1–5). In *How to Write History* (23), Lucian advises against elaborate prefaces, as well as long works without any preface at all, and criticizes those who think "Darius and Parysatis had two sons" is not a preface; it is a preface in its effect (*dunamei*).

19. G. B. Nussbaum, 96–146; cf. J. K. Anderson (1970), 67–83.

20. For an introductory survey of a confusing period of history, see Fine, 526–604.

21. Gomme, Andrewes and Dover, 437–444.

22. For the ending of Thucydides, see Connor (1984), 210–230.

23. Most of all Henry; cf. 49: "So far from finding any conceptual relation between the two works, however, we are at a loss to discover much evidence that Xenophon was acquainted with Thucydides' history or came under its influence in any respect."

24. Münscher, 93–95; cf. Baden.

25. In the *Cyropaedia* Xenophon reserves this special effect for comic and contemptible characters, a stylistic trait to be discussed in Chapters 7 (on Croesus) and 8 (on Araspas).

26. Cf. a similarly ambivalent victory over the Catilinarian conspirators in Sallust, *Catiline*, 61: friend and foe, victor and vanquished are mingled in similar confusion. The account of Sallust's reading of Xenophon in Münscher, 82–83 needs revision.

27. Cf. *all' egô ennoêsas pote* (*Constitution of the Lacedaemonians*, 1.1), *euthus epeidê anegerthê prôton men ennoia autôi empiptei* (*Anabasis*, 3.1.13), *ennoia poth' hêmin egeneto* (*Cyropaedia*, 1.1.1).

28. For the relationship between Isocrates and Xenophon, see Hirsch, 57–60; on the literary influence of Isocrates, cf. Momigliano (1971), 49–52.

29. Hirsch, 46–57.

30. Agesilaus is the third member of a trio of ideal leaders thought to inspire the literary *persona* of Cyrus; cf. Hirsch, 67–69 for other sources. We shall find that each member of this trio has

been improved upon or surpassed in some significant way; though reminiscent of others, Cyrus will amount to much more than the sum of Socrates, Cyrus the Younger, and Agesilaus.

31. E.g., 4.1.2–6, 7.5.72–86.
32. See Hirsch, 39–55.
33. On the title *apomnêmoneumata* ("things related / told from memory"), see Momigliano (1971), 52; *commentarii* is the correct Latin translation (cf. Aulus Gellius, 14.3: *libri quos dictorum et factorum Socratis commentarios composuit*).
34. See Higgins, 21–43; Erbse; Strauss (1972); Gigon, vol. 2, 191.
35. Such wonder or surprise (the verb *thaumazô* and related forms) is typical of the openings of Isocrates' treatises.
36. Momigliano (1971), 52–54; cf. Leo, 90–94; Dihle; cf. von Fritz, 326–332.
37. Bakhtin (1981), 130–146.
38. *Memorabilia*, 3.11; cf. Tatum (1983), 142–210.
39. Cf. Higgins, 154 and note 86: "the form of the *Memorabilia* becomes all the more appropriate, since it belonged, as a *logos Sokratikos*, to the realm of mimetic literature (cf. Aristotle, *Poetics*, 447b, 9–20) and so had as one object to speak and work upon the reader in just the same way as Socrates' discussions had worked upon his listeners and interlocutors."
40. A major point in Plato's version; see *Apology*, 28d–29b. As Leo Strauss notes (1970, 88–89), Socrates in Xenophon is a patriot and a just man in civil life, but not the warrior he claims to have been, according to Plato. Even in the Platonic passage in question, Socrates' point is not simply that he was a good soldier; the rhetorical effect of mentioning his military service serves to deepen the outrageous similarity implied between himself and the greatest of heroes, Achilles (28b–d: "like Achilles"), and bring out the ironic differences between them.
41. The technical treatises take pains to show the relevance of the practical arts to the political life of those who practice them; cf. *On Hunting* (*Cynegeticus*), 12.1, where practicing the art of the hunt leads straight into practicing the arts of *Aretê* (Virtue) (12.18–22), and *The Cavalry Commander* (*Hipparchichus*), where the training of horses and of the men who ride them are of equal concern; cf. J. K. Anderson (1961). For an explanation of the different spellings *paideia* and *paedia*, see Chapter 3, note 12.
42. Lukács (1983), 60–62, 71–73; Ortega y Gasset, 143–144; Bakhtin (1981), 45–49.
43. As Hoïstad notes, Xenophon's antidemocratic view of the

world sharpened the contrast hc was able to draw between his ideal ruler, and all the rest of the world composed merely of *archomenoi*, "ruled ones," in a general sense. To put it another way, the *Cyropaedia* instructs us, its readers, in the arts of a personal dictatorship. The rest of humanity—the background to Cyrus's achievements, as well as whatever action and plot the narrative possesses—is of no importance whatever. It is not the world that matters, but rather Cyrus, the shaper of that world. Hoïstad, 73–94, esp. 77–82.

44. Cf. McKeon, 238 for a similar process in the early English novelists.

45. Cf. Plato, *Republic*, 4.419aff.; Aristotle, *Politics*, 3.1.1274b, 4.1.1289a.

46. The basic strategy of the *Oeconomicus* is to fuse education for public and private arts together; thus the manager of a household and his wife have much to learn from the Persian King and Queen (4). Cf. the analysis of these reciprocal arts in Strauss (1970), esp. 166–177, on the education of the household officer (*episkopos*) in political arts, and 205–210, on the art of farming as a means of training the kingly man.

47. And then made figurative again by Cyrus at 8.2.14. Plato subjects all of this to a devastating deconstruction in the *Laws* (to be discussed in Chapter 10).

48. A similar exercise in intertextuality is offered us in the *Hiero*. It is remarkable for its exposition of what is to be gained from tyranny as a form of government, but the faults of tyranny can be discussed here only implicitly; reference to Xenophon's other works, especially the *Memorabilia* and *Oeconomicus*, is required. See Strauss (1948), 50–62.

CHAPTER THREE

1. Parker, 4–5; cf. Lukács (1983), 19–29; Eagleton (1976), 27–34. The last chapter of the *Cyropaedia* (8.8) reflects Xenophon's struggle with the consequences of creating a romance (to be treated in Chapter 10).

2. Cf. Hans R. Breitenbach, 1709–1721; Montgomery, 133–143; Hägg (1971), 291–305.

3. Hägg (1983), 5–80; Smith, 210–234; Kermode, 127–152.

4. For a recent discussion of the end of the *Odyssey*, see Wender.

5. The phrase *eti kai nun* ("even at present," "and still today") is a stylistic tic of the *Cyropaedia*; cf. Delebecque (1957), 395–396, and Hirsch, 69 and note 25 (92–93). Besides the intertextual relationships he creates with his own works (the presence of Socrates, Agesilaus, Cyrus the Younger and others in the *Cyropaedia*), this phrase is Xenophon's principal means of tying the remote, fictional world he is creating to present-day realities. The pervading theme that the Persians still do it (whatever "it" may be) made his fictions into something that shaped contemporary Persia.

6. For his *philanthropia* and the political uses of seeming to be good, see esp. 8.2 (discussed further in Chapter 9), and cf. Machiavelli, *Prince*, xvii ("Of Cruelty and Mercy, and Whether It Is Better to Be Loved Than Feared, or the Contrary").

7. The perfunctory nature of Cambyses' speech is even more apparent when one knows the genuine *paideia* about tyranny in the *Hiero*. Cf. Strauss (1948), 63–79; Andrewes; Fine, 100–125.

8. On the *mithra* cf. Hirsch, 120–122.

9. See Momigliano (1977), 25–35 ("Eastern Elements in Post–Exilic Jewish and Greek Historiography").

10. On the function of the *mithra*, Gershevitch, 26–44; for evidence of Cyrus's cultivation of Zoroastrianism, cf. Boyce, 50–53.

11. Gershevitch, 75.

12. The variation in spelling is due to convention: whereas *paideia* is a transliteration of the Greek, *paedia*, as in *Cyropaedia*, is the Latin spelling of the same word.

13. Herodotus, 3.91; cf. Pritchard, 315–316, and Hirsch,171–173.

14. Cf. 1.2.2 (*epaideuthê en tois Persôn nomois*). Any noble peer (*homotimos*) could be educated by these laws, and Cyrus is careful to praise them on more than one occasion (1.5.11, 8.7.9–10), but there was only one Cyrus. As we shall see, the *nomoi* of the Persians do surprisingly little to explain how he achieved what he did; cf. Higgins, 46. This aspect of the *Cyropaedia*'s design is also an object of Plato's critique (Chapter 10, below).

15. Cf. Aristotle, *Rhetoric*, 1354b, 18, 1414b, 19ff.

16. E.g., the elaborately staged debate at 7.5.4–8.1.8, where Cyrus and his lieutenants talk their way through the formulation of his postwar policies. It is not the case that he does not know what to do; he only wants his subjects to persuade him to do what he intends to do in any case.

17. Cf. his later meticulous preparations before battle with the Assyrians at 6.2.1–37 and 6.4.12–7.1.22.

18. Cf. 6.1.1 (*toiauta . . . dialegomenoi*).
19. On recapitulation (*anakephailaiôsis*) as a typical narrative technique of later Greek romances, see Hägg (1971), 327–332. The difference is that Xenophon recapitulates something we actually hear about for the first time.
20. Another stylistic tic, *hôsper eikos* ("as is fitting," "as one would expect"), is a favored marker; like *eti kai nun* (note 5, above) it underscores the plausibility of an event. Xenophon usually employs it at the end of a scene, or as a way of rounding off a sequence.
21. As discussed in Chapter 2. Both the *Cyropaedia* and the *Memorabilia* are theoretically capable of infinite expansion between their opening and closing passages, because the program of neither work commits Xenophon to a life story in the literal sense of biography.
22. Hans R. Breitenbach, 1707–1708.
23. Higgins, 55.
24. See Redfield, 60–67 (on "plot as knowledge"). As Avery has observed, Herodotus constructs his portrait of Cyrus by means of polarities of success and failure, so that the ultimately tragic outcome of Cyrus's career becomes an instructive response to his earlier successes (Avery, 546). Instead of following the Herodotean technique of happiness leading to unhappiness, Xenophon constructs a pattern whereby early success leads ultimately to still more success—for his readers (he hopes) as much as for Cyrus.
25. Bernadete, 213 and Immerwahr, 161–167.
26. Cf. Lang, 67: " 'look to the end' is as basic to Herodotean narrative style as it is to his historical interpretation."
27. E.g., 8.1.17, 8.1.39, 8.1.40, 8.2.14, 8.2.15, 8.3.1, 8.6.16; cf. the rhetorical questions of the *Agesilaus* (e.g., "And what of his strategy after he had received the army and had sailed out?") (19); cf. also 3.1, 4.15.17, 7.4, 7.7, 9.1, and esp. 11.1: "I want to go back and summarize his virtue again, so that my praise of it may be more easily remembered."
28. Cf. *Catiline*, 58.
29. Xenophon adapted this technique of naming and not naming his characters from Herodotus; cf. *Histories*, 1.51 (on a certain man at Delphi who falsified temple offerings, of whom Herodotus says that he knows his name, but will not mention it [*ouk epimnêsomai*], presumably because one who is wicked does not deserve the *kleos* [fame, enduring memory] which inclusion in the *Histories* will confer). The technique is one which later novelists

adapted to their own use, though not even the most devious improves on what Xenophon devises here. There will be further remarks in Chapter 8 on the naming of characters in the Panthea affair; cf. Hijmans.

30. Thereby he resembles the cruel Persian monarchs of Herodotus' *Histories*, Astyages and Cambyses (the name of both the grandfather and the son of Cyrus the Great); cf. Olmstead (1923), 81–98 and 645–655.

31. Frye (1957), 187.

32. The interweaving of such characters begins in Homer; e.g., the contrasting pairs of Paris and Helen and Hector and Andromache in *Iliad*, 6, and the even more elaborate counter-example of the House of Atreus, which runs in elaborate counterpoint to the House of Odysseus throughout the *Odyssey* (1.32–43, 3.253–336, 11.405–464, 24.191–202). For a later novelist's adaptation of this technique, see Tatum (1979), 69.

33. Cf. Frye (1957), 195: "The characterization of romance follows its general dialectic structure, which means that subtlety and complexity are not much favored. Characters tend to be either for or against the quest. If they assist it they are idealized as simply gallant or pure; if they obstruct it they are caricatured as simply villainous or cowardly. Hence every typical character in romance tends to have his moral opposite confronting him, like black and white pieces in a chess game."

CHAPTER FOUR

1. Cf. Rosenberg, 8–10 and 115–43 and also Greenblatt, 68 (for the distance between the public *persona* and the private self in a Renaissance self-fashioner like Sir Thomas More).

2. *Cyropaedia*, 1.2.3. The divisions are *paides* (boys) to the age of sixteen or seventeen, *ephêboi* (youths) to twenty-five, *teleioi andres* (mature men) to fifty, and *geraiteroi* (elders above the age of fifty).

3. Cf. Herter, esp. 149 (on the Astyanax scene, *Iliad*, 6.446–473): "Wir dürfen hier von der ersten Kinderszene der griechischen Dichtung sprechen, aber das Kind spielt nicht um seiner willen seine Rolle, sondern in höheren Interesse des Ganzen."

4. This ancient view contrasts sharply with later portraits of childhood, especially in the modern era; cf. Olney, esp. 118 on modern autobiography and its portrayal of the young: "There is no

evolutionary law operative in the development of personality; it is discontinuous in its myriad transformations, which are unpredictable, abrupt, irregular; and far from there being a single personality or character for each man, there are multiple characters and possibilities—which is the logic of depth psychology and schizophrenia as well as the logic of multiple literary personae. Autobiographers who adhered, at least implicitly, to the old psychology, Franklin and Thoreau—wrote about a personality that was defined, completed, and comprehended before the writing began." As Momigliano observes, the situation in antiquity was fundamentally different from the modern view Olney has defined: "Autobiography is now the most subjective kind of self–expression. We expect confessions, rather than factual autobiographies, whereas we expect factual information rather than subjective effusions in biography. The most elementary facts about ancient biographical and autobiographical writing are a warning that this may not have been so in Greece and Rome. There was a close relation, if nothing more, between *bios* and *encomium*. On the other hand autobiographical commentaries were often written for the direct purpose of being used as raw materials by historians. Whereas biographers were free to be encomiastic, autobiographers seem to have been bound to be factual—at least in certain cases" (Momigliano, 1971, 15).

    5. Cyrus's table-talk is part of a long tradition in the art of manipulation through seemingly innocent conversations in a relaxed setting. The power of rulers, even at their ease, is never far from anyone's mind, no matter what they may profess; cf. Greenblatt, 53–73. In later symposium scenes of the *Cyropaedia* (2.1 and 8.4.1–27), Cyrus mixes seriousness and laughter (*spoudaia* and *geloia*) to encourage his men to the good, and as a means of settling serious business in a relaxed way. A sure sign that he has little of his ego invested in these exercises is that his lieutenants do not hesitate to tell him to his face that his is a frigid kind of wit (*psychros* 8.4.23).

    6. Cf. Tompkins, esp. 226 and note 67.

    7. Hoïstad, 83.

    8. Plutarch, *Alexander* 1.2–3 (on the *sêmeia tês psychês* or distinctive signs of a person's soul); cf. also Polybius, 10.24.

    9. The Persian Cyrus may have been like this, but Xenophon's character is also a beneficiary of the sophists' controversy over *nomos* and *physis* (the arbitrariness of conventional restraints on human nature and conduct; cf. Guthrie, 55–133), and cf. also Herod-

otus' famous comment on the relativity of cultural values (3.38), as well as his account of Egyptian customs (2.35–36).

10. Cf. Aristotle, *Rhetoric*, 2.12.16: the young are witty and fond of laughter, because wit is an educated or cultivated insolence (*pepaideumenê hybris*).

11. Plato's *Lysis* is a brilliant portrayal of adolescent psychology. To speak in terms of Aristotle's analyses of the characteristics of youth and old age, Cyrus has both the generosity and spontaneity characteristic of the young (*Nicomachean Ethics*, 8.3.5–6, *Rhetoric*, 2.11.3–16), and the mind of an older person, who prefers friendships that will bring some advantage or profit to him (*Ethics*, 8.3.4, *Rhetoric*, 2.12.13–16).

12. Note that Xenophon tells the tragic version of the hunt that kills a king's son in the story of Gobryas; his son was murdered by the evil Assyrian prince on a hunt (4.6.1–11).

13. Cf. 8.1.34–39 (on hunting as a preparation for war), *On Hunting*, 12–13 (a violent postscript attacking those who would dare question this precept), and Anderson (1985).

14. Especially when we compare it with the extraordinary analogies of the prologue (Chapter 2) or the fantastic speech of Cyrus's lieutenant Chrysantas on centaurs and horsemanship at 4.3.15–21.

CHAPTER FIVE

1. Cf. Geertz, 28: "to rework the pattern of social relationships is to rearrange the coordinates of the experienced world. Society's forms are culture's substance."

2. Chapter 2.
3. Chapter 10.
4. Chapter 3.
5. Cf. Harris, 308–342 and Schusky, 55–57. In a patrilineal system for the transmission of authority, the paternal uncle might view the brother's child as a potential rival for accession to a status his brother has already claimed. But a maternal uncle like Cyaxares is already blocked from accession to the status Cambyses confers on Cyrus. What is striking about Cyrus is the way he imposes himself on even Cyaxares' legitimate status as the heir of Astyages. He subverts Cyaxares' legitimate position of authority, even as he affirms clearly the patrilineal system for the transmission of authority from his own father Cambyses. In effect, Cyrus

replaces Cyaxares as the son of Astyages. Cf. Harris, 309: "Kinship is the ideology of domestic life, the most important 'mirror' of the world of primitive man."

6. Bremmer, 186; cf. Garbáty, 233: "the basic condition necessary for the evolution of an avunculate in the sense of the uncle-nephew relationship as we see it in epic, heroic literature (which did not, after all, represent a cross section of society, but mirrored the activity of an upper class), was that of a noble, wealthy polygamous society involving a low confidence of paternity." Such conditions do not pertain for an uncle in the position Cyaxares occupies.

7. In Lincoln's words, McClellan had "the slows"; cf. Thomas Williams, 147–178.

8. Cyaxares' savage temper (4.5.12, 4.5.19) is a family trait borrowed from the Herodotean Astyages' father Cyaxares, or from Astyages himself; cf. Herodotus, 1.73.

9. Cyrus employs the same tactic of postponement in his response to Croesus (7.2.5, discussed below in Chapter 7).

10. All three of these future allies are introduced in relatively short order: Gobryas at 4.6.1–10, Panthea at 4.6.11, and Gadatas (through the report of Gobryas) at 5.2.8. Each of them makes the texture of Xenophon's fiction livelier, and each widens the scope of Cyrus's education in a significant new way.

11. Delebecque (1978), 130, note 1.

12. 6.1.1–6, 6.3.2, and esp. 8.5.17–19.

CHAPTER SIX

1. For strategy as a metaphor for rhetorical organization, see Cicero, *Letters to Atticus*, 5.2.2; Plutarch, *Moralia*, 755d, Dionysius of Halicarnassus, *Rhetoric*, 9.8. Since language is a means to power, words can naturally be conceived of as instruments of power as easily as soldiers and cavalry in a formation.

2. See Sander Goldberg, 112–121. In this instance, Cambyses is not being in the least metaphoric: *poiein* ("to fashion") and *poietês* ("fashioner," "maker") are merely the general terms for an activity which "poet" and "poetry" describe by a semantic narrowing in usage; cf. the Scots word "makar," a poet or ballad–writer.

3. Cf. 1.6.26–40 and *Prince*, 18. These passages will be shock-

ing only to those who do not see how this advice fits into the larger schemes of Xenophon's and Machiavelli's projects.

4. And not in the sense of a genuine artist; for the wrong mixture of an artistic temperament in a political context, see Griffin, 143–163.

5. *De Sophisticis elenchis* (*On Sophistical Refutations*), 33; 182b, 33–183a, 13.

6. Cf. the discussions of Croesus' efforts to exploit conventional piety in 7.2 (Chapter 7) and Cyaxares' easygoing attitude to the demands of his office (Chapter 5).

7. E.g., the portrait of Euthydemus in *Memorabilia*, 4.2, 4.3, and 4.5. Plato's *Euthydemus* (not the same young man, but a sophist skilled in eristics) dramatizes the difference between the Socratic and eristic methods, cf. Hawtrey, 11–23.

8. Cf. also *Discourses* 2, 13: "Xenophon, in his Life of Cyrus, calls attention to the necessity for deceit . . . (he) shows that without such frauds Cyrus could not have attained the greatness he did attain." As Mansfield (1979), 226 observes, "Xenophon was not an historian but a writer of fiction who taught the necessity of fraud in the guise of an historian"; cf. Strauss (1958), 139. And as Frye observes, fraud also plays an important role in romance; cf. Frye (1976), 65–93.

CHAPTER SEVEN

1. Herodotus 1.29–33, 1.86–91; *Oeconomicus*, 4.6–5.1; *Hiero*.

2. Lefèvre, 290ff; cf. Hirsch, 77–78, and esp. Sage, 87 and 107.

3. See Immerwahr, 154–167; cf. also Lattimore, and Bischoff.

4. A nineteenth-century German scholar compared this encounter to the meeting of Wilhelm I and Napoleon III at Sedan, where a civilized conclusion was made to the Franco-Prussian War. I am inclined rather to compare it to a meeting between Napoleon I and Talleyrand; cf. Cronin, 443–44.

5. As Lefèvre observes, "for you can do it" (*kai gar dunasai poiêsai*) is an archaic formula that suggests Croesus is praying to a god; in effect, Croesus is replacing Apollo, the god who did not help him as much as he could have, with Cyrus, a man promoted by Croesus' flattery to the status of the "god," who can (Lefèvre, 293).

6. Cf. Hans R. Breitenbach, 1721; Lefèvre, 294–295; Higgins, 52–54; Sage, 84.

7. Cf. Antisthenes' comment on the *êthos* of Heracles and Cyrus: both are *philoponoi*, lovers of hard work (Dio Chrysostom, *Orations*, 5.109); cf. Dittmar, 58–76.

8. Higgins, 53; cf. 7.3.10–14.

9. Sage, 100.

10. Aside from a passing comment in the Budé edition (Delebecque [1978], 59, note 2), the first sustained discussion of the manipulative aspects of Croesus' character is Sage, 71–133; cf. esp. 105: "What seems, on the surface, to be stupidity and disarming candor may in fact be carefully staged by a shrewd Croesus who is attempting to maximize his favorable treatment at Cyrus's hands."

11. *Kuron eboa* (7.2.5). The verb *boaô* ("call out," "summon with a loud cry") is better rendered by "Crésus . . . appelait Cyrus à grands cris" (Budé) than "he called for Cyrus" (Loeb). Note that Herodotus' Croesus calls out Solon's name three times in anguish (1.86.3–4)—yet another indication of the fundamental difference between the two versions of the meeting.

12. 5.3.6.

13. Cf. Bakhtin (1981), 86–110. For the disastrous implications in tragedy that come from linking oneself with *tychê*, cf. Knox, 159–184, and esp. 176–180 (on Oedipus as "the child of fortune"; *Oedipus Rex*, 1080).

14. In this scene, as elsewhere, these Persians are thoroughly Hellenized—a tendency already apparent in characterizations of Barbarians in earlier Greek literature; cf. Bacon, 63 and 167–172; Long, 129–156.

15. Cyrus employs a similar tactic in his leading question to Panthea at 7.3.12 ("To whom do you wish to taken?"), discussed below in Chapter 8.

16. The oracle's reply is a joke for the reader at Croesus' expense, as comparison with other responses will show; see Fontenrose, 269–354, esp. 294 and 303–304.

17. Cf. comments on the assassination of Jason of Pherae (*Hellenica* 6.4.31) in Chapter 2 and on the fall of Araspas (5.1.18) in Chapter 8.

18. The prologue: "We have investigated who this man was in his ancestry [*genea*], what nature he possessed [*physis*] and what sort of education [*paideia*] he enjoyed that he so greatly excelled in governing men" (1.1.6); the end of the excursus on Persia's laws: "we shall now narrate the deeds of Cyrus from his childhood onwards [*ek paidos*]," (1.2.16); Croesus' flattery: "for I thought I was

able to wage war against you, who are in the first place being born
[*gegonoti*, cf. *genea*] from the gods, then growing up [*pephukoti*, cf.
physis] in a line of kings, and finally a person who has practiced
virtue from childhood onwards [*ek paidos aretên askounti*],"
7.2.24. Croesus' flattery of Cyrus is at once an exaggeration of his
ancestry and a revision of the less fortunate *genea*, *paideia*, and
physis of the Herodotean Cyrus; cf. Lefèvre, 291 and Sage, 97.

CHAPTER EIGHT

1. For a more developed and more poignant representation of
the changes monarchy can work in human relationships, see
Henry IV, Parts I and II for Alexander's experience, cf. Badian.

2. Compare the similar concentration of multiple roles in the
character of Dido in the *Aeneid*. In one sense, this kind of com-
plexity is a result of the artist's imagination, which in Vergil's case
is capable of applying an unlimited number of perspectives to a
single role. But in another sense the astonishing compression of
many prior character types into a single character like Dido is a
consequence of the ideology of the work in which she appears. We
suspect that it was first Aeneas who existed, and then Dido, whose
characterization is drawn to complement and complicate the por-
trait of Aeneas. Dido is evocative of many Homeric and tragic her-
oines (as well as of historical figures such as Arsinoe and Cleopa-
tra), because she is all of those characters reduced to one character,
at once: the woman who is the other, the one who aids, impedes,
or otherwise plays a crucial role in the career of the hero of the
poem.

3. Trenkner, 26; Perry, 168; cf. Haight, 22–29.

4. Cf. 1.4.26 and 5.1.2 (where Araspas is named for the first
time). Artabazos' naming is postponed in similar fashion, but
when he is named in Book 4, it is not immediately clear who he
is. Xenophon's adaptation of this Herodotean technique is not al-
ways carried through with the finesse of a later novelist like Apu-
leius. His workmanship can be traced out in the introduction of
this slightly mysterious character.

In 1.4.27–28 (the *paidikos logos*), Artabazos is identified as
"the Mede who claims kinship with Cyrus"; then at 4.1.22–24
and 5.1.24–26 he reappears as "the one who once said he was Cy-
rus's kinsman and kissed him," a rather long-winded periphrasis
that requires a reasonably sharp memory of an earlier moment in

the text. At 5.3.38 Cyrus finally names him: "Next let Artabazos follow at the head of Persian peltasts." But who is Artabazos? Without an allusion to "the one who claimed to be Cyrus's kinsman" we do not have a clue as to who he is, especially since he is in the company of others who are named only here and who play no role whatever in the *Cyropaedia*: Andamys, Embas, Artuchas, Thambradas, Datamas, Madatas, Rhambacas, Alceunas (5.3.38–41). "Artabazos" and "the one who once claimed to be a kinsman of Cyrus" finally intersect at 6.1.9, in a debate Cyrus stages on the continuation of the war.

5. Cf. 4.6.11, where we learn of "a most beautiful tent" *kallistên skenên*] and a woman, who is said to be "the most beautiful [*kallistê*] in Asia"; as a prize of war she initially has the same status as a tent. Then she is identified as "the wife of Abradatas of Susa" (5.1.2–8).

6. See Schaps, esp. 329; cf. Gould, esp. 43–52.

7. Cf. McKeon, 212ff.: in romance, true nobility always finds a way to show itself; disguise only confirms the internal nobility whose external signs have been removed, as here, by temporary misfortune.

8. Argyle and Cook, 1–34, 58–97.

9. Cf. Machiavelli, *Prince*, 19: "What makes him hated above all . . . is to be rapacious and a usurper of the property and the women of his subjects. From these he must abstain, and whenever one does not take away either property or honor from the generality of man, they live content and one has only to contend with the ambition of the few which may be checked in many modes and with ease." This is a point of view completely at odds with the experience of romance in which Eros rules; cf. Carson, 77ff.

10. Chapter 7, above.

11. See Shell, 11–61, esp. 17–19; cf. Bernadete, 25.

12. Carson, 83.

13. Plato's version of the myth of Gyges turns it into a dialectical examination of the problem of justice, with the conflicts among Candaules, Gyges, and Candaules' wife condensed into one person. In Glaucon's version of the myth (*Republic*, 2.359b–360b), an ancestor of Gyges discovers the magic ring that enables its wearer to make himself visible or invisible by turning the ring on his finger. This power enables its wearer to do what he pleases, and thus centers the moral choice of acting justly or unjustly in one person's consciousness. In Glaucon's version, Gyges commits adultery with the king's wife, assassinates the king, and takes the

throne for himself. Thus the ring of Gyges would be a fine test of a person's capacity to act justly or unjustly.

14. Araspas is seized by love and driven to proposition her (*lêphtheis erôti tês gynaikos ênagkasthê prosenegkein logous autêi*) (6.1.31). To send this kind of message (*logous prospherein*) is the mark of a lover in later romantic contexts; cf. Xenophon of Ephesus, 3.12.4 (Kyno to Habrocomes), Apollodous, 2.3.1 (Sthenoboea to Bellerophon) and 3.13.3 (Astydameia to Peleus). The sequence of moving from efforts to persuade by argument or prayer to threats of force (*peithein* and *anagkazein*) (6.1.33) is also typical of later erotic writers (and of erotic scenes in unerotic writers); e.g., Parthenius, *Love Stories* (*Erotika Pathemata*), 18; Xenophon of Ephesus, 4.5.2 and 5.4.5; Livy 3.44, 4.38; Plutarch, *Moralia*, 257ff., 258a, 272f; cf Braun, 40 and notes 88–89.

15. Cf. Dover, 81–100.

16. At the end of Xenophon's *Symposium* (9.7), the interlocutors are so aroused by their discussion of Eros that the married men rush home to their wives and the unmarried men turn to their prostitutes; cf. the end of the tales about the boy of Pergamum and the widow of Ephesus in Petronius' *Satyricon*, 90 and 112, and the shocking finale of certain tales in Apuleius' *Golden Ass* (1.20, 2.20, and Books 9 and 10, passim).

17. Cf. a similar linguistic hybridization of hero and heroine in Apuleius' *Cupido* and *Psyche*.

18. Cf. McKeon, 38: "Like 'romance love,' the striking importance of naming in romance may be associated with 'telling the truth' by means that are rooted in the empirical but empowered by an essentialist authority. The power of names is their power to signify lineage; not only the genealogical essence of family, but the etymological mystery that lies at the heart of words themselves."

19. See *Memorabilia*, 1.2.13 and Plato, *Symposium*, 203d and *Phaedrus*, 237d; cf. *Republic*, 439d and *Laws*, 896d.

20. Delebecque (1978), 36 and note 1 (on 6.4.2).

21. Cited approvingly by Plutarch in his essay on inoffensive self-praise (*Moralia*, 545b). Like Xenophon's apologetic aside on the *polylogia* (talkativeness) of the boy Cyrus (1.4.3; Chapter 4, above), this authorial intrusion reveals how high a standard Xenophon has for Cyrus; he rarely finds anything to criticize in the conduct of the hero he has created. Such brief moments may or may not reflect an actual historical fact about Cyrus. Their main purpose is to create an aura of authenticity, as if Xenophon were reassuring his readers that Cyrus is not *completely* without flaws.

22. Anderson (1970), 165–91; cf. Holden, vol. 1, lii–liii; vol. 3, 196–197; Ludwig Breitenbach, *ad* 7.1.29–32: "ähnliches" ("similar").

23. Ortega y Gasset, 156.

24. Chapter 5, above.

25. On funerals and antifunerals, see Redfield, 180–186.

26. Delebecque, III (1978), 61, notes 2 and 3.

27. Sidney (1987), 399.

28. As will be apparent, I find unlikely the theory that these episodes in the *Cyropaedia* inspired the adolescent education that seems to be the subject of the *Ninos* fragments (Weil).

CHAPTER NINE

1. Cf. 1.6.45: "You may learn from what has happened in history. For many men who seemed most wise have persuaded states to start a war against others, and the states so persuaded were destroyed. Many men have made others great, both individuals and states; and when they have made them great, have suffered the worst kinds of evils at their hands. And many who might have treated people as their friends and done them favors and received favors from them, have received their just rewards from these people because they preferred to treat them like slaves rather than as friends. Many were not content to live happily in enjoyment of their own shame, have lost even what they had, because they wanted to be lords of everything. And many, when they gained the wealth they so much desired, have been ruined by it." Cambyses sketches out the dangers of a new kingdom, and Cyrus's conduct in Books 7 and 8 may be conceived of as an answer to the potential problems his father foresees.

2. Cf. *Oeconomicus*, 21; on tyranny as a faulty political order in the *Hiero*, see Strauss (1948), 50–62.

3. "He had no regard whatever for gold or silver or fancy clothes, but considered all of these things worthless, except in so far as he could give them away and curry favor" (Dio Chrysostom, *Orations*, 5.109; cf. Julian 7.219d). This testimony from later antiquity reflects the calculated generosity described in Ezra 1 and 6.3–5, which is much closer to the historical Cyrus; cf. Olmstead (1948), 52–58.

4. On the politics of spectacle and the judicious use of wealth, see for example Millar, 28–40 and 189–201; Strong (1973), and Bender, 14–78.

5. Orgel, 42–43 (quoting McIlwain, 43); cf. Jonathan Goldberg, 113–119, and the comments of Cambyses to Cyrus at 1.6.22–23. Cyrus observes that nothing is more efficient in governing others than to seem to be wiser than the ones ruled (*phronimôteron dokein einai tôn archomenôn*). Cambyses pushes Cyrus's idea further: the shorter road to achieving this is really to be wise about the things one wants to seem to be wise about.

6. Cf. the discussion of father and son as metaphors for organizing the empire in Chapter 3.

7. Cf. the discoveries of the boy Cyrus discussed in Chapter 4, and Tompkins, 226: "The similarity between contemporary critical theory and the criticism of antiquity, if such a similarity exists, lies not in the common focus on literature's audience . . . but rather in the common perception of language as a form of power."

8. 2.1.1–3, 2.3.17–24, 3.2.25, 5.2, 8.4. This is also supremely characteristic of the monarchs of the Renaissance. See Jonathan Goldberg, 1–55 for different but equally intelligent uses of spectacle by Elizabeth I and James I; cf. Greenblatt, 166–169.

9. Thus the monuments and palaces of Cyrus's successors Darius and Xerxes, described in Olmstead (1948), 272–288.

10. The show was only good if it worked; cf. the comments of Orgel, 88–89 and Jonathan Goldberg, 240 on King Charles I.

11. Cf. Griffin, 119–42, and Boethius, 94–128.

12. Arrian, *Anabasis of Alexander*, 4.7.4–14; cf. Brunt, I, 532–544.

13. Cf. 7.5.38–47 with *Symposium*, 9.7.

14. Cf. the outline of symmetrically conceived characters at the end of Chapter 3. The display of *philanthropia* is one of the qualities most admired in Cyrus (8.6, 1.1); it is also a reputation which Cambyses advises his son to cultivate as part of his project of ruling other men (1.6.24–25). It is not important whether this feeling is genuine or contrived; the point is that it persuades others that Cyrus cares for them. Cf. Treu.

15. Gobryas' account of his son's death is an occasion for a rare excursion into mimetic stylistics. His recital is broken by sobs; he begins several sentences but cannot complete them: "For he who was my only son, a fine and noble one, master, one who loved me and respected me as much as any son could to make his father happy . . . him, this present king . . . when the old king, the father of the present ruler, invited my son to his court intending to give him his daughter in marriage . . . and I let him go, flattered that I should see my son married then to the king's daughter . . . then the man who is now the king invited him to go hunting with him

and gave him permission to do his best in the chase, for he considered that he was a much better horseman than my son, and when a bear came out, they both gave chase, and the one who is presently ruler let fly his spears—would that he never had—but my son threw his spear—he should not have—and brought down the bear" (4.6.3). This attempt at a narrative underscores the pathos of Gobryas' situation and, as a narrative technique, may be compared to the single long sentence Xenophon elsewhere uses for comic effect; cf. the discussion of Jason of Pherae (Chapter 2), Croesus (Chapter 7), and Araspas (Chapter 8). Gobryas is as sympathetic as they are contemptible. Gobryas and his son thus represent the tragic experience of Croesus and his son Atys, who is slain by the suppliant Adrastus in Herodotus (1.34–45). A romantic, positive revision of the story is given to Cyrus (above, Chapter 4), which is here balanced by the Herodotean fate of Gobryas (4.6.2–7).

16. Other notable beneficiaries of Cyrus's pity are the Egyptians who kill Abradatas (6.1.41), and Panthea (7.3.14).

17. 8.5.17–20; cf. the dynastic marriage of Alexander and Roxane for similar *raisons d'état* in Arrian, *Anabasis of Alexander*, 4.19–20.

18. *Odyssey*, 4.120–305; cf. 2.3.5 (Chrysantas is *anêr oute megas oute ischuros idein, phronêsi de diapherôn*, "a man not large nor imposing to look at, but distinguished by his wisdom").

19. *Odyssey* 14.81–184. Cf. 2.3.7 (Pheraulas is *kai to sôma kai tên psychên ouk agennei andri eioikôs*, "not unlike a noble man in his body and in his soul").

20. There is some anticipation of this kind of lieutenant in the portrait of Clearchus in the *Anabasis*, though he is notably more limited than Chrysantas; cf. *Anabasis* 1.3, 1.5, and esp. 2.5, where Clearchus is outwitted by the far cleverer Tissaphernes.

21. "A Letter of the Authors" (23 January 1589).

22. Chapter 3.

23. The prestige of Cicero and his adaptation of the speech in the *De Senectute* account for this; cf. the discussion in Chapter 2 of the influence of the tag *imago iusti imperii* from *Ad Quintum Fratrem*, 1.1.

24. Cf. Plato, *Apology*, 40d–e and *Phaedo*, 118a; Hirsch, 178. The precise degree of Xenophon's use of ancient Persian sources remains an unsolvable issue. While Ferdowsi draws on traditional materials that run back to Cyrus, everything is filtered through Islam and a text composed a thousand years after the *Cyropaedia*; see Momigliano (1975), 123–150.

25. E.g., Warner and Warner, vol. 1, 119.
26. Zeus and Hestia: 1.6.1, 3.3.21, 7.5.57, 8.7.3. The *magoi*: 9.6.11, 5.5.4, 7.3.1.
27. Warner and Warner, vol. 1, 335–336.
28. Cicero actually uses only a small part of Cyrus's speech; *De Senectute*, 22/79–81 is like 8.7.17–22.

CHAPTER TEN

1. Burke, 1.
2. For the symmetrical design typical of romance, see Frye (1957), 186–206 and Chapter 3.
3. See Connor (1984), 63–75.
4. Thus Henry Holland summarizes 8.8 in his father's translation of 1632: "How after the death of Cyrus all his ordinances were perverted. The author's discourse concerning the government of the Persian kings after Cyrus." Similarly, the *Bibliothèque* (December 1775), 62: "Xenophon, in sum, appears here (sc. 8.8) to have had no other goal than to respect history, which attests that the character of the Persians began to be corrupt following the epoch of the conquests of Cyrus"; and ibid., 63: "The eighth and last book of the *Cyropaedia* (a work, as we have said, prolonged beyond its own merits, but acquitted of this fault by the beauty of its details) contains exhortations to obedience, his final illness, and the corruption of the Persians after his death." Maurice Ashley links the last chapter with actual political experience as well: "The arts that Cyrus used with private men, and with whole nations, in order to gain them to his purpose, were certainly right; but this does not prove that that purpose of his was honest. In like manner all his regulations with respect to the establishment of his scheme of tyranny were as certainly rightly contrived to serve that end; but yet this is no proof that such tyranny is not most unjust, unequal, and barbarous establishment. And when the foundation and ruin of the empire of Cyrus is directly ascribed to a green government; when his own education under such a government appears to be the foundation of all the virtues he has; and when the effects of his empire erected are declared to be a general defection from all virtue in the people, and the misery of the prince's own family; then let anyone judge, whether the moral of this fable of Xenophon's does decide in favour of tyranny."

5. The state of the question prior to 1880 is summarized by Eichler, 1–5.

6. Walter Miller, 2.438–439.

7. Eichler, 75–87.

8. Cf. esp. his analysis of the frequency of the particle *mên* and related clusters on pp. 10–15; this stylistic marker was later reconfirmed by Denniston, 347.

9. Cf. Bizos, xxvi–xxxvi; Delebecque (1978), 172.

10. Thus the vexed interpolation of the *Constitution of the Lacedaemonians* (13): "If someone should ask me whether the laws of Lycurgus seem to me to remain even now unmoved, By Zeus I could absolutely not say this." Such editorial second thoughts appear in various forms throughout Xenophon's work. He likes to appeal to someone else to finish what he has done, to disagree with him, to check his facts, and, if they are so minded, to do better.

Let this be written by me up to this point. The things that came after these events perhaps will be the concern of another. (*Hellenica*, 7.5.27)

But if anyone thinks that he will have great difficulties if he has to practice horsemanship in this way, let him reflect that men in training for gymnastic contests face troubles far more numerous and exacting than the most strenuous exercises in horsemanship. (*Cavalry Commander*, 8.5)

If anyone is surprised at my frequent repetition of the exhortation to work with god, I can assure him that his surprise will diminish, if he is often in peril, and if he considers that in time of war his enemies plot and counterplot, but seldom know what will come of their plots. There is no one else that can give counsel in such times but the gods. (Ibid.; cf. *Cyropaedia*, 1.6.44–46)

But if anyone wants to own a horse suitable for parade, with a high and showy action, such qualities are by no means to be found in every horse; but it is essential that he should have plenty of spirit and a strong body. (*On Horsemanship*, 11.1)

If any of the men who pursue virtue has ever encountered anyone more helpful than Socrates, that man, I believe, has a right to be called the happiest man alive. (*Apology*, 34)

Notes

Notes

ort>88888888888888888888888888888888888888888888888888888888888888888888888888888888888888888888888888888888 put, ut cetera, ipse scripsit; opusculum est, non operis particula; Cyrupaediae appendix est nec tamen quidquam ad illam addit aut, unde fidem ei habeamus, continet. Paulo post eam confectam scriptus est. Quid Xenophontem moverit ad istas obiurgationes nescio." ("Xenophon himself wrote the eighth chapter to Book 8 of the *Cyropaedia*, along with everything else; it is a small project in its own right, not an extension of the main work; it is an addition to the *Cyropaedia* and yet it neither adds anything to it, nor gives us any cause to take its comment seriously. It was written a short time after the main work was finished. I have no idea what may have moved Xenophon to write this invective") (Eichler, 87).

23. Cf. Chapter 2.

24. Cf. Higgins, 59: "perfect polity must have struck him as a willful delusion. And so in the *Kyroupaideia* he wrote an epic novel whose noble protagonist may—but only may—instruct, though his deeds are as grass. For all its high confidence, for all its mighty exploits, the *Kyroupaideia* retains a poignance Homer would have known, the sad sense that all things pass."

25. In this respect he exemplifies what Lentricchia calls "conservative fictionalism": "One of the difficulties with the opposition of fiction and reality is that it severely and unnecessarily narrows artistic options by enforcing an all-too-predictable dialectic. Reality is horrible; it drives us into satisfying worlds of our own making. But the poet, with his prized faculty of self-consciousness, knows his fictions not to be 'true'; however unsatisfactory reality may be, as a mature and sane individual (who will not dwell in fantasy), the poet is forced to 'open up' his fiction to reality and to face the hard truth. Once he has done that, his sense of the real is renewed, but such renewal is (how could it be otherwise?) a terror-inspiring occasion. The poet is driven back to fiction-making—and so on and so forth. The point is that with reality ontologically privileged, the poet will always be driven to self-ironic critique of the process of fiction-making. Yet that same privileging of the real is a privileging of the horror; in an effort to preserve his being, so goes the logic of conservative fictionalism, the poet will necessarily be driven back to fiction-making" (Lentricchia, 56).

BIBLIOGRAPHY

ADKINS, Arthur. *Merit and Responsibility. A Study in Greek Values.* Oxford, 1960.

VON ALBRECHT, Michael. *Meister der römischen Prosa, von Cato bis Apuleius.* Heidelberg, 1971.

ANDERSON, Graham. *Philostratus. Biography and Belles Lettres in the Third Century A.D.* London, Sydney, and Dover, N.H., 1986.

ANDERSON, J. K. *Ancient Greek Horsemanship.* Berkeley and Los Angeles, 1961.

————. *Military Theory and Practice in the Age of Xenophon.* Berkeley and Los Angeles, 1970.

————. *Xenophon.* New York, 1974.

————. *Hunting in the Ancient World.* Berkeley, Los Angeles, and London, 1985.

ANDREWES, Antony. *The Greek Tyrants.* New York, 1963.

ARGYLE, Michael, and Cook, Mark. *Gaze and Mutual Gaze.* Cambridge and New York, 1976.

ARIÈS, Philippe. *Centuries of Childhood. A Social History of Family Life.* Translated by Robert Baldick. New York, 1962.

ARON, Raymond. *Clausewitz, Philosopher of War.* Englewood Cliffs, N.J., 1985.

ASHLEY, Maurice, translator. *Cyropaedia, or The Institution of Cyrus.* Third edition. London, 1770.

AVERY, Harry C. "Herodotus' Picture of Cyrus," *American Journal of Philology* 93 (1973): 529–46.

BACON, Helen H. *Barbarians in Greek Tragedy.* New Haven, 1961.

BADEN, Hans. *Untersuchungen zur Einheit der Hellenika Xenophons.* Hamburg, 1966.

BADIAN, Ernst. "Alexander the Great and the Loneliness of Power," in *Studies in Greek and Roman History*. London, 1964, 192–205.

BAILEY, D. R. Shackleton, editor. *Cicero: Epistulae ad Quintum Fratrem et M. Brutum*. Cambridge, 1980.

BAKHTIN, M. M. *The Dialogic Imagination. Four Essays by M. M. Bakhtin*. Caryl Emerson and Michael Holquist, translators. Michael Holquist, editor. Austin, 1981.

———. *Speech Genres and Other Late Essays*. Vern W. McGree, translator. Caryl Emerson and Michael Holquist, editors. Austin, 1986.

BARKER, William, translator. *The School of Cyrus. William Barker's Translation of Xenophon's Cyropaedia (London, 1567)*. James Tatum, editor. New York, 1988.

BENDER, James P. *Spenser and Literary Pictorialism*. Princeton, 1972.

BERGER, Harry, Jr. "Mutabilitie Cantos: Archaism and Evolution in Retrospect," in *Spenser: A Collection of Critical Essays*. Harry Berger, Jr., editor. Englewood Cliffs, N.J., 1968, 146–76.

BERNADETE, Seth. *Herodotean Enquiries*. The Hague, 1969.

Bibliothèque Universelle des Romans (various editors). Paris, July 1775–June 1789.

BINGHAM, Caroline. *The Making of a King. The Early Years of James VI and I*. London, 1968.

BISCHOFF, Hans. "Der Warner bei Herodot," in *Herodot*. Darmstadt, 1961, 302–9.

BIZOS, Marcel. *Xénophon. Cyropédie. Livres I–V*. Paris, 1971–1973.

BOETHIUS, Axel. *The Golden House of Nero. Some Aspects of Roman Architecture*. Ann Arbor, 1960.

BOILEAU-DESPRÉAUX,. Nicholas. *Les Héros du roman. Dialogue de Nicolas Boileau-Despréaux*. Thomas B. Crane, editor. Boston, 1902.

BOLOTIN, David. *Plato's Dialogue on Friendship. An Interpretation of the Lysis, with a New Translation*. Ithaca and London, 1979.

BOWERSOCK, G. W. *Greek Sophists in the Roman Empire*. Oxford, 1969.

BOWIE, E. L. "Greeks and Their Past in the Second Sophistic," in *Studies in Ancient Society*. M. I. Finley, editor. London and Boston, 1974, 166–209.

———. "The Greek Novel," in *The Cambridge History of Classical Literature*, vol. 1. P. E. Easterling and B.M.W. Knox, editors. Cambridge, 1985, 683–98.

BOYCE, Mary. *Zoroastrians. Their Religious Beliefs and Practices.* London and Boston, 1979.

BRAUN, Martin. *Griechischer Roman und Hellenistische Geschichtschreibung.* Frankfurt, 1934.

BREITENBACH, Hans R. *Xenophon von Athen* (Pauly's Realencyclopädie der classischen Altertumswissenschaft, vol. IX, A2). Stuttgart, 1966.

BREITENBACH, Ludwig. *Xenophons Kyropaedie.* Leipzig, 1878.

BREMMER, Jan. "The Importance of the Maternal Uncle and Grandfather in Archaic and Classical Greece and Early Byzantium," *Zeitschrift für Epigraphik und Papyrologie* 50 (1983): 173–86.

BRETT, R. L. *The Third Earl of Shaftesbury. A Study in Eighteenth-Century Literary Theory.* London, 1951.

BROWN, Truesdell S. *Onesicritus. A Study in Hellenistic Historiography.* Berkeley and Los Angeles, 1949.

BROWNLEE, Kevin, and Marina Scordilis Brownlee, editors. *Romance. Generic Transformations from Chretien de Troyes to Cervantes.* Hanover and London, 1985.

BROWNLEE, Kevin. "Jean de Meun and the Limits of Romance," in Brownlee and Brownlee, *Romance*, 114–34.

BRUNT, P. A., translator. *Arrian. History of Alexander and Indica*, in two volumes. Cambridge, Mass., and London, 1976.

BURKE, Kenneth. *The Philosophy of Literary Form.* Second edition. Baton Rouge, 1967.

CARSON, Anne. *Eros the Bittersweet.* Princeton, 1986.

CAWKWELL, George L. Introduction to *Xenophon: A History of My Times (Hellenica).* Rex Warner, translator. Harmondsworth, 1978, 7–46.

CHRISTENSEN, Arthur. *Les Gestes des rois dans les traditions de l'Iran antique.* Paris, 1936.

COHEN, Ralph. "Afterword. The Problems of Generic Transformation," in Brownlee and Brownlee, *Romance*, 265–80.

CONNOR, W. Robert. *Thucydides.* Princeton, 1984.

———. "Historical Writings in the Fourth Century B.C. and in the Hellenistic Period," in *The Cambridge History of Classical Literature*, vol. 1. P. E. Easterling and B.M.W. Knox, editors. Cambridge, 1985, 458–71.

COUSIN, Victor. *La Societé francaise au XVIIe siècle, d'après le 'Grand Cyrus' de Mlle de Scudéry*. Fourth edition. Paris, 1873.

COX, James M. "Jefferson's *Autobiography*: Recovering Literature's Lost Ground," in *Autobiography: Essays Theoretical and Critical*. James Olney, editor. Princeton, 1980, 123–45.

COX, Patricia. *Biography in Late Antiquity. A Quest for the Holy Man*. Berkeley, Los Angeles, and London, 1983.

CRONIN, Vincent. *Napoleon*. New York, 1972.

CUENIN, Micheline, editor. *Les Précieuses ridicules. Documents contemporains*. Paris and Geneva, 1973.

CULLER, Jonathan. *On Deconstruction. Theory and Criticism after Structuralism*. Ithaca and London, 1982.

DANKOFF, Robert, translator. *Yusuf Khass Hajib: Wisdom of Royal Glory (Katadsu Bilig). A Turkish-Islamic Mirror for Princes*. Chicago and London, 1983.

DELEBECQUE, Edouard. *Essai sur la vie de Xénophon*. Paris, 1957.

―――. *Xénophon. L'art de la chasse*. Paris, 1970.

―――, editor. *Xénophon. Cyropédie III: Libres VI–VIII*. Paris, 1978.

DE MAN, Paul. Introduction to Jauss, *Toward an Aesthetic of Reception*, vii–xxv.

DENNISTON, J. D. *The Greek Particles*. Oxford, 1934.

DHOUDA. *Manuel pour mon fils*. Pierre Riche, editor. Paris, 1975.

DIHLE, Albrecht. *Studien zur Griechischen Biographie*. Göttingen, 1956.

DITTMAR, Heinrich. *Aeschines von Sphettos*. Berlin, 1912.

DOVER, K. J. *Greek Homosexuality*. Cambridge, Mass., 1977.

DREWS, Robert. *The Greek Accounts of Eastern History*. Cambridge, Mass., 1973.

DRYDEN, John. *Aureng-Zabe* (1676). Frederick M. Link, editor. Lincoln, 1971.

EAGLETON, Terry. *Marxism and Literary Criticism*. Berkeley and Los Angeles, 1976.

―――. *Literary Theory. An Introduction*. Minneapolis, 1983.

EDELSTEIN, Ludwig. *Plato's Seventh Letter*. Leiden, 1966.

EICHLER, Gustav. *De Cyrupaediae capite extremo*. Dissertation. Leipzig, 1880.

ERBSE, Hartmut. "Die Architectonik und Aufbau von Xenophons *Memorabilien*," *Hermes* 89 (1961): 261–87.

ERMARTH, Elizabeth Deeds. *Realism and Consensus in the English Novel*. Princeton, 1983.

FARBER, Joel. "The *Cyropaedia* and Hellenistic Kingship," *American Journal of Philology* 100 (1979): 497–514.

Bibliography 279

FEHLING, Detlev. *Amor und Psyche. Die Schöpfung des Apuleius und ihre Einwirkung auf das Märchen: eine Kiritik der romantischen Märchentheorie.* Wiesbaden, 1977.

FIEDLER, Leslie. *What Was Literature? Class Culture and Mass Society.* New York, 1982.

FIGGIS, John Neville. *The Divine Right of Kings.* Second edition. Cambridge, 1922.

FINE, John V. A. *The Ancient Greeks. A Critical History.* Cambridge, Mass., and London, 1983.

FONTENROSE, Joseph. *The Delphic Oracle.* Berkeley, Los Angeles, and London, 1978.

FORCIONE, Alban K. *Cervantes' Christian Romance. A Study of Persiles y Sigismundo.* Princeton, 1972.

———. *Cervantes and the Humanist Tradition. A Study of Four Exemplary Novels.* Princeton, 1982.

FORSTER, E. M. *Aspects of the Novel.* New York, 1927.

FRAME, Donald M., translator. *The Complete Essays of Montaigne.* Stanford, 1965.

FREEMAN, Douglas Southall. *Lee's Lieutenants,* vol. 1. New York, 1974.

VON FRITZ, Kurt. Review of Dihle's *Studien zur Griechischen Biographie, Gnomon* 28 (1956): 326–32.

FRYE, Northrop. *Anatomy of Criticism.* Princeton, 1957.

———. *The Secular Scripture. A Study of the Structure of Romance.* Cambridge, Mass., and London, 1976.

GALLET-GUERNE, Danielle. *Vasque de Lucène et la Cyropédie à la cour de Bourgogne (1470).* Geneva, 1974.

GARBÁTY, Thomas J. "The Uncle-Nephew Motif: New Light into its Origins and Development," *Folklore* 88 (1977): 220–35.

GEERTZ, Clifford. *The Interpretation of Cultures.* New York, 1973.

GERSHEVITCH, Ilya. *The Avestan Hymn to Mithra.* Cambridge, 1959.

GIBBON, Edward. *The History of the Decline and Fall of the Roman Empire,* 1776–1788.

———. "Mémoire sur la Monarchie des Mèdes," in *The Miscellaneous Works of Edward Gibbon,* vol. 3. London, 1814, 56–149.

GIGON, Olof. *Kommentar zum Ersten Buch von Xenophons Memorabilien.* Basel, 1953.

GLEASON, C. W., editor. *Selections from Xenophon's Cyropaedia.* Boston, 1897.

GODENNE, René. *Les Romans de Mlle de Scudéry.* Paris, 1983.

GOLDBERG, Jonathan. *James I and the Politics of Literature.* Baltimore and London, 1983.

GOLDBERG, Sander. *The Making of Menander's Comedy.* Berkeley, Los Angeles, and London, 1981.

GOMME, A. W., Andrewes, A., and Dover, K. J. *A Historical Commentary on Thucydides,* Book VIII. Oxford, 1981.

GOULD, John. "Law, Custom and Myth: Aspects of the Social Position of Women in Classical Athens," *Journal of Hellenic Studies* 100 (1980): 38–59.

GREENBLATT, Stephen. *Renaissance Self-Fashioning from More to Shakespeare.* Chicago and London, 1980.

GRIFFIN, Miriam. *Nero: The End of a Dynasty.* New Haven and London, 1985.

GROTE, George. *History of Greece.* London, 1846–1856.

GUTHRIE, W.K.C. *A History of Greek Philosophy,* Vol. III: *The Fifth Century Enlightenment.* Cambridge, 1969.

HADOT, P. "Fürstenspiegel," *Reallexicon für Antike und Christentum.* Stuttgart, 1950. Vol. 8, 555–632.

HÄGG, Tomas. *Narrative Technique in Ancient Greek Romances.* Stockholm, 1971.

———. *The Novel in Antiquity.* Berkeley and Los Angeles, 1983.

———. "*Callirhoe* and *Parthenope*: The Beginnings of the Historical Novel," *Classical Antiquity* 6 (1987): 184–204.

HAIGHT, Elizabeth Hazelton. *Essays on Ancient Fiction.* New York, 1936.

VON HALLBERG, Robert, editor. *Canons.* Chicago and London, 1984.

HARRIS, Marvin. *Culture, Man, and Nature. An Introduction to General Anthropology.* New York, 1971.

HAWTREY, R.S.W. *Commentary on Plato's Euthydemus.* Philadelphia, 1981.

HEALE, Elizabeth. *The Faerie Queene. A Reader's Guide.* Cambridge, 1987.

HEISERMAN, Arthur. *The Novel Before the Novel.* Chicago and London, 1977.

HELD, Julius S., editor. *Rubens and the Book. Title Pages by Peter Paul Rubens.* Williamstown, 1977.

HENRY, W. P. *Greek Historical Writing. A Historiographical Essay Based on Xenophon's Hellenica.* Chicago, 1967.

HERTER, Hans. "Das unschuldige Kind," *Jahrbuch für Antike und Christentum,* 4 (1961): 146–62.

HIGGINS, William E. *Xenophon the Athenian. The Problem of the Individual and Society of the Polis.* Albany, 1977.

HIJMANS, B. L., Jr. "Significant Names and their Function in Apuleius' *Metamorphoses*," in *Aspects of Apuleius' Golden Ass,* B. L. Hijmans, Jr. and R. van der Paardt, eds. Groningen, 1978, 107–22.

HIRSCH, Stephen W. *The Friendship of the Barbarians. Xenophon and the Persian Empire.* Hanover, N. H., and London, 1985.

HOÏSTAD, Hagnar. *Cynic Hero and Cynic King. Studies in the Cynic Conception of Man.* Uppsala, 1948.

HOLDEN, Hubert A. *The Cyropaedia of Xenophon.* Commentary in 4 volumes. Cambridge, 1890.

HOLUB, Robert C. *Reception Theory. A Critical Introduction.* London and New York, 1984.

HUGHES, Thomas. *Tom Brown's School Days.* Sixth edition. New York, 1891.

HUME, David. "On the Balance of Power," Essay VII in *Essays Moral, Political, and Literary.* Eugene F. Miller, editor. New York, 1985, 332–41.

HUNGER, Herbert. *Die Hochsprachliche Profane Literatur der Byzantiner.* Munich, 1978.

IMMERWAHR, Henry R. *Form and Thought in Herodotus.* Cleveland, 1966.

JAEGER, Werner. *Paideia. The Ideals of Greek Culture,* vol. 3. Oxford, 1943.

JAMESON, Fredric. "Magical Narratives: Romance as Genre," *New Literary History* 7 (1975): 135–63.

JAUSS, Hans Robert. *Toward an Aesthetic of Reception.* Timothy Bahti, translator; with an Introduction by Paul de Man. Minneapolis, 1982.

JENKYNS, Richard. *The Victorians and Ancient Greece.* Cambridge, Mass., 1980.

JOHNSON, W. Ralph. *Darkness Visible. A Study of Vergil's Aeneid.* Berkeley, 1976.

KENNEDY, George. *The Art of Rhetoric in the Roman World.* Princeton, 1972.

KERMODE, Frank J. *The Sense of an Ending. Studies in the Theory of Fiction.* Oxford, 1966.

KERN, Edith. "The Romance of Novel/Novella," in *The Disciplines of Criticism,* Peter Demetz, Thomas Greene, and Lowry Nelson, Jr., editors. New Haven and London, 1968, 511–30.

KNOX, Bernard M.W. *Oedipus at Thebes.* New Haven, 1957.

LANG, Mabel L. *Herodotean Narrative and Discourse*. Cambridge, Mass., and London, 1984.

LATTIMORE, Richmond. "The Wise Adviser in Herodotus," *Classical Philology* 34 (1939): 24–35.

LEFÈVRE, Eckerd. "Die Frage nach dem *Bios Eudaimon*: Die Begegnung zwischen Kyros und Kroisos bei Xenophon," *Hermes* 99 (1971): 283–96.

LENNOX, Charlotte. *The Female Quixote. The Adventures of Arabella* (1752). Sandra Shulman, editor. London, 1986.

LENTRICCHIA, Frank. *After the New Criticism*. Chicago and London, 1980.

LEO, Friedrich. *Die Griechisch-römische Biographie nach ihrer Literarischen Form*. Leipzig, 1901.

LERNER, Gerda. *The Creation of Patriarchy*. New York and Oxford, 1986.

LESKY, Albin. *Geschichte der Griechischen Literatur*. Third edition. Munich, 1971.

LEVY, Reuben, translator. *A Mirror for Princes. The Qabus Nama by Kai K'us Iskandar, Prince of Gurgan*. London, 1951.

———. *The Epic of Kings. Shah-Nama, the National Epic of Persia by Ferdowsi*. Chicago, 1967.

LEWALSKI, Barbara K. *Paradise Lost and the Rhetoric of Literary Forms*. Princeton, 1985.

LICHTHEIM, Miriam, editor. *Ancient Egyptian Literature. A Book of Readings*. Berkeley, Los Angeles, and London, 1973.

LONG, Timothy. *Barbarians in Greek Comedy*. Carbondale and Edwardsville, 1986.

LUKÁCS, Georg. *The Theory of the Novel*. Anna Bostock, translator. Cambridge, 1973.

———. *The Historical Novel*. Hannah and Stanley Mitchell, translators. Lincoln and London, 1983.

McDOUGALL, Dorothy. *Madeleine de Scudéry. Her Romantic Life and Death*. London, 1935.

MACHIAVELLI, Niccolò. *The Discourses (Discourses on the First Decade of Titus Livy)*. Leslie J. Walker and Brian Richardson, translators, with an Introduction by Bernard Crick. Harmondsworth, 1970.

McILWAIN, C. H., editor. *Political Works of James I*. Cambridge, Mass., 1918.

McKEON, Michael. *The Origins of the English Novel 1600–1740*. Baltimore and London, 1987.

MALLOWAN, Max. "Cyrus the Great," in *The Cambridge History* of Iran, vol. 2. Ilya Gershevitch, editor. Cambridge, 1985, 392–419.

MANSFIELD, Harvey C., Jr. Machiavelli's New Modes and Orders. A Study of the Discourses on Livy. Ithaca and London, 1979.

———, ed. The Prince. Niccolo Machiavelli. A New Translation with an Introduction. Chicago and London, 1985.

MARCHANT, E. C., editor. Xenophontis Opera Omnia. Tomus IV. Institutio Cyri. Oxford, 1910.

MARROU, H. I. History of Education in Antiquity. George Lamb, translator. Madison, 1982.

MATTHIESSEN, F. O. Translation: An Elizabethan Art. Cambridge, 1931.

MILLAR, Fergus. The Emperor in the Roman World. Ithaca, 1977.

MILLER, Nathan. FDR: An Intimate History. New York, 1983.

MILLER, Walter, translator. Xenophon. Cyropaedia. Cambridge, Mass., and London, 1914.

MOMIGLIANO, Arnaldo. The Development of Greek Biography. Cambridge, Mass., 1971.

———. Alien Wisdom. The Limits of Hellenization. Cambridge, 1975.

———. Essays in Ancient and Modern History. Middletown, Conn., 1977.

MONTGOMERY, Hugo. Gedanke und Tat. Zur Erzählungstechnik bei Herodot, Thukydides, Xenophon und Arrian. Lund, 1965.

MORROW, Glenn R. Plato's Cretan City. A Historical Interpretation of the Laws. Princeton, 1960.

———. Plato's Epistles. Indianapolis, 1962.

MÜNSCHER, Karl. Xenophon in der griechisch-römischen Literatur. Philologus Supplementband 13. Leipzig, 1920.

MURRAY, Oswyn. Peri Basileias. "Studies in the Justification of Monarchic Power in the Hellenistic World." D. Phil. thesis (unpublished). Oxford, 1971.

NUSSBAUM, G. B. The Ten Thousand. A Study in Social Organization and Action in Xenophon's Anabasis. Leiden, 1967.

NUSSBAUM, Martha C. The Fragility of Goodness. Luck and Ethics in Greek Tragedy and Philosophy. Cambridge, 1986.

OLMSTEAD, Albert T. History of Assyria. New York and London, 1923.

———. History of the Persian Empire. Chicago and London, 1948.

OLNEY, James. "Autos. Bios. Graphein: The Study of Autobiographical Literature," South Atlantic Quarterly 77 (1978): 113–23.

ORGEL, Stephen. *The Illusion of Power. Political Theater in the English Renaissance.* Berkeley, Los Angeles, and London, 1975.

ORTEGA Y GASSET, José. *Meditatons on Quixote.* Evelyn Rugg and Diego Marin, translators. New York, 1961.

PANGLE, Thomas L., translator. *The Laws of Plato.* New York, 1980.

PARKER, Patricia. *Inescapable Romance. Studies in the Poetics of a Mode.* Princeton, 1979.

PARRY, Edward Abbott, editor. *The Love Letters of Dorothy Osborne to Sir William Temple, 1652–1654.* New York, 1901.

PEPYS, Samuel. *The Diary of Samuel Pepys,* vol. VII (1666). Robert Latham and William Matthews, editors. London, 1972.

PERRY, Ben Edwin. *The Ancient Romances. A Literary-Historical Account of Their Origins.* Berkeley and Los Angeles, 1967.

POCOCK, J.G.A. *The Machiavellian Moment. Florentine Political Thought and the Atlantic Republic Tradition.* Princeton, 1975.

———. "The Machiavellian Moment Revisited: A Study in History and Ideology," *Journal of Modern History* 53 (1981): 49–72.

PRITCHARD, James B., ed. *Ancient Near Eastern Texts Relating to the Old Testament.* Second edition. Princeton, 1955.

PUCCI, Pietro. *Odysseus Polutropos. Intertextual Readings in the Odyssey and the Iliad.* Ithaca and London, 1987.

RAMSAY, André-Michel. *Les Voyages de Cyrus.* Paris, 1727.

REARDON, B. P. *Courants littéraires grecs des IIe et IIIe siècles après J.-C.* Paris, 1971.

———, editor. *Erotica Antiqua. Acta of the International Conference on the Ancient Novel.* Bangor, Wales, 1977.

REDFIELD, James M. *Nature and Culture in the Iliad. The Tragedy of Hector.* Chicago, 1977.

RENZA, Louis A. *"A White Heron" and the Question of Minor Literature.* Madison and London, 1984.

ROHDE, Erwin. *Der Griechische Roman und seine Vorläufer.* Second edition. Leipzig, 1900.

ROSENBERG, Charles E., editor. *The Family in History.* Philadelphia, 1975.

SAGE, Paula Winsor. "Solon, Croesus, and the Theme of the Ideal Life." Dissertation (unpublished). Johns Hopkins, 1985.

SCHAPS, David. "The Woman Least Mentioned: Etiquette and Women's Names," *Classical Quarterly* 27 (1977): 323–30.

SCHLAM, Carl C. *Cupid and Psyche. Apuleius and the Monuments.* University Park, Pa., 1976.

SCHUSKY, Ernest L. *Manual for Kinship Analysis.* New York, 1965.

SCHWARTZ, Eduard. *Fünf Vorträge über den Griechischen Roman.* Berlin, 1943.

DE SCUDÉRY, Georges. *Les Femmes illustres ou les Harangues heroiques de M de Scudery avec les veritables portraits de ces heroines, tirez des medailles antiques.* Paris, 1664.

DE SCUDÉRY, Madeleine. *Artamène ou le Grand Cyrus.* Paris, 1649–1653.

SHACKLETON, Robert. "The Impact of French Literature on Gibbon," in *Edward Gibbon and the Decline and Fall of the Roman Empire.* G. W Bowersock, John Clive, and Stephen R. Graubard, editors. Cambridge, Mass., and London, 1971, 207–18.

SHELL, Marc. *The Economy of Literature.* Johns Hopkins, 1978.

SHOWALTER, Jr., English. *The Evolution of the French Novel.* Princeton, 1972.

SIDNEY, Sir Philip. *Selected Prose and Poetry.* Robert Kinbrough, editor. Madison, 1983.

———. *The Countess of Pembroke's Arcadia (The New Arcadia).* Victor Skretkowicz, editor. Oxford, 1987.

SIMPSON, William Kelly. *The Literature of Ancient Egypt.* New Haven and London, 1973.

SMITH, Barbara Herrnstein. *Poetic Closure. A Study of How Poems End.* Chicago, 1968.

STADTER, Philip A. *Arrian of Nicomedia.* Chapel Hill, 1980.

STARK, Freya. *Alexander's Path.* London, 1958.

STERNE, Laurence. *The Life and Opinions of Tristram Shandy.* Graham Petrie, editor, with an Introduction by Christopher Ricks. Harmondsworth, 1967.

STRAUSS, Leo. *On Tyranny. An Interpretation of Xenophon's Hiero.* New York, 1948.

———. *Thoughts on Machiavelli.* Chicago and London, 1958.

———. *Xenophon's Socratic Discourse. An Interpretation of the Oeconomicus.* Ithaca and London, 1970.

———. *Xenophon's Socrates.* Ithaca, 1972.

STRONG, Roy. *Splendour at Court: Renaissance Spectacle and Illusion.* London, 1973.

——— *The Cult of Elizabeth. Elizabethan Portraiture and Pageantry.* London, 1977.

STÜCKRATH, Jörn. *Historische Rezeptionsforschung. Ein kritischer Versuch zu ihrer Geschichte und Theorie*. Stuttgart, 1979.

SUMMERSON, John. *The Classical Language of Architecture*. London, 1964.

TASSO, Torquato. *Discourses on the Heroic Poem*. Mariella Cavalchini and Irene Samuel, translators. Oxford, 1973.

TATUM, James. *Apuleius and the Golden Ass*. Ithaca and London, 1979.

TATUM, James, translator. *Plautus: The Darker Comedies*. Baltimore and London, 1983.

THESLEFF, H. "The Interrelationship and Dates of the *Symposiums* of Plato and Xenophon," *Bulletin of the Institute of Classical Studies* 8 (1978): 79–84.

TODOROV, Tzvetan. "The Origin of Genres," *New Literary History* 8 (1976): 159–70.

―――. *The Poetics of Prose*. Richard Howard, translator. Ithaca, 1977.

TOMPKINS, Jane P. "The Reader in History," in *Reader-Response Criticism from Formalism to Post-Structuralism*, Jane P. Tompkins, editor. Baltimore and London, 1980, 201–32.

TRENKNER, Sophie. *The Greek Novella in the Classical Period*. Cambridge, 1958.

TREU, M. "*Zur Clementia Caesaris*," *Museum Helveticum* 5 (1948): 197–217.

VATAI, Frank Leslie. *Intellectuals in Politics in the Greek World*. London, Sydney, and Dover, N.H., 1984.

VERRALL, Arthur W. *Euripides the Rationalist*. Cambridge, 1895.

WARNER, Arthur George and Edmund Warner, translators. *The Shahnama of Firdavsi*. London, 1905.

WEIL, H. "La Ninopédie," in *Études de Littérature et de Rhythmique grecques*. Paris, 1902, 90–106.

WELLEK, René, and Warren, Austin. *Theory of Literature*. Second edition. New York, 1956.

WELLEK, René. "Zur Methodischen Aporie einer Rezeptionsgeschichte," in *Geschichte: Ereignis und Erzählung*, Reinhart Koselleck and Wolf-Dieter Stempel, editors. Munich, 1973, 515–517.

WENDER, Dorothea. *The Last Scene of the Odyssey*. Leiden, 1978.

WIELAND, Christoph Martin. *Werke*, Volume 3: *Poetische Jugendwerke*. Fritz Homeyer, editor. Berlin, 1910.

WILLIAMS, Neville. *Thomas Howard, Fourth Duke of Norfolk*. London, 1964.

WILLIAMS, Thomas Harry. *Lincoln and His Generals*. New York, 1952.

WINKLER, John J. *Auctor & Actor. A Narratological Reading of Apuleius' Golden Ass*. Berkeley, Los Angeles, and London, 1985.

WLOSOK, Antonie. "Amor and Cupido," *Harvard Studies in Classical Philology* 79 (1975): 165–79.

WOODRUFF, Paul, translator. *Plato. Hippias Major*. Indianapolis and Cambridge, 1982.

YAVETZ, Zvi. "The *Res Gestae* and Augustus' Public Image," in *Caesar Augustus. Seven Aspects*. Fergus Millar and Erich Segal, editors. Oxford, 1984, 1–36.

INDEX

Abradatas, 21, 95–96, 164, 178, 179–82, 253n. *See also* Cyrus the Younger; Panthea
Achilles, 57, 91
Achilles Tatius, 20
acting, *passim*. *See also* Cyrus; theatricality
Agesilaus, 50–52, 53, 55, 58, 149, 190, 238, 254n, 255n
Agesilaus (Xenophon), 51–52, 258n
Aglaïtadas, 199–200
Alcibiades, 53
Alexander the Great, 5, 11–12, 34, 193, 197, 238–39, 246n, 247n, 270n
Anabasis of Alexander (Arrian), 247n, 254n, 270n
Anabasis (Xenophon), 4, 12, 41–45, 53, 61, 89, 90, 92, 116, 250n
Andromache, 179–80. *See also* Panthea
animals, 61–62. *See also* fiction, Xenophon's art of: analogy; hunting; ruling and being ruled
Antisthenes, 38, 264n
apaideutoi (uneducated persons). *See* education
Appollonius of Rhodes, 243n
Apology of Socrates (Plato). *See* Plato
Apology of Socrates (Xenophon), 38
Apuleius, 20, 25, 174, 235, 248n, 265n, 267n
Araspas, 20, 95–97, 157, 164, 168–79, 203, 265n, 267n. *See also* Panthea; fiction, Xenophon's art of: characterization; fiction, Xenophon's art of: long sentences

archein kai archesthai (to rule and to be ruled). *See* ruling and being ruled; fathers and sons
Archilochus, 146
archomenoi (subjects), 69. *See also* ruling and being ruled
Aretina or The Serious Romance. *See* MacKenzie, Sir George
Ariosto, 24
Aristophanes, 54, 144, 204
Aristotle, 12, 42, 136, 192, 235, 247n
Armenian king, 95–96, 135–39, 200, 232. *See also* ceremony, uses of; theatricality
Aron, Raymond, 34
Arrian, 18, 254n
Artabazus, 95–96, 97, 173–75, 178, 190, 195, 198, 203, 206, 265n, 266n. *See also* Araspas; eros, uses of; fiction, Xenophon's art of: characterization; lieutenants
Artamène ou le Grand Cyrus. *See* *Le Grand Cyrus*; de Scudèry, Madeleine
Ascham, Roger, 12
Ashley, Maurice, 29–31, 250n, 271n
Assyrians, 98, 151–52; king (father), 92–93, 208; king (son), 93, 110, 115–16, 153, 189–90, 201–2, 261n. *See also* fiction, Xenophon's art of: characterization; romance
Astyages, 88, 95–100, 107–11, 102–6, 190, 197
Astyages (in Herodotus), 100–111, 259n, 262n
Augustus, 10, 34, 190, 196, 204

INDEX LOCORUM